BUILDING
THE
BORDERLANDS

NUMBER TWENTY-TWO:
ENVIRONMENTAL HISTORY SERIES
DAN L. FLORES, GENERAL EDITOR

BUILDING
THE
BORDERLANDS

A TRANSNATIONAL HISTORY OF IRRIGATED COTTON
ALONG THE MEXICO-TEXAS BORDER

CASEY WALSH

TEXAS A&M UNIVERSITY PRESS
COLLEGE STATION

Library of Congress Cataloging-in-Publication Data

Walsh, Casey.
Building the borderlands : a transnational history of irrigated cotton along
the Mexico-Texas border / Casey Walsh. — 1st ed.
p. cm. — (Environmental history series ; no 22)
Includes bibliographical references and index.
ISBN-13: 978-1-60344-013-4 (cloth : alk. paper)
ISBN-10: 1-60344-013-5 (cloth : alk. paper)
1. Cotton farmers—Mexican-American Border Region—History.
2. Cotton trade—Mexican-American Border Region—History.
3. Irrigation farming—Mexican-American Border Region—History. I. Title.
HD8039.C662M589 2008
338.1′735109721—dc22
2007037686

CONTENTS

LIST OF ILLUSTRATIONS

Photographs

Maps

Graphs

ACKNOWLEDGMENTS

This book owes its existence to a great number of people and institutions. The central questions about cotton, development, and state formation were formulated in graduate seminars at the New School for Social Research. Deborah Poole got me started on the dissertation and helped me finish. Bill Roseberry died as I was writing, leaving me with unpaid intellectual debts and great sorrow. In Matamoros I was welcomed by the staff and researchers at the Colegio de la Frontera Norte, and by the Familia Vivanco. I would like to thank Cirila Quintero, Arturo Zarate, Jaime Mendoza, and Elizabeth Cueva for their support. In Valle Hermoso the Familia Acosta shared their home with me, and Doctor Renato Vázquez shared his vast knowledge of the region. In Mexico City the CIESAS provided me with an institutional home during the initial fieldwork, and Roberto Melville convinced me of the importance of studying water. I thank the *compañeros* at the Center for U.S.-Mexican Studies at the University of California San Diego for beach barbecues, Wednesday seminars, and bowling. Support from the Universidad Iberoamericana has allowed me to follow this project through to the end. I thank my colleagues in the Graduate Anthropology Program at the Ibero for their support, and especially Roger Magazine for always pushing me to take my anthropology just a little bit farther. Luis Aboites, at the Colegio de México, read the dissertation from start to finish, and his comments guided the transformation of the dissertation into a book. Thanks, Luis, for your patience. Steve Striffler and Sterling Evans read the manuscript and provided excellent suggestions. Financial support for the research and writing of this book was provided by: the New School for Social Research; the National Security Education Program; the Social Science Research Council; the Fulbright Program; the Rockefeller Archive Center; the Center for U.S.-Mexican Studies at UCSD; and the Universidad Iberoamericana. I thank my parents William and Catherine Walsh for their love and support while I follow my star. Finally, I thank my wife and colleague, Emiko Saldívar, and our daughters Amaya and Naomi, for accompanying me across so many political, intellectual, and emotional borders.

BUILDING
THE
BORDERLANDS

CHAPTER 1
INTRODUCTION: SOCIAL FIELDS OF COTTON

"*¡Era la jungla!* [It was the jungle!]," exclaimed Doña Elisa, telling of her arrival in the summer of 1939 to the dense mesquite thickets of rural Matamoros, just south of the Mexico-U.S. border at Brownsville.[1] She and her brothers accompanied their parents and hundreds of other Mexican *repatriados* (repatriates) from Texas to a new irrigation system being built by Mexico's federal government in the delta region of the Río Bravo, or Rio Grande, as it is known in the United States. Her parents had heard of the wonderful possibilities offered by the new zone from the Mexican officials who traveled that spring through the cotton belt of East and Central Texas, announcing their government's intention to give away land to Mexican colonists with experience in farming cotton. They decided to enlist in the government plan, and in May headed south with their belongings, in a caravan of buses, trucks, and cars, through the dry ranchlands south of San Antonio to the fertile agricultural zone of the Río Bravo/Rio Grande Valley, crossing the bridge into Mexico at Matamoros. It was the Great Depression, and the repatriates were impressed by the bounty of food provided to them by the Mexican government. "Piles of ham sandwiches," recalled Don Benito, who was sixteen at the time, "on store-bought white bread!"[2]

The travelers were met on the other side of the bridge by Eduardo Chávez, the energetic young engineer directing the construction of the irrigation and flood control works by the Secretary of Communications and Public Works (Secretaría de Comunicaciones y Obras Públicas, or SCOP). After spending a night in an empty warehouse that, in a few more months, would be stacked to the rafters with part of the region's cotton harvest, the group continued their journey southward. Leaving Matamoros, the repatriates saw large expanses of newly cleared lands, where many of those who had already fled Texas due to economic depression and nativist politics were working as day laborers in verdant cotton fields, or were building the government's hydraulic works. Once past the agricultural zone, the convoy followed a narrow path (*brecha de anteojo*) cleared by the SCOP engineers into the vast subtropical scrub forest that covered most of northern Tamaulipas. After pulling their vehicles time and again out of the thick mud left by the summer rains, they finally arrived at their new home, a clearing deep in the forest with a sign announcing the "Colonia

Office of Repatriation, Matamoros, Tamaulipas, 1939. *Courtesy of the Archivo General de la Nación, Mexico. Fondo Presidentes, Ramo Lázaro Cárdenas, 508.1/490, caja 593.*

18 de Marzo" (18th of March Colony), named for the day on which, one year earlier, Mexico's oil industry was nationalized by Pres. Lázaro Cárdenas.

Despite strong sentiments of optimism and patriotism, the repatriates soon discovered that their new lives as cotton farmers in Mexico were not to be easy ones. Snakes, mosquitoes, intolerable heat, and illness plagued the colonists, who were housed in buildings with tin roofs during those first, scorching summer months. The water they were given was bad, Doña Elisa continued, telling of how she had to pour it through a piece of cloth to rid it of debris before boiling it. Her father and brothers painstakingly cleared their 12.5-hectare plot of land with just a pick and an ax: "*trabajo de lágrimas* [tearful work]," she said. Her American citizenship enabled her to support their efforts by working legally in Brownsville, first in a laundry and later in a doctor's office. Her role in the family project to establish a homestead in Mexico was to bring money and supplies down to their farm in the colony on weekends. Those repatriates such as Doña Elisa and Don Benito that stayed to clear and farm the land saw the bitter struggles of the early 1940s turn into triumphant prosperity as the region grew during the later 1940s and 1950s. The cotton produced in the region commanded high prices from the end of World War II until about 1960, spurring rapid growth and the transformation of the colony into the town and municipality of Valle Hermoso. "I came as a young man with hope, energy, a screwdriver, and a pair of pliers, and I have built a fortune here," Don Benito told me proudly in impeccable English. Despite his success he has not cut his ties with the country in which he was born. His daughter was educated in Texas, but returned

Caravan of repatriates, heading south from Matamoros, 1939. *Courtesy of the Archivo General de la Nación, Mexico. Fondo Presidentes, Ramo Lázaro Cárdenas, 508.1/490, caja 593.*

to Mexico to work in the family law practice. They both occasionally return to the United States for vacations.[3]

Like Don Benito and his family, Doña Elisa has lived her entire life straddling the border between the United States and Mexico. Her parents were from the northern Mexican states of Nuevo León and San Luis Potosí, and during the Revolution (1911–1920) they migrated to work in the cotton fields around Pryor, Texas, where she was born in 1915. Lacking working papers, her father had difficulty finding a job during the Depression, and, given the opportunity by the Cárdenas government (1934–1940), he chose to return to Mexico rather than become a citizen of the United States. Although her brothers moved back to Texas a few years after they arrived at the colony, they maintain family ties through frequent visits, usually on the occasion of a wedding, anniversary, birthday, or civic celebration. Her parents stayed on in the Matamoros region, cultivating cotton on the 12.5-hectare parcel given to them by the federal government.

"*Mi papa era patriota, muy de su época* [My father was a patriot, very much of his era]," Doña Elisa's husband Fernando explained to me.[4] When U.S. Census workers came to their house in Brownsville in 1929, his father saw it as a choice between U.S. citizenship and deportation. He chose neither, and instead moved his family across the river to Matamoros of his own accord, where they joined the swelling crowd of *repatriados.* Like many of those *repatriados,* a few years later Fernando got a job working for Eduardo Chávez on the SCOP's Valle Bajo Río Bravo flood control and irrigation project. When Chávez left the region, Fernando returned to

Repatriate truck, stuck in the mud on the road to the Colonia 18 de Marzo. *Courtesy of the Archivo General de la Nación, Mexico. Fondo Presidentes, Ramo Lázaro Cárdenas, 508.1/490, caja 593.*

Brownsville to earn a good wage operating heavy machinery for the Port of Brownsville. During the summer harvest he would unload the trains from Matamoros that brought cotton to the storage and dock facilities of the port, and during the rest of the year he would continue to load stored cotton as well as other agricultural products produced in the Texas Valley onto ships bound for the United States, Japan, and Europe. He later married Doña Elisa, and settled in Valle Hermoso. Now retired, Don Fernando enjoys government pension benefits from having worked in both countries.

As we sat chatting in their front yard, Don Fernando spoke to me in Spanish, but Doña Elisa spoke her "native" English, flavored with a Mexican accent that merged with a Texan drawl. None of these designations of place alone reflects who Doña Elisa is: she is at once Mexican, a U.S. native, and Texan. Although she has lived in Valle Hermoso for most of her life, Doña Elisa still identifies herself and her family as many do in that part of the borderlands: "Mexican from Texas," or "Tex-Mex." Even "Tex-Mex" fails to describe the *fronterizo* (borderlands) status of her grandson, Rogelio, who lived in an apartment at the back of the house. He explained to me, with a different accent from that of his grandmother, that he had just moved from Alabama to Valle Hermoso to take care of his grandparents, and was commuting daily to his job as a carpenter building houses on the Texas side of the Valley.[5] There was plenty of work to be had, he said, as the booming construction business turned irrigated vegetable fields into housing for urban workers and retirees. By building

The Colonia 18 de Marzo. *Courtesy of the Archivo General de la Nación, Mexico. Fondo Presidentes, Ramo Lázaro Cárdenas, 508.1/490, caja 593.*

houses on the agricultural lands cleared by previous generations whose labor turned the border into an agricultural emporium, he was continuing and extending the border crossings of his parents, grandparents, and great-grandparents.

Border crossings such as those made by Doña Elisa, Don Benito, Don Fernando, and Rogelio are central to life and livelihood in northern Mexico and the southwestern United States, and they are at the heart of the Valle Bajo Río Bravo irrigated agricultural development project and the regional society that grew up in the delta region of the Río Bravo/Rio Grande in northern Tamaulipas during the twentieth century. Living in Valle Hermoso, I saw how the people cross the border to secure jobs, education, government support, and other resources, or to visit family members or participate in community activities. Sometimes people cross the border simply because they feel they can "breathe more easily" on the other side. What was not immediately evident in the way people in the Bajo Río Bravo spoke of their experiences, however, is that these border crossings contribute to large-scale processes and projects of capital accumulation and state formation. Taken together, the multitude of people who settled the land, built the irrigation works, and financed, cultivated, and processed the cotton in northern Mexico's irrigation districts formed regional societies with distinctive class formations and political cultures.

The Valle Bajo Río Bravo project, of which the "Colonia 18 de Marzo" was an element, was one of many regional irrigated agricultural development projects built by the government in the river valleys of northern Mexico after the Revolution.[6] The Mexican state concentrated its development efforts in the northern borderlands for a number of reasons. First, agricultural, industrial, and mining enterprises were already flourishing in the region because it was connected to the infrastructure, capital, and commodity markets of the United States. Second, capitalist development had generated a large class of skilled but politically volatile migrant workers in the borderlands, which Mexican state officials viewed as a problematic but politically, economically, racially, and culturally valuable resource. Third, the availability of this labor was matched by the availability of land and water in that thinly populated region. In choosing the north as the object of its development efforts, the Mexican state reinforced a process, already under way, of irrigating and settling the semiarid binational border region, displacing livestock ranching as the primary economic activity, and moving cotton production from the old cotton belt of the southern United States into this new area.[7] State financial and technological investment in the borderlands strengthened the popular conceptualization of the north as more developed: more mechanized, more European and American, more white, more civilized, harder working, and more productive. Many of the social and cultural characteristics that define the Mexico-U.S. borderlands today, as well as the popular imagination of that area, originated or were strengthened during the cotton age—the age of "white gold."

This book is an anthropological history of irrigated cotton society in the borderlands. In the chapters that follow I show that the planning, construction, colonization, and subsequent florescence of the irrigated cotton zone in the delta region of the Río Bravo is one episode in a long story of capitalist development and state formation in the Mexican borderlands. After the Mexican Revolution the emergent postrevolutionary state sought to settle landless sharecroppers and migrant rural workers on expropriated *hacienda* land in northern Mexico, and to irrigate that land with the water of the rivers that punctuate the arid landscape of the region. Following the examples set by the Laguna region, in the drainage of the Nazas and Aguanaval rivers in the states of Durango and Coahuila, and Mexicali region, in the delta of the Colorado River in Baja California, many of these new irrigation districts were dedicated to cotton. The Mexican government's promotion of cotton agriculture in its northern borderlands reinforced a shift of cotton production away from the southern United States, and the expansion of investment by U.S. cotton capital in Latin America. The Anderson Clayton Company was particularly important in financing and organizing Mexico's cotton agriculture after the Revolution, and it was given a leading role during the administration of Lázaro Cárdenas in the project to nationalize cotton farms in the Laguna and Mexicali regions, and to expand cotton production for export by building and colonizing an irrigation system in the Valle Bajo Río Bravo.

The irrigation, migration, and cotton politics of the Mexican government were backed ideologically by notions of racial, cultural, social, political, and economic development. These ideas about regional development changed over time, and found expression in the social formations and political cultures of cotton zones such as the Valle Bajo Río Bravo. But plans for the creation and colonization of irrigated cotton zones in the borderlands were not formed in a vacuum, and were not simply imposed by the government and U.S. capital. Rather, these blueprints were a response and adaptation to the particular social and environmental conditions that existed in those regions. By focusing on the complex dynamics of this process, this book shows how global and national forces interacted with regional forces to give borderlands society and culture its particular shape and attitude. In the Valle Bajo Río Bravo, struggles to define region and development continued to shape the efforts of various social and state actors to control the benefits of cotton production throughout the age of white gold (1945–1960).

The detailed history of cotton development in northern Mexico shows that political economy and culture must be viewed together in order to understand the building of the Mexico-U.S. borderlands. It chronicles the actions and interactions of particular groups and individuals—regional and national government officials, migrant workers, cotton businessmen, small farmers, and others—as they struggled to make livelihoods, push forward political projects, increase profits, and shape the world according to their ideas. By describing this history in detail, this book shows how the state's development projects and the world's cotton markets shaped the lives of the people in the region, and, just as important, how those people gave shape to capitalism and state formation as it was lived in the borderlands.

Social Fields of Cotton

Regional, national, and global histories of cotton are woven into the book from start to finish, and this work builds on a tradition of anthropological commodity studies that places emphasis on long-term dynamics of capital accumulation, state formation, the constitution of social classes, migration, resource extraction, and environmental change.[8] From about 1880 to about 1960, cotton was the quintessential crop of the Mexico-U.S. borderlands, the production of which involved much of the region's agricultural land, capital, and labor, and generated similar social conditions throughout the binational region. Cotton production attracted and depended upon large amounts of private and state capital for irrigation infrastructure, agricultural financing, and industrial processing; a stable, settled population of landholders; and great numbers of migrant workers. Borderlands cotton was also the focus of intense development efforts by state and private actors aimed at providing and managing all these elements of production. Despite the generalities in the mode of cotton production and developmental attention, wide variety existed in the ways that labor, capital, and natural resources were provided and organized socially in the different agricultural zones scattered throughout the binational borderlands.[9] In striving to reflect at once both the unity and diversity of human society, this book pays close attention to the specific ways that the global political economy of cotton took shape as regional processes of class and community formation within the particular social and environmental conditions of northern Mexico and the southwestern United States.

The concept of "social field" helps to clarify and condense the relationships between environment, political economy, and culture that are described in the book. The term has a long history in anthropology, and rather than attempt a thorough genealogy I will touch upon some of the ways the term is useful for understanding the social, spatial, and temporal aspects of commodity studies such as this one.[10] A central task of anthropological political economy is analysis of the relations of production and power that structure society.[11] Evoking Marxian concepts of "mode of production" and "social formation,"[12] the idea of the social field directs attention to a wide but historically specific array of protagonists and the power-laden, web-like connections between them, and militates against attributing too much power to just one actor, or collapsing all the actors and inequalities into a one-dimensional discursive space. Pierre Bourdieu elaborates on the relational social dynamics that constitute "fields": universes of concrete things, agents and the relations between them, that comprise specific social spaces marked both by diversity and individuation as well as logics that unify and delimit. Thus there can be very general or very specific fields, which change over time: fields of production such as the field of soft drinks; fields of social classes; a field of the dominant class (which could include a large number of fractions); the field of modern art; the field of consumption; even the field of fields.[13]

The people, practices, and discourses of irrigated cotton development analyzed in this book must be understood as part of a historically changing social field, composed of the productive political relations among a range of actors occupying unequal positions of power in variably configured but nonetheless material geographies. The metaphor of social field suggests "the field": the place where anthropologists have traditionally lived and studied. The discipline has long defined itself among the social sciences and humanities by privileging fieldwork, as well as the ethnographic description of fieldwork sites, which provides the authority of immediacy to anthropological texts. In the last few decades, trends toward the transnationalization of capital and the creation of supranational political and economic regions such as those formalized by the European Union and the North American Free Trade Agreement have stimulated an expansion in the scale of anthropological research, and the inclusion of multiple research loci.[14] At the same time that the scale of anthropological research has been reconfigured, anthropologists have gained a stronger appreciation for the highly constructed character of the spatial units of analysis used by earlier generations. The precepts of "area studies" are now being challenged as a growing awareness of the processes of globalization, diaspora, and migration stirs a general interrogation of the boundedness of cultures, states, classes, races, and spaces.[15] In anthropology, these critiques revitalize a long-standing interest in acculturation and cultural contact, but take the additional step of questioning the fixity of the units that are coming into contact.[16] In thinking about cotton and regional development in the Bajo Río Bravo, I stress the historical constitution of regional societies and spaces, viewing them as precipitates of processes of capital and state formation. I discuss the projects and processes through which culturally specific ideas about "region" have found expression in a regional social field in the Mexican borderlands.

Changes in anthropological notions of space and scale have been accompanied by a deeply processual approach that has introduced historical methods and research agendas into the discipline. The historical turn in anthropology has questioned the location and character of fieldwork by incorporating archival and documentary research, which is usually carried out in cities and towns, among the papers that make up historical archives that are, more often than not, accumulated by governments, businesses, or other organizations. Anthropological approaches to history have interrogated temporal notions of development. The version of development thought that surged in the United States after World War II and was used to organize the political and economic reconstruction of Europe, Asia, and southern countries came into question by the 1970s as the stability of commodity and currency prices crumbled.[17] Armed with tools of discourse theory, anthropologists have set about challenging the premises and goals of development thought and intervention, and pointing out the paradoxes of their often unintended effects.[18] Research on the objective historical processes of development at work in the constitution of social fields must now recognize that ideas about such historical processes form part of the historical processes of development. As we shall see, the language and ideology of development ("developmentalism") played a key role in the creation and colonization of irrigation systems in the Mexican borderlands and, in particular, the delta region of the Río Bravo/Rio Grande.

To understand the history of cotton in the irrigation districts of the Mexico-U.S. borderlands, the physical, environmental dimensions of the concept of social field need to be stressed. Recently anthropologists have taken a newfound interest in the heterogeneous and necessarily local expression of global phenomena in particular environments, marking an advance from political economy approaches, strong in the 1970s and 1980s, toward a more ecumenical political ecology.[19] To capture these environmental dynamics, I suggest that an important idea of "field" might be the most readily accessible one: the image of cultivated land. In northern Mexico, as is the case wherever Spanish is spoken, the word for field (campo) refers to "countryside" (el campo), or the particular fields where one or another crop is grown: fields of cotton (campos de algodon), for example. Fields have specific geographical and environmental characteristics: soil types, temperatures, exposure to sun, rainfall and drainage, winds, plants and animals that live in them, and so on. When the anthropological concept of the social field as a set of human groups, relationships, and processes is superimposed on this one, the image of the field as a natural setting is transformed into that of a landscape where "nature" is an actor, and political ecologies of production, power, and meaning stand out.[20] Because the concept of social field captures these emerging social, spatial, historical, and ecological perspectives, it is particularly useful in the effort to create more robust anthropological political economies.

Irrigation, Agriculture, and Society

Aridity defines the Mexico-U.S. borderlands, and this book shows the fundamental importance of water to the history of the region. Irrigation systems have long been a preferred venue for studying the state, particularly in Mexico. A key founding inspiration was the pioneering work of Karl Wittfogel, who built a theory of the causal relation between irrigation and state formation by welding the findings of archaeologists and historians to the theoretical suggestions made by Karl Marx and Max Weber concerning "Asiatic" societies.[21] Wittfogel's central argument was that the construction and operation of prehistoric irrigation systems in places like Mesopotamia, the Nile, and China required a centralized bureaucracy to mobilize massive amounts of labor, which in turn was supported by irrigated agriculture. Julian Steward, Eric Wolf, and Ángel Palerm used Wittfogel's ideas to explore the relationship between irrigated agriculture and the rise of complex state societies with urban centers in Mexico.[22] Critiques of this theory of hydraulic society came from various directions. On the one hand, historians and archeologists found evidence that irrigation systems were built by states that already existed, effectively reversing the causal direction posited by Wittfogel.[23] Another kind of argument came from those who felt that Wittfogel got his ideas about the "Asiatic mode of production" wrong, or who simply didn't like his anticommunism. Finally, scholars provided evidence of irrigation systems where water was managed democratically, or by a weak state rather than a bureaucratic or despotic one.[24]

Although scholars have largely discredited Wittfogel's theory, politics and power remain at the center of research on water management in Mexico, Latin America, and elsewhere. Debating "oriental despotism" is no longer on the agenda, but historians and archaeologists still find important connections between the long-term expansion of state power and the control of water.[25] Law is an obvious domain of state activity, and historians, in particular, have dedicated energy to understanding the importance of law in the negotiation of control over hydraulic resources.[26] Other research has placed attention on the local forms of organization and management of irrigation systems, and the processes of centralization, rationalization, and discipline by which these local arrangements are subjugated to national or colonial government power.[27] Detailed regional studies have shown that the image of the irrigation system as the carefully engineered creation of an all-powerful state does not reflect the importance of local actors and environments in the constitution of irrigated social fields.[28]

In this book I describe how the hydrological dynamics of the Río Bravo/Rio Grande, and the landscape of that river's delta, shaped efforts to turn the region into an irrigated agricultural emporium. The Río Bravo/Rio Grande, like most arid-lands rivers, has always had dramatic flood stages during the hurricane season of late summer. On the Mexican side of the Río Bravo/Rio Grande delta in the 1930s, a combined flood control and irrigation system was built using levees, floodgates, and reservoirs that followed and accentuated the region's topography and the river's flood patterns, diverting and storing excess waters and channeling them to the agricultural fields. Even when a large dam and canal system superceded the earlier levee and floodgate system in the early 1950s, the new irrigation system utilized the flood method, and so the fields around Matamoros continued to receive periodic inundations. Cotton was exceptionally well suited to these flood patterns, and to the hybrid landscape that was built in the Río Bravo/Rio Grande delta. The history of water and cotton shows how the social formation that took shape to produce and process this crop was connected in this way to the environment of the region, itself a human artifact produced dialectically and historically through the actions and decisions of the region's inhabitants.[29]

The move from analyzing total state power to studying local irrigated landscapes and social fields is consistent with a general historical movement from centralization/state control to decentralization/private control of water resources around the world. The twentieth century was the century of massive hydraulic works, and the governments of Mexico and the United States built irrigation systems in almost every adequate location in the arid lands that form the border region.[30] As this happened, local systems were subjugated to national systems. The debate over despotic state formation and irrigation, so important to Mexican anthropologists in the 1940s and 1950s, took place in this context of massive spending on hydraulic works by a one-party state and the destruction or reconfiguration of countless local productive adaptations as lakes and marshes were drained, rivers dammed, and aquifers tapped. At the end of the twentieth century, governments and international financing institutions such as the World Bank and the International Monetary Fund shifted their hydraulic philosophy from one of centralized, state-led development to one of local control.[31] In Mexico in the 1990s, at a time when state revenue for costly hydraulic infrastructure was limited, legal reforms were carried out to privatize the management and operation of irrigation systems by handing them over to their users. Anthropologists have followed these tendencies, and a resurgent interest in water and irrigation has centered on small-scale, sustainable systems that provide an alternative to large-scale systems, as well as possible models for the restructuring of irrigated agriculture.[32]

Because the anthropology of water was born in the debates over "oriental despotism" and state formation, because problems of scarcity have led to serious conflicts,[33] and because of the recent legal and organizational changes in water management,[34] more energy has been dedicated to studying the politics of water than to understanding the changing social uses of water. Commodity studies, with their fundamentally economic and ecological approach to understanding the histories of particular social fields, are capable of linking bureaucratic rationalization, discipline, despotism, local organization, centralization, and other concepts used to discuss the politics and power of water to the basic issue of social reproduction. The focus of this book on the productive, social use of water for irrigated cotton agriculture rescues, in some ways, the posture taken by Ángel Palerm in his studies of agriculture, irrigation, and society in Mesoamerica.[35] Rather than concentrate on despotic state power or even politics, Palerm used ethnographic data to show how different uses of land and water resulted in different agricultural yields and population densities. He combined this information with archaeological evidence to make an argument for the connection between irrigation, agricultural surplus, urbanization, and, finally, complex societies marked by social differentiation and states. In the cultural ecology of Ángel Palerm, power is understood as the politics of producing and distributing goods in human landscapes with particular land-water-labor systems, rather than the politics of organizing and using water itself.

The lessons learned from the literature on irrigation and state formation are relevant to a more recent discussion among historians and anthropologists interested in the importance of popular culture to the formation of the postrevolutionary state in Mexico.[36] Stimulated in different ways by Antonio Gramsci and Michel Foucault, these scholars present a strong argument that the state, rather than an institution or central locus of power, should be seen as power embodied and enacted in quotidian settings and in the realm of the culture. One result of the florescence of this "new cultural history"[37] within the bounds of the historiography of the Mexican state is that definitions of "culture" have been generated that are saturated with political power, but mostly devoid of production.[38] In these accounts, the state is more cultural than economic, and "culture" is more symbolic and "artifactual" than processual and generative. In the detailed history of social fields of cotton presented in this book, I hope to correct those imbalances. After the Revolution, the leaders of the formative Mexican state mounted a strong cultural project to reinforce national power on the northern border, but they assumed that this cultural and political development could only be achieved through the expansion of cotton production for export.

The management of agricultural labor was a key element of state formation in the borderlands. During the rule of Porfirio Díaz (1877–1910), the expansion of agriculture, mining, and industry in northern Mexico and the southwestern United States drove the formation of a sizable, highly mobile, and politically volatile class of semiproletarianized Mexican workers in the borderlands.[39] This labor force formed the rank and file of the northern armies that fought, and won, the Mexican Revolution (1910–1920). The postrevolutionary state's irrigated development and colonization projects were aimed at rooting these people to the land, and it was assumed that this would make them productive and politically quiescent middle-class citizens. At the same time that they posed a threat and constituted a problem, migrants were also considered to be a resource because of the industrial work skills and discipline they had acquired in the plantations and factories of the borderlands. By making these workers into small farmers and fulfilling their productive capacities, government planners hoped to convert them into responsible citizens who would form the basis of state power.

To achieve these developmental goals the government sought to capture the water of the international rivers—the Río Bravo (or Rio Grande, when seen from the United States) and the Río Colorado—with dams and canals, and use it for the production of cotton. Mexico's National Irrigation Commission, created in 1926, planned and built regional societies from the ground up, where the state could provide and manage all the physical and social infrastructure necessary to create rural Mexico anew: health care, sanitation, electricity, housing, education, and so on. Because it was a strong earner of dollars, was the basis of textile industries, promised to support the formation of a small-farmer agricultural society, and brought with it a host of associate industries (gins, oil presses, factories to make soap and livestock feed, livestock production, etc.), cotton was viewed as the development crop *por excelencia*. Moreover, cotton exports provided the government with the tax revenue it needed to implement its material, cultural politics of state formation in the borderlands. By looking beyond the ideologically charged pronouncements of these governments (and the positive and negative readings of those pronouncements) to the productive politics of water, labor, and cotton, we find state formation to be a fundamentally economic process and project.

Though this book explores the political economy of cotton, this does not mean that culture is excluded, but rather that culture is seen as an integral and material part of the social field of cotton. One of the great achievements of Marxist anthropology has been precisely this unification of political economy and culture,[40] and in this book I argue that languages and ideas of development, region, and race shaped society, economy, and culture in the borderlands. Recent anthropological and historical research on race and racism in Latin America has described the multiplicity of meanings within racial discourse, and has shown that racial categories, terms, and identities such as *mestizo* and *indio* have been constantly reworked by all kinds of social actors through material, political struggles that also pivot on class, region, nation, and gender.[41] Although development is an idea inseparable from the biological and cultural concept of evolution that holds such a central place in popular and scientific thought in the nineteenth and twentieth centuries,[42] little concern has been given to the connections between race and development. Ideas about biology and race permeated the development discourse of the Mexican federal government, and these racialized development ideas shaped the construction and colonization of irrigation zones in northern Mexico between 1926 and 1940. The inhabitants of northern Mexico were presumed to be culturally, biologically, socially, and economically more advanced than their compatriots in the central and southern regions, which gave them a patina of "whiteness" in the gaze of the mostly northern Mexican government leaders. This popular conception of the *mestizo* and *criollo* "whiteness" of the north was articulated, theorized, and codified in the work and writing of the politicians, engineers, and social scientists who contributed to development planning in the Valle Bajo Río Bravo irrigation zone. The history of irrigated development in the borderlands shows how these ideas took material form in state projects to create regional spaces and racialized social fields.

Arguments, Sections, and Chapters

The evidence, analysis, arguments, and narrative style presented in this book, as well as the methods used in the research phase, bridge the disciplines of anthropology and history, and engage themes important to scholars in both Mexico and the United States. In writing for an interdisciplinary, transnational audience with varied scholarly practices and standards, I was forced to make difficult decisions and compromises, with the knowledge that the book might not live up fully to the expectations of any one audience. Different disciplines do things differently. Historians may be satisfied by the detail of the evidence presented, but may find that the theoretical discussions distract attention from the narrative. Anthropologists might appreciate the theoretical reflections, but question the preponderance of archival evidence over interviews and observation. Those interested in the political economy of development might find the attention to local history excessive. Even within the disciplines of anthropology and history there will be readers who find the book short on political economy and long on culture, or the other way around. The same issues arise between scholars of Mexico and Latin America, and those who study U.S. history. Cotton is a theme that U.S. historians—especially historians of the South and Southwest—will be quite familiar with, but that is barely studied in Latin America. Revolution and state formation are topics of intense interest in Mexico, but hardly as much so in the United States. The themes of water and race have attracted more attention in the history of the U.S. West than they have in the history of northern Mexico.

Despite these differences, I have tried to construct a text that respects and engages both history and anthropology, as well as literature from both Mexico and the United States. To reduce confusion, in-text citations were eliminated and endnotes were used exclusively. Historians will most likely be comfortable with this, but social scientists may find that following the discussion of relevant literature in the endnotes is a bit cumbersome. The book, then, is an invitation to enter into a dialogue: between history and anthropology, between theory and evidence, between past and present, between archival research and ethnography, between political economy and culture, and between the national and regional intellectual traditions in Mexico and the United States.

The book is divided in two parts. The first (chapters 2 and 3) provides an understanding of the larger context of cotton capitalism and state formation in northern Mexico, and the second (chapters 4 to 8) discusses how this history unfolded in the Valle Bajo Río Bravo. Chapter 2 ("Cotton and Capitalism in the Borderlands, 1820–1920") demonstrates the usefulness of telling histories that follow a particular commodity—in this case, cotton. Cotton was a plant native to the river valleys of the semiarid borderlands, but it was not an important commercial crop in that

region until the Union blockade of southern cotton during the U.S. Civil War created global fiber shortages and turned the Mexican north into a nexus of the world
cotton economy. I show that the flow of cotton from Confederate Texas to Matamoros and then to European consumers resulted in an accumulation of capital in
northern Mexico that laid the basis for regional textile industries and commercial
cotton agriculture. The new Laguna cotton zone that was built after 1880 was considered the model of agriculture-based development for subsequent irrigated cotton
schemes in northern Mexico, but the Mexican Revolution (1910–1920) made it clear
that the formation of a highly mobile and politically volatile mass of cotton workers could have dramatic unplanned consequences. The Mexican governments that
assumed power after the Revolution sought to take advantage of favorable trends
in the world cotton economy by stimulating production of the fiber in borderlands
irrigation systems, a move that was also designed to ameliorate political conflict by
settling landless agricultural workers as small farmers.

The effort to increase cotton production in the borderlands was a project of
state formation aimed at reducing political instability and "civilizing" the semiproletarianized inhabitants of northern Mexico. In chapter 3 ("Developmentalism in
Northern Mexico, 1910–1934") I discuss the efforts by postrevolutionary Mexican
governments to create regional cotton-producing agricultural societies in the northern borderlands by settling migrant workers in irrigation systems. I trace a change in
the philosophy and practice of state-led development in Mexico from a laissez-faire
stance to an interventionist one. Because of ideological conviction, and financial and
political limits to the power of their governments, Presidents Francisco Madero and
Alvaro Obregón placed the agency of development in the historical process of evolution. The tendency toward greater state agency in the process of development led to
the creation in 1926, by the government of Plutarco Elias Calles, of the Mexican National Irrigation Commission (Comisión Nacional de Irrigación, or CNI). Calles's
land and water politics were backed by a vision of an agrarian north populated by
a class of small farmers constituted by rehabilitated former *rancheros* (ranchers)
and migrant workers. Anthropologist Manuel Gamio's stress on the racial-cultural
dimensions of "integral regional" development played an important role in shaping
the vision and blueprints of the CNI, and I discuss the anthropologist's relationship
with the institutions and actors of the Calles government. Finally, I show the importance of these ideas about integral regional development in the creation of one such
cotton-producing agricultural zone in the northern borderlands, the "Don Martín"
irrigation system in the states of Coahuila and Nuevo León.

Chapters 4 through 8 form the second large section of the book, in which I
describe the delta region of the Río Bravo, placing attention on land tenure and
use, the emerging cotton economy, social class formation, and development thought
within that historically dynamic social field. Patterns of land tenure and use established between 1780 and 1900 changed as cotton ranching gave way to commercial
cotton agriculture, and, in the 1930s, a particular conjuncture of regional, national,

and international ideas, events, and processes paved the way for the implementation of long-standing plans to turn the Mexican side of the delta into a cotton emporium. These plans were drafted and constantly redrawn to confront the particular contingencies of the social field of cotton development as it materialized in the region, but nevertheless formed the basis of land reform, colonization, the remapping of regional space, and the constitution of new social categories and subjects.

Chapter 4 ("Land and Labor in the Río Bravo/Rio Grande Delta, 1780–1930") describes how patterns of land use and tenure based on kin relations and communal resource management formed the basis of a regional mode of production and social formation in the Río Bravo delta, and how that mode of production and social formation changed with the advent of commercial agriculture in the first few decades of the twentieth century. By 1930, this uneven transition on the Mexican side of the border had generated deep social divisions, which would provide room for the developmental intervention of the federal government in the region during the crisis years of the Great Depression (1929–1940). The extraordinary conditions of the crisis years served as a catalyst for state development intervention in the Valle Bajo Río Bravo. As we shall see in chapter 5 ("Crisis and Development in the Valle Bajo Río Bravo, 1930–1935"), the U.S. government responded to the crisis of the world cotton economy with price supports and acreage reduction measures, which served to reduce supply and boost prices. This provided a structure of opportunity for development-minded state officials in Latin America, who responded with efforts to promote cotton production both for export and for burgeoning domestic textile industries. When, in the early 1930s, the Valle Bajo Río Bravo was hit by a succession of devastating floods and a wave of return migration from the United States, the Mexican government revived dormant plans for developing an irrigated cotton zone in the region. The Cárdenas government, in particular, set land reform and agriculture as priorities, and, in order to facilitate its development plans, negotiated an alliance with a regional political bloc consisting of rural and urban, popular and elite sectors in Matamoros. In 1935 flood control and irrigation works were begun by the Secretary of Communications and Public Works, under the direction of Francisco Múgica and Eduardo Chávez.

Between 1935 and 1939, the Cárdenas government moved forward with plans to develop the Valle Bajo Río Bravo. Chapter 6 ("*Cardenista* Engineering, The Anderson Clayton Company, and Rural Unrest in the Río Bravo Delta, 1935–1939") argues that state-led irrigated cotton development in the Bajo Río Bravo should be seen as a process of negotiating power and resources between a host of actors both within and outside the region. Rather than a unilateral enactment of a government "blueprint," *cardenismo* in this stretch of the borderlands was a process of negotiation through which the state sought to implement a collectivist, industrial vision of agricultural society within the bounds established by the government's dependency on foreign cotton capital as well as the political resistance of regional social actors. Following the expropriations of cotton plantations in the Laguna and Mexicali areas during 1936 and 1937, Cárdenas negotiated a deal with the Anderson Clayton Company by which the U.S. cotton giant agreed to finance and commercialize Mexico's public-sector (*ejido*) production in exchange for a guaranteed profit share. With the cotton economy under the trusteeship of the Anderson Clayton Company and the federal government, and the agricultural development project in construction in the Valle Bajo Río Bravo, Cárdenas plotted an ambitious course to expand Mexican cotton exports tenfold. Chapter 7 ("Repatriation in the Río Bravo Delta, 1935–1940") explains that because of serious resistance to collectivization in the region, and when it became clear that skilled cotton farmers were needed to pilot the expansionist cotton program, the government scuttled its collectivist vision in favor of a plan to settle Mexicans repatriated from the United States in colonies of property-owning small farmers.

During the late 1930s and early 1940s, the planning and creation of an agricultural landscape in the hinterland of Matamoros inhabited by cotton-producing small farmers was carried along by a strong narrative of regional development propagated by the state. This discourse and practice of historical progress and regional community gained strength as it was reproduced by farmers, workers, and regional leaders in the years that followed. Chapter 8 ("Defining Development in the Río Bravo Delta, 1940–1963") discusses the expansion of cotton production and cotton society in the Valle Bajo Río Bravo, and traces the ongoing struggle among regional and federal government actors to define, and control the benefits of, this regional development. In 1944 the federal government sought to assert control over the marketing of the burgeoning Matamoros cotton crop, but met with fierce resistance from the emergent class of regional cotton merchants and industrialists. Both sides in this struggle used the language of regional development to solidify cross-class alliances within the region in support of their efforts to control the cotton economy.

After 1945, the Matamoros cotton economy boomed. The expansion of the world economy in the postwar years was provoked by U.S. government foreign aid spending and, in the case of cotton, continued domestic price supports and acreage restrictions by the U.S. Department of Agriculture. Despite the immense amount of wealth generated by cotton production in the Valle Bajo Río Bravo, there was a severe lack of public services in rural areas, and in 1950 the small farmers settled during the Cárdenas period mounted a campaign to secure benefits of development such as electricity, water, schools, and telephones. As they fought for municipal independence against a political group led by the cotton industrialists of Matamoros, the inhabitants of the region around Valle Hermoso gave new definitions to the concepts of regional community and historical development. Although the secession was successful, changes in U.S. cotton policy led to the demise of cotton production in the Valle Bajo Río Bravo by 1960. Despite the passage of forty years since the cotton boom turned bust, memories and histories of the "age of white gold" are still strong, and the language of regional development continues to define political culture in the region today.

PART I

THE BORDER, MEXICO, AND THE WORLD

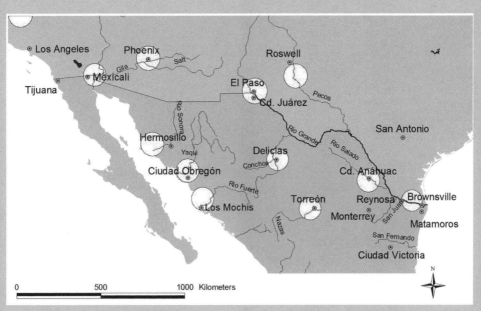

Irrigated cotton zones, 1900–1960.

CHAPTER 2
COTTON AND CAPITALISM IN THE BORDERLANDS, 1820–1920

During the eighteenth and nineteenth centuries, *mestizo* and indigenous peasants from Mesoamerica settled near water sources throughout northern Mexico and the southwestern United States, learning to live with aridity and battling nomadic groups of indigenous people.[1] This long history of peasant communities in northern Mexico notwithstanding, what came to define the region in the late-nineteenth and twentieth centuries was the growth of railroads, mining, and commercial agricultural enterprises, and social formations characterized by a regional bourgeoisie and a large, migratory class of "semi-industrial, semi-agricultural" workers.[2] In an oft-cited essay about the "peculiarities" of northern Mexico, Barry Carr argued that many of the men who led the armies of the Mexican Revolution (1910–1920) and rose to national power as a result of the fighting came from this northern bourgeoisie. Their liberalism, entrepreneurialism, racism, and anticlericalism were forged in those conditions "peculiar" to northern Mexico, and the northern character of these men guided the formation of the state, society, and economy after the Revolution.[3]

In this chapter I discuss the emergence of this new borderlands society by tracing the history of cotton in the region. Cotton, cultivated by an army of migratory workers, was central to the constitution of systems of production and social classes in Mexicali and the Imperial Valley, El Paso and Ciudad Juarez, the Comarca Lagunera in Durango and Coahuila, the area around Corpus Christi, the Salt River Valley in Arizona, the San Joaquin Valley in California, the Yaqui and Mayo river valleys in Sonora, the Río Conchos in Chihuahua, and the Matamoros and Brownsville region where the Río Bravo empties into the Gulf of Mexico. Cotton production in the borderlands was characterized by large plantations and migrant labor, by industrial production techniques and mechanization, by massive irrigation systems and the rationalization of space, by a struggle to control the waters of the international rivers, and by huge demands for capital met by both private and state investment. I highlight three dimensions of this history. The first is the regional, national, and international political economy of cotton. The social dimensions of irrigated cotton agriculture—labor, its settlement, and migration—will also be discussed. The third dimension is the creation of irrigation zones, and the struggle to control the waters of the international rivers shared by the United States and Mexico. By following cotton we move beyond the limits of the locality to confront the "regional particularities" of a larger domain—the borderlands.[4] At the same time, the story of cotton in the borderlands forces us to avoid reproducing the boundedness of community studies on the scale of region. Instead, to understand cotton production in the Mexico-U.S. borderlands we must take into consideration global systems of textile production involving cotton agricultural zones, cotton markets, industrial centers, capital, and imperial states that extend their web-like connections across the planet. I follow the fiber around the globe in order to discuss the social relations of the people organized within global networks of cotton production, exchange, and consumption.

Although cotton is native to the borderlands, it was not its status as an indigenous plant that placed it at the center of the evolution of capitalism in the region, but rather the integration of the borderlands into global systems of industrial textile production. The emergence in Mexico of a textile industry during the nineteenth century, promoted by federal and state governments, in turn generated demand for fiber, which, despite serious efforts to establish commercial cotton agriculture, was met by imports from the southern United States. The Union blockade of Confederate exports during the Civil War in the United States (1861–1865) caused a severe shortage of cotton fiber in the textile centers of the northern United States and Europe, as well as Mexico. In this context, the dramatic intensification of overland cotton commerce between the U.S. South and northern Mexico led to the accumulation of capital in the city of Monterrey. When trade fell off after the war, merchant capitalists reinvested in local textile industries and cotton agriculture. Along with important land reforms, this capital investment laid the basis for the growth, after 1885, of the Laguna region as the first major irrigated cotton zone in the Mexico-U.S. borderlands.

The lasting effect of the cotton famine was to demonstrate to textile industrialists and their government allies their dependence on U.S. cotton sources. Insecurity about cotton supplies led the governments of Europe to expand cotton production in colonized areas such as Egypt, India, and the Sudan, and to seek new sources in nation-states such as Mexico and Brazil. The search for new cotton sources gained further impulse after 1900 from the destruction caused by the boll weevil in the old cotton belt of the U.S. South. The delta region of the Colorado River, shared by California and Baja California, was opened to cotton production at that time, and when the demand for cotton created by World War I (1914–1918) combined with the availability of labor generated by the migration northward of Mexicans seeking to escape the violence of Revolution (1910–1920), that border agricultural zone boomed. After World War I, shifting global trade relations and the dynamic of the cotton market further accentuated the migration of cotton production westward and southward from the old cotton belt of the U.S. South. Presented with favorable market conditions, Mexican and U.S. authorities sought to expand cotton production in the river valleys of the borderlands by taming the waters of the Río Bravo/Rio Grande and Colorado river systems with hydraulic projects and international treaties. The state-led irrigated cotton development projects of the Mexican borderlands were intended to be engines of progress for the region and nation, and to provide lands on which to colonize landless and migrant workers as small farmers.

Colonial Ecologies

To understand how cotton came to dominate borderlands society and economy after 1880 we must first look at the relationship developed by the inhabitants of the region with their environment before irrigation and commercial agriculture was introduced. Most of northern Mexico is very dry, except for the two big mountain chains which run north-south. Seasonal rain in the Sierra Madre Occidental fills the rivers of the Pacific slope and those that drain into the interior. Moisture from the Gulf of Mexico results in late-summer rainfall on the eastern slope of the Sierra Madre Oriental. The occasional tropical storm or hurricane will slam into the Gulf Coast, or the southern end of the Baja California peninsula, Sinaloa and Southern Sonora. Before they were controlled by massive hydraulic works in the early years of the twentieth century, the flows of rivers of the borderlands followed a fairly predictable pattern. With relatively little organic matter to hold the water in the desert soil, rainwater would barrel down the river courses, scouring out canyons and overflowing the banks when it reached the delta regions. The river systems of the Colorado, the Río Bravo/Rio Grande, the Yaqui, the Mayo and Fuerte, and the Aguanaval and Nazas of the Laguna region followed this pattern during the rainy season, while the dry season reduced these rivers to a trickle.

Before the arrival of the Spaniards, much of the borderlands, like desert environments elsewhere, supported a plethora of small, nomadic groups of people who made their living from gathering and hunting. Often these groups would settle for a while during the drier months around a perennial water source, and resume their movement during the wetter months. In the hot river delta areas of the borderlands a form of flood-recession agriculture was practiced that responded to the cyclical pattern of flooding and desiccation typical of rivers in arid zones. When storms or snowmelt brought silt-laden waters flooding down the river, the inundation watered and fertilized the soil. Small-scale irrigation works were also built by indigenous groups to aid irrigation in the floodlands. After the water receded, these lands were planted with corn, squash, and other food crops. In the higher elevations, sedentary, complex societies practiced irrigated agriculture, built urban centers, and engaged in significant trade with central Mexico. Canals and ditches watered crops in the region long before Spaniards, criollos, and indigenous immigrants arrived with their knowledge of irrigated farming.[5]

The colonists of the eighteenth century are credited with bringing the agricultural cultivation of cotton to the borderlands.[6] Long before Europeans arrived, however, wild cotton, which reached heights of 20 feet and produced fiber annually for five years or more, was gathered to make textiles. Cotton has a few qualities that allowed it to thrive in the riverine environments of the borderlands, and that continue to make its cultivation in the region attractive. The first set of qualities has to do with water. Cotton has an extremely deep taproot, which enables it to continue to soak up water when the surface of the soil is dry. Thus the cotton plant is well suited to the cycles of flooding and drought that characterized these rivers. After a deep period of flooding, the plant is able to mature without subsequent rainfall or flooding. In fact, its fibers are often damaged by excessive rain, especially during the period of maturation just before and during picking, when the cotton bolls open up and the fiber is exposed.

Other conditions found in the borderlands also support the cultivation of cotton. First, the whole area lies roughly at a latitude of about 30 degrees north, which is sufficiently far north to experience marked seasonal changes in temperature, and in the length of the days. The cold winters in the borderlands combat the proliferation of insects. Most of the borderlands area experiences at least a few nights of frost each year, which kills insects, their eggs, and larvae. Also, the long, cloudless, extremely hot summer days provide the plant with the sunlight needed for it to create useable energy through photosynthesis. Because of the lack of water in the atmosphere, at night the temperatures fall markedly. Cool, short nights during the growing season reduce the plant's "dark respiration," the process by which photosynthesized material is lost at night. Taken together, these geographical and climatic conditions of the borderlands contributed to high yields for Mexican cotton production in the late-nineteenth and twentieth centuries. Of course, for capitalist cotton agriculture to flourish in the arid borderlands, these natural advantages had to be complemented by monumental human effort.[7]

Mexican Industrial Development and the World Cotton Trade

Although cotton is indigenous to the borderlands, to understand the emergence of commercial cotton agriculture during the late-nineteenth and twentieth centuries we must follow our commodity far from the region, to the centers of the textile industry in Europe, the United States, and central Mexico. For it is the industrial centers that generated the demand for fiber, provided the material reward for its supply, and dressed the whole transaction in the new clothes of empire. Despite the intense interest in the history of the textile industry in Europe, the cotton-producing areas of the world and their links to the metropolitan centers are not nearly as well understood. Although, as Allen Isaacman and Richard Roberts state, "raw cotton was the single most important item of commerce in the Atlantic basin in the nineteenth century," its production and trade outside of the southern United States and Europe are only just beginning to receive the attention they deserve.[8]

Cotton agriculture in Mexico has always been linked to textile production. Even before the arrival of the Spaniards, cotton produced in the coastal areas of Veracruz was woven by local artisans into cloth that was used for trade and tribute with the

Aztec empire. The weaving of these fine and scarce textiles for trade gave way during the colonial period to the mass production of coarser cotton *manta* that was made into the clothing worn by the majority of Mexicans. The leaders of the new republic, guided by the model of development represented by England's textile industry, aimed to replace artisan forms of cotton cloth production with factory production. With the independence from Spain secured in 1821, prominent figures such as Estevan de Antuñano and Lucas Alamán encouraged the federal government to support a national textile industry. Federal tariffs were established to protect the nascent cotton industry in the 1820s and 1830s, and the rise of Antonio Bustamante to national power in 1830 brought with it the establishment of the Banco de Avío, which sought to use public funds to modernize production techniques.[9] Private capital, both Mexican and foreign, was also crucial to the financing of the fledgling industry. From its birth as an independent nation, then, Mexico had decided upon a state-supported industrial development program—a program that also promoted domestic cotton agriculture and was intimately linked to world markets for capital, cotton fiber, and manufactures.

As early as 1838, just eight years after embarking upon the cotton textile development program, it became clear that Mexico's production of cotton fiber was inadequate to the demands of the expanding industry. Between 1830 and 1850 it was common that only 50 percent of the installed capacity of the textile industry was being used at any one time, due to a lack of fiber. This industry was also quite limited in its geographical scope, with most factories located in Puebla, most fiber originating in nearby Veracruz, and the manufactures largely consumed in the altiplano surrounding Mexico City. By 1843, 80 percent of Mexican cotton fiber came from Veracruz, but Mexico's cotton cultivators were supplying less than 20 percent of what was needed by the textile industry. The rest was imported from New Orleans and East Texas.[10]

The failure of the new Mexican Republic to produce enough fiber for its own textile industries generated two responses: at the same time that the smuggling of contraband cotton from New Orleans and Texas boomed, developmental efforts were made to stimulate cotton agriculture at home. From about 1800 on, most of the world's cotton was grown in the southern United States. Mexico's industrialists sought U.S. cotton because of its good quality and the fact that the textile machinery they imported from France and England was designed to process the particular fiber lengths of the U.S. product. National leaders established protectionist tariffs in the hope that high domestic prices would stimulate national production of cotton fiber, but U.S. cotton, produced by slaves, was cheap and abundant, and those tariffs combined with slack enforcement to make contraband cotton a hugely profitable business. Protectionist policies were also established by regional elites interested in guarding their own textile industries against this growing federally supported industry in Puebla, but, again, these measures often served no more than to increase the movement of contraband.

The fiscal and legal measures designed to stimulate national fiber production did not achieve their end, and Alamán met this failure with a proposal to colonize the coastal areas where cotton grew and where population was scarce. According to local historians of the Río Conchos region in Chihuahua, Alamán also considered that area for a cotton-producing colonization project. This proposal bore insignificant results, but can be seen as an early attempt to overcome the limits of an agricultural landscape dominated by *haciendas,* for the most part, and indigenous communities. Despite the ongoing scarcity in cotton fiber, the *haciendas* were not motivated by import tariffs to increase production. They chose to maintain scarcity instead, and profit from the artificially high prices secured by the state's intervention. Indigenous communities, on the other hand, were more likely to defend their land against incursions by the *haciendas,* and produce food for their own consumption rather than cotton for outside markets. Given the situation, Alamán proposed to colonize medium-sized parcels of land with foreign colonists who, he argued, would be more entrepreneurial than the *hacendados* and the *comunidades.* Although Alamán was a conservative, he embraced the strategy of liberals who had been impressed by the agrarian development of the United States. This development vision of a Mexican landscape of small farmers dedicated to commercial cotton agriculture would continue to influence agrarian politics through the 1930s.[11]

Cotton Famine, Civil Wars, and Foreign Intervention: 1861–1865

In the 1860s a constellation of international and domestic events dramatically changed the course of Mexico's cotton agriculture, trade, and industry, and set the conditions for the growth of regional cotton societies in northern Mexico during the reign of Porfirio Díaz (1876–1911). The most important event was the Civil War in the United States (1861–1865), which prevented most of the cotton produced in the cotton belt of the southern United States from leaving port. During the first 60 years of the nineteenth century, the southern United States produced almost all of the cotton used by the industrial centers in England, France, Germany, and the northeastern United States, and much of that used in central Mexico. Although the U.S. mainland exported almost no cotton in the eighteenth century, when the cotton gin was invented in 1793 it became profitable to separate the seed from the lint of the short-staple upland varieties that grew well in that area. The expansion of cotton in the United States was rapid: between 1790 and 1810, U.S. cotton production increased by 6000 percent. With this expansion the United States rapidly came to dominate the world market in the fiber: by 1810 England received 50 percent of its cotton from the United States, and by 1830, about 80 percent. France, too, followed the demand-side pressure of its burgeoning textile industries and became dependent on U.S. cotton. By 1860 that country was purchasing 93 percent of its cotton from the United States.[12]

The U.S. economy also depended on its southern cotton exports. In fact, in the early nineteenth century, cotton accounted for around 40 percent of the nation's total exports, and generated much of the foreign currency that financed the industrialization of the country.[13] The industrial growth and territorial expansion of the United States made it a debtor nation until World War I, and its huge cotton exports served to balance payments with Europe. Surpluses were unheard of in the United States, as the European textile industries were fed by U.S. fiber and because cotton sales to Europe kept the importing economies healthy by equalizing their balance of payments. The South also produced the raw material for the industrialization of the northern states. In the South, cotton was the lifeblood of the economy, and the basis of the plantation system, which provided, through slavery, the enormous amount of labor needed for the harvest.

Disruption to the cotton trade caused by the U.S. Civil War had a huge impact on the world's textile industries and cotton agriculture. When the war began in 1861, the northern states imposed a naval blockade on the southern states, in order to keep their cotton from reaching market. This was largely successful, and after the stocks of cotton accumulated previously in Europe ran out, a "famine" of cotton fiber struck European industry. The southern Congress in Richmond countered with decrees prohibiting the export of the fiber and even mandating its destruction, measures aimed at forcing England and France—its biggest customers—to defy the Union blockade, resume trade, and recognize the Confederate government. At that time the English were actively trying to get the Mexican government to pay back loans that were in default. Although they were desperate for cotton, they chose to intervene neither politically nor commercially in the Civil War on behalf of the Confederates, nor to secure cotton through military intervention in Mexico. Instead, they maintained their support for the Union, scrambled for supplies of the fiber from India, Egypt, and elsewhere, and began a long-term effort to secure and establish new sources of the fiber in their colonies and in other, independent nations. The French were perhaps even more dependent on U.S. cotton, and the same shortages hit their industry, causing widespread unemployment and hunger in 1862–1863. Unlike the British, they were ready to intervene militarily in the western hemisphere in order to guarantee a steady cotton supply. Paris officials even proposed to the governor of Texas that his state form an independent republic under the protection of France. The control of cotton sources was one reason why, in 1862, France invaded Mexico and set up an imperial government.[14]

As in England and France, the textile industry in Mexico depended on U.S. cotton fiber and was threatened by the disruption of trade caused by the Civil War. To make matters worse, Mexico was already suffering through its own civil war. Conservatives and liberals had been at odds since Independence. When liberal Benito Juárez became president and introduced a new constitution in 1857 matters disintegrated further, and by 1858 the country was wracked by open warfare. In 1862 French troops invaded Mexico in support of centralist opponents of Juárez's liberal government, and in 1864 Maximilian was installed as the ruler of the French imperial government in Mexico. After a series of military defeats, Juárez was chased to the thinly populated expanses of northern Mexico, where he continued to raise support for his cause, usually by conceding political and economic favors to local populations. The northern elite saw in Juárez's federalism an opportunity to ease trade restrictions, enforce the autonomy of regional civil administration, and ensure the strength of state militias. Northern liberalism, with its roots in the settlement and colonization projects of the Bourbon era, was given strong impetus during the Mexican Civil War.[15]

The French hoped to use Mexico in the way that the British used India, alleviating shortages at home by importing its cotton fiber. Envisioning itself as a manufacturing center, and Mexico as a consumer market, France encouraged the production of raw cotton in Mexico and discouraged the manufacturing of textiles there. Despite their liberalism in other aspects of rule, the French increased the number of tariffs, and made them more complicated. With tariffs commonly above 100 percent of the price of the goods, and a government too weak to control its borders, contraband surged. Much of this trade originated in New Orleans, and coastal ships were outfitted with Mexican flags to protect them while they transported their goods to phantom factories on the coast of Veracruz, where phony labels of origin were affixed before fiber and cloth entered further into the country. The surge in contraband provoked by French imperial policy was further accentuated by the cotton famine, when the price of raw cotton doubled. Needless to say, the bales of blockaded cotton stacked up in southern ports must have been extremely attractive to enterprising Mexican merchants, who had ready markets in Europe as well as in Mexico.[16]

Mexico's experience with the cotton famine was also strongly conditioned by the fact that it shared a long, porous border with the southern United States. During this period in the early 1860s textiles were brought to Mexico as usual from the northeastern United States and Europe. Southern cotton fiber, on the other hand, was forced to take new routes to Mexico. The only way for cotton to leave the South was to either run the Union's naval blockade, or to travel south through Texas. Confederate cotton, which before had left Galveston and New Orleans for destinations on the shores of Veracruz, was now shipped south along the Gulf Coast by steamer or overland by ox-cart to Matamoros, where it was re-exported. Despite the complicated route and the difficulties in getting the cotton from the mouth of the Río Bravo/Rio Grande to the ships waiting offshore, this trade soon reached truly massive proportions. By early 1863 some two hundred ships were waiting for cargo off the coast at any given moment, and a number of European countries had established consulates in Matamoros's improvised port town of Bagdad. The British customs houses in London counted imports of 3 million pounds (6000 bales) by 1863, 22.5 million pounds (45,000 bales) by 1864, and 84.5 million pounds (169,000 bales) by the end of the war All told, it is estimated that Matamoros shipped about 20 percent of all the cotton that left the Confederate states: the rest ran the Union blockade. In return, foodstuffs and other goods needed by the South were paid for in cash or cotton, and shipped from northern Mexico overland through Texas.[17]

Cotton and Capital Formation: The Monterrey-Laguna Axis

Almost overnight, in the early 1860s Mexico's isolated northern borderlands were refashioned as a geopolitical base for Mexican liberalism, a hub of the global cotton economy, and the center of an incipient regional process of industrial capital formation. The money accumulated through the wartime cotton trade on the border was reinvested in textile industries in Monterrey, Nuevo León. Demand for fiber generated by these industries in turn prompted the rise of commercial cotton agriculture in the nearby Laguna region of Coahuila and Durango. The Laguna region would become the prototypical cotton region in northern Mexico, and plans to create irrigated cotton zones elsewhere in the north—Mexicali and Matamoros, for example—aimed to replicate its growth by providing the same elements found there: railroads, irrigation, colonization. The history of the Laguna region also shows how the growth of irrigated cotton agriculture led to the formation of a class of landless, underemployed migrant workers and generated revolutionary social conditions in northern Mexico. Let us, then, follow the threads of cotton history from the border to Monterrey, and to the Laguna.

In 1850 the Comarca Lagunera, or Laguna, was an area of shallow lagoons formed by the drainage of two intermittent rivers of the Sierra Madre Occidental— the Nazas and the Aguanaval—into the interior desert of northern central Mexico. Beginning in the 1850s, the groundwork was established that would make the Laguna a booming center of commercial agriculture and industry, and the most important cotton region in Mexico. The liberal fiscal measures dictated by the provincial government of Nuevo León under Santiago Vidaurri in the late 1850s encouraged the growth of legal commerce, which led to the accumulation of merchant capital (such as that of the Madero family) in the urban centers of Monterrey and Saltillo. At the same time, simmering tensions between *hacendados* and *campesinos* in the Laguna came to a head in the early 1860s. When Juárez, vanquished to the north by the alliance between the French and conservatives, passed through the Laguna region, he broke up *haciendas* and distributed land and water rights to smallholders. The government of Coahuila also made significant land reforms at this time. By bringing land out of the possession of the *haciendas,* these changes set the conditions for the emergence of a speculative real estate market, and a more dynamic form of production in the region.[18]

With the end of the U.S. Civil War, cross-border trade again dwindled to a trickle. The Juárez liberals effectively destroyed Vidaurri's regionalist political and military apparatus in the mid-1860s, and tariffs, banditry, and Indian attacks again made commercial trade in the northeast a dicey prospect. When the border fell back from the boom of the 1860s into the entropy of the 1870s, Monterrey merchant capitalists who had amassed wealth from the trade of the previous decade looked closer to home for investments. One of the main opportunities was in the area of cotton textiles. The creation of regional textile industries was common all over Mexico in the 1860s and 1870s, part of a decentralization of industry that the cotton famine further stimulated. With the decline of the cotton trade and the insecurity of borderlands commerce after 1865, fledgling northern industrialists sought to establish local sources of fiber. Evaristo Madero, for example, left Monterrey in 1869 to settle in Parras, Coahuila, where he purchased the *hacienda* El Rosario, which counted a textile mill among its holdings. He refurbished the mill, and set about generating regional sources of fiber for his new business, investing especially in the newly opening Laguna region.

Cotton is an expensive crop to produce. Even if the farmers of the Laguna were producing local varieties of cotton in the 1870s, and not investing in modern machinery or improved seeds, the cotton harvest still demanded a considerable amount of labor, which had to be bought with cash. Monterrey merchants began loaning money to Laguna growers with steep interest, in order to secure a supply of cotton for their emerging textile industry. Many of these agricultural producers failed to pay the loans, which resulted in the concentration of Laguna property in the hands of the emergent Monterrey bourgeoisie. Although the concentration of capital, industry, and land in the hands of a regional bourgeoisie was an important prerequisite for the emergence of a dynamic industrial cotton agriculture in the Laguna, the products of the region still lacked access to larger markets, as well as the capital and legal structure needed to establish a regional irrigation system. These obstacles would be overcome during the Porfiriato.[19]

The efforts of Porfirio Díaz to reach national power kept the northeast in turmoil for much of the 1870s. However, by 1880 he had established relative peace in the country and was assembling a political machine that would rule Mexico for the next thirty years. With order established, it was not long before investment picked up. Díaz offered development companies huge tracts of land in return for surveying the countryside. Foreign investors were given assurances by the Díaz regime of returns on their investments, at a time when capital in the metropolitan centers of Europe and North America was searching for new markets. Railroads constituted one of the biggest, earliest arenas for investment, and North Americans eager to connect the hinterland of Mexico and its resources to the existing U.S. rail grid began construction of two lines in 1880. The creation of railroads enabled the profitable expansion of mining and agriculture.[20]

The railroad changed everything for the Laguna. In 1884 the Mexican Central linked the region to both Mexico City and the U.S. border town of El Paso, and in 1888 the Mexican International crossed the region from east to west. With the problem of transportation largely surmounted, regional capitalists were able to move forward with integrated production schemes. The Madero family sent young Francisco Madero to the Laguna to establish a cotton farm that would implement and utilize industrial production techniques, improved seeds, and irrigation. This farm would supply the Madero textile mills and others in Monterrey. Other important regional investors included the Terrazas family of Chihuahua, the Treviños, and the

Reyes family of Nuevo León and Coahuila. These landowners and others increased the surface area in the Laguna dedicated to cotton production 400 percent between 1880 and 1890.[21]

While the dramatic growth of the Laguna region was based to a degree in the accumulation of regional capital during the cotton famine, from 1880 onward national and foreign investment in the region was also extremely important to development. The railroad is, of course, the most obvious example of the importance of this "outside" investment to regional development, but there was also a great deal of foreign money plowed into the region in the form of irrigation works, cotton seed, land rents and purchases, machinery, and wages. As William K. Meyers shows, much of the best land upriver was, by 1903, owned by Spanish families and the British and U.S. stockholders of the Compañía Agrícola, Industrial y Colonizadora del Tlahualillo. Together these actors held 135,000 hectares of Laguna property, irrigated by extensive canal systems. The Tlahualillo company planned to settle foreign colonists and build the largest irrigation system in Mexico, and the federal government cooperated in the effort by approving the colonization plan and establishing a new federal water law for the specific purpose of superseding local water-use rights and administering the Laguna's water in a more centralized manner. This was industrial agriculture at its most rational, and it was almost entirely dedicated to cotton production.[22]

Cotton production in the borderlands gave rise to a new, socially unstable migrant worker class. To understand how this happened we must examine briefly the productive process involved, the labor demands, and the way that labor was provided for socially, through regimes of land tenure and migration. The logic behind the industrial, mechanized cotton production common to the southwestern United States and northern Mexico was to have fewer farmers cultivate more land for less money, thereby making cotton more profitable. Nevertheless, the perseverance of the manual aspects of cotton production meant that a vast amount of labor was needed, albeit for specific moments in the production process. The soil must be prepared, irrigated, and sown during the winter, and some months later in the spring the plants must be thinned ("chopped") and weeds removed. However, before mechanization came along in the 1960s, the most labor-intensive moment was the harvest, or *pizca*. Due to the aridity of the north, there was very little regional population to do this work, and the cotton regions suffered a chronic labor shortage. The only way to provide this casual labor was through an enormous mobilization of agricultural workers.

In his study of the Laguna, William K. Meyers describes three general types of agricultural workers that served the region's cotton plantations: resident workers, temporary workers (*trabajadores eventuales*), and migrant workers. Each plantation had a core group of resident workers who lived on the property and performed most of the basic work. Because of their skills and the scarcity of labor, these workers commanded relatively good wages, although the plantation owners were careful not to let resident workers establish independent means of subsistence on their land. It took three or four people to pick what one person could plant, and during harvest time labor was at a premium. The part-time *trabajadores eventuales* who lived in the region were not sufficient in number to pick the crop, forcing planters to seek additional workers imported from southern and central Mexico. Given the great need for a reserve labor pool in the region, many of these migrant workers settled in the region and sought employment on the cotton plantations during times of peak labor shortages. These workers then joined the ranks of the *eventuales,* taking other jobs in the industries, mines, and railroads of the region when not involved in cotton agriculture, and living in informal, improvised settlements on the fringes of the plantations. Perhaps because they were dependent on these part-time workers, plantation owners and small farmers were at the same time hostile to them and eager to keep them available, and the two groups joined forces to pass laws to keep labor contractors from operating in the region and luring their workers away.[23]

The labor demands of cotton production helped give rise to the Mexican Revolution in the borderlands. With the vertiginous development of the 1880s, cotton agriculture boomed and labor streamed into the Laguna, lured both by the highest wages in Mexico and active recruitment campaigns mounted by *hacendados.* The new railroads facilitated the movement of these workers, and between 1880 and 1910 the rural population increased 400 percent. During the two-month picking season some eighty thousand workers occupied the fields. Some returned to their homes afterward, while others continued on to work in the railroads, mining, and agriculture of northern Mexico and the southwestern United States. In fact, by 1910 the Laguna had become just one stop on international migrant labor circuits that included the cotton harvest of Texas and the harvests of California. When production fell, unemployment and social unrest grew among these workers. In 1907 a combination of water scarcity in the Laguna and a global economic crisis brought a wave of violence, political activity inspired by the liberal-anarchist ideas of the Flores Magón brothers, and rebellion. The numbers of unemployed people in the Laguna expanded with the return of migrant workers from the United States, prompting federal and state authorities to ship them to other parts of Mexico to defuse tensions in the region. These marginally employed cotton workers formed the ranks of the northern revolutionary armies beginning with Francisco Madero's uprising in 1910, and violence increased in direct proportion to the decrease in work for this semi-agricultural, semi-industrial mass.[24]

World War I, the Mexican Revolution, and Cotton Development: Mexicali, 1900–1920

Beginning around 1860, cotton—its commerce, confection, and cultivation—became the motor of capitalist development in northern Mexico, tying the borderlands into global flows of capital, labor, and goods that extended from the southern United States, to Central Mexico, England, and France. The presence of the global cotton economy in Mexico was also evident in the various national and regional conflicts of the second half of the nineteenth century, and the occupation of the country by the French. The consolidation of industrial society and commercial agriculture along the Monterrey-Laguna axis between 1885 and 1905 is a central part of this history of cotton. A series of global and regional factors combined around the turn of the century to prompt other areas of northern Mexico and the southwestern United States to start down this development path, confirming the expansion of cotton production from the old cotton belt of the southern United States to the irrigated river valleys of the borderlands.

In 1892 the boll weevil crossed the border from Mexico at Brownsville, Texas, and in three years had reached the latitude of San Antonio. In 1894 the U.S. Department of Agriculture responded to the rapid spread of the pest with the first of a long series of studies, but by 1901 the boll weevil had arrived at the Trinity River, Galveston, and Houston. Losses in the main cotton-producing counties of Texas were as high as 50 percent, and the likelihood that the weevil would spread and cause extensive damage throughout the old cotton belt of the southeastern United States reinforced the opinion of textile industrialists and the government that new sources of the fiber had to be found.[25] In Europe, fears about the boll weevil combined with the realization that world commodity markets had become too complex and unstable for the mercantilist trade policies in effect since the 1870s. As a result, joint private-public efforts were made to secure dependable sources of cotton. The British Cotton Growing Association was formed in 1902 by a group of British textile industrialists, and similar organizations came together in France, Germany, Russia, Italy, and Portugal to promote cotton agriculture abroad, especially in colonies or dependencies whose production and trade the industrialists felt they could control through colonial government agencies.[26]

The efforts in Europe to stimulate and secure new sources of cotton fiber generated interest in producing cotton in new agricultural zones of the southwestern United States. This coincided with the arrival of irrigation technology to many of the arid zones of the borderlands, especially those near the established cotton area of East and South Texas. On the Texas side of the Río Bravo/Rio Grande[27] delta, for example, water pumped from the river was used to dramatically expand cotton production during the first years of the twentieth century, creating what was described at the time as a "Magic Valley." In 1902 the U.S. federal government became directly involved in building irrigation projects in the borderlands with the passage of the Reclamation Act, which established the Reclamation Service. Some of the earliest irrigation projects—the Rio Grande Federal Reclamation Project in New Mexico and Texas, for example—were dedicated entirely to cotton. In the Lubbock-Amarillo region of West Texas, during the first two decades of the twentieth century centrifugal pumps began to tap the Ogallala aquifer, converting dry cattle rangeland to cotton agriculture. These were regions where land was relatively cheap and level, which allowed for large-scale mechanized production.[28]

The binational delta region of the Río Colorado—what would become Mexicali and the Imperial Valley—was opened to agricultural production and colonization around the turn of the century as well, and soon became a major cotton zone. For the first four decades of the twentieth century most of the land on the Mexican side of the delta, and much of it on the U.S .side as well, was owned by the Colorado River Land Company (CRLC), a company formed by wealthy entrepreneurs from Los Angeles and San Francisco with the idea of building irrigation works and selling land to colonists. Many of the ten thousand colonists settled in the Imperial Valley between 1902 and 1906 had recently arrived from the boll-weevil-infested southern cotton belt, and were disposed to produce cotton. With the colonization of the Imperial Valley and the building of the Colorado River Irrigation Canal, the U.S. Department of Agriculture (USDA) opened up an experimental station just north of Yuma, Arizona, dedicated to developing new varieties of scarce long-staple cotton that would grow well in the irrigation zones that the Bureau of Land Reclamation planned to build in the Southwest. The main impetus behind organized cotton production in the Imperial Valley, however, was CRLC general manager H. H. Clarke. Clarke hired some twenty agricultural experts to teach the new colonists how to grow irrigated cotton, and the CRLC oversaw the financing, ginning, and marketing of the crop. Between 1910 and 1920, the CRLC was also directly involved in farming cotton, and in the manufacture of cottonseed products. Cotton secured a foothold in the Imperial Valley due to a serious reduction of the 1909 long-staple cotton crop in Egypt, which sent English textile industrialists scrambling to find other sources of the rare fiber. The damage caused by the boll weevil to the short-staple cotton crop in the old cotton belt of the southern United States further ensured the success of Imperial Valley cotton, and soon the Imperial Valley was being referred to as "the Egypt of America."[29]

Movements in the international political economy of cotton greatly stimulated the expansion of production in Mexicali from 1915 to 1920. With the onset of World War I in 1914, foreign trade was reduced and the United States experienced a temporary glut of cotton; U.S. industry picked up some of the slack, however, and the federal government bought surplus cotton to keep the prices up. Although the demand and price of cotton fiber did not immediately respond to the outbreak of hostilities in Europe in 1914, cotton prices on the New York exchange went from 9 cents a pound in the 1914–1915 season to 29.6 cents in 1917–1918. This trend peaked in 1919–1920, when cotton reached 38 cents a pound before crashing down to 17.9 cents the next year.[30]

With its irrigation system functioning and the railway to Mexicali completed in 1909, a few growers from the Imperial Valley began to invest in cotton in the Mexican side of the delta in 1913–1914, planting 4400 acres (1782 hectares) and producing 3700 bales. This acreage almost tripled during the following season, and by 1919–1920 it had expanded to 40,000 acres (16,200 hectares) and 54,000 bales. Despite the price drop of 1920, Mexicali farmers continued to plant around 50,000 or 60,000 acres (20,000–25,000 hectares) of cotton until the Depression of 1929, when production plummeted. The war had similar effects elsewhere in the U.S. borderlands. For example, in the nearby Salt River Valley of Arizona (where Phoenix is today), the wartime cotton demand caused a complete transition from small farms producing a variety of crops for a regional market, to large commercial cotton enterprises. In one of the many "conjunctural" moments that characterize the history of cotton development in the borderlands, the establishment of transportation and irrigation infrastructure coincided with a boom in prices to produce a rapid period of regional growth.[31]

As was the case in the Laguna twenty years earlier, a main obstacle to the expansion of cotton production in the delta region of the Río Colorado was the absence of people. Extreme temperatures, lack of rainfall, and distance from central Mexico made Mexicali an unpopular place to live. In 1910, Mexicali had only 1600 inhabitants, most of whom were irrigation or railroad workers and those who provided services to those two groups. Despite these obstacles, the owners of the CRLC sought to turn the Colorado River delta into a booming speculative real estate market, as they had done for the Los Angeles area.[32] Around 1910 the CRLC began renting land in 100,000-acre lots to smaller development companies, who were given ten years to bring the land into production. Cotton was the only crop permitted, and the renting companies were responsible for turning over half their crop, and for building much of the necessary infrastructure within their rented properties. These smaller development companies then sublet plots of 150 to 400 hectares to individual farmers. Initially the labor needed by these large farms was provided by importing Chinese and Japanese workers and renters. In 1908, the first year of irrigated production, immigrant workers cultivated 2800 hectares, a number that rose to 4400 hectares in 1914. By 1915 Chinese workers comprised nearly 42 percent of Mexicali's population. Revolutionary disturbances during these years spurred many Mexicans to head to the southwestern United States, and these new arrivals gradually displaced the Chinese and Japanese workforce in the emergent cotton zone of the Colorado River delta. A shipping line was opened that brought Mexican workers from the ports of Sonora and Baja California Sur to the mouth of the Colorado River, and by 1920 the influx was large enough to allow for the cultivation of 40,000 hectares of cotton, and the production of almost 80,000 bales. This flow of Mexican labor to the region made the importation of Asian workers an unnecessary expenditure. Furthermore, during the Revolution and the 1920s, a particularly nasty anti-Chinese movement erupted in northern Mexico. Sonora's ruling political class carried this anti-Chinese politics to national power after the Revolution, and in 1923 the federal government prohibited not only Chinese immigration, but the immigration of all foreign manual laborers.[33]

The Migration of Cotton Production in the 1920s

During the decade that bore witness to the horrors of World War I and the Mexican Revolution, long-term structural changes in the international political economy of cotton became clearly evident. The most important of these trends was the

geographical shift of cotton production from the old cotton belt of the southern
United States to new producing areas in other parts of the world. After 1916 cotton
production boomed in the U.S. Southwest, and headed south across the border to
Mexico and other countries in Latin America. Moreover, the stage was set for the
countries of Latin America, Africa, and Asia to wrest control of the world's markets
away from the United States over the next few decades. These long-term changes
would take material form in the Mexico-U.S. borderlands through the construction
and colonization of new irrigation zones dedicated to cotton production.

At the root of the relocation of cotton production was the changing position
of the United States in world trade. Before World War I, the United States was a
debtor nation that exported huge amounts of cotton to finance territorial expansion,
the development of industry, communications infrastructure, and other aspects of
growth. As we have seen, by 1880 U.S. cotton accounted for 75 percent of the consumption of foreign industries, and much of the world's textile industry was geared
to process the short-fiber upland cotton varieties. This amounted to a dependence
that foreign industrial countries were not comfortable with, and gradually the
United States lost ground to other producers such as India, Egypt, and Brazil. Still,
in 1910 the United States controlled 53 percent of foreign raw cotton markets, and
cotton accounted for 25 percent of the country's total exports—by far the single
largest source.[34]

During World War I the United States went from being a debtor nation to
a creditor nation. The countries of Europe, eager to strengthen their industries
after the fighting ended, needed even more raw cotton than before, and, as always,
they looked to the United States. At the same time however, the U.S. government
maintained tariffs that stimulated domestic industries and made the importation
of foreign-made industrial products prohibitively expensive. Largely dependent on
U.S. cotton, and unable to sell their manufactures or raw materials in the United
States, buyers outside the United States were forced to export gold to the United
States, or to borrow dollars in U.S. credit markets to finance the supply of fiber to
their industries. Despite moves by these buyers to find or create other sources of
cotton, between 1915 and 1929 the United States extended more than 15 billion dollars of credit, much of it to supply foreign industries with the fiber. After World
War I, these unfavorable terms of trade combined with strong cotton prices to stimulate an expansion of the crop outside of the old cotton belt in the U.S. South. In 1919
and 1920, the war, Reconstruction, and the damages wrought by the boll weevil sent
prices up to near 40 cents a pound in the U.S. markets, which, because the United
States was by far the largest producer, set prices for cotton around the world. During
the 1915–1920 era, the boll weevil caused an average of 200 million dollars of damages a year, driving production costs up, fiber quality down, and rural southerners
in search of better fortune elsewhere. Adding to the problem, a postwar depression
in 1920–1922 sent many migrant cotton pickers headed back to Mexico, where the

fighting had just ended. Others were stranded in the United States, or in Mexico's northern border cities and towns.[35]

Because of the destruction wrought by the boll weevil and the postwar depression, U.S. cotton production fell from some 13 million bales before World War I to about 10 million bales in 1923, during which time exports fell from about 8 million to 5 million bales. Despite the fact that less cotton was produced on each farm, the recent expansion of cotton agriculture into new areas west of the Mississippi—West and South Texas in particular—meant that total production climbed steadily through the late 1920s. These new western areas suffered less from the boll weevil, and were usually irrigated, which resulted in extraordinarily high yields per hectare. In most cases cotton farms in the western areas were larger than those in the South, which allowed them to benefit from economies of scale. In California, for example, the opening of cotton production in the San Joaquin Valley spurred a threefold increase of cotton in the state from 1921 to 1925. Dwindling supplies on the world market gave a boost to cotton prices from 1922 to 1925, but the individual farmer in the old cotton belt of the United States, suffering from lower yields and higher costs, did not gain from this price surge.[36]

Countries other than the United States also felt the shortage of cotton fiber brought on by small U.S. harvests in the early 1920s. Because the United States was by far the largest producer, trends there were felt in producing and consuming countries around the globe, regardless of the particular conditions of those countries. For example, levels of production might increase in Mexico, but global fiber prices still responded to the fate of the U.S. crop. For foreign cotton-exporting countries, this provided the possibility of increasing production without prices falling. Of course, it also meant that a small crop could coincide with lower prices. Faced with these conditions, governments of cotton-producing countries responded to differences in supply and demand by raising or lowering tariffs on raw fiber and textiles. National projects to stimulate cotton production were adopted by both producing and consuming countries (such as Spain, Japan, Australia, Brazil, and Argentina) that sought to take advantage of the decreasing ability of the United States to hold onto its overseas cotton markets. In areas where the force of commodity markets did not hold sway, industrial powers such as Great Britain, France, and Belgium mounted efforts to turn colonized populations into cotton farmers, or to bring colonial subjects that were already producing cotton within the orbit of European markets. For example, the agricultural land dedicated to cotton in India rose from 8.1 million hectares in 1921 to 11.34 million in 1925. The famous Gezira scheme of Sudan was created during this time to provide cotton for British industry.[37]

Cotton production expanded greatly in some countries of Latin America during the 1920s. Peru's famed "Tanguis" variety sold well in European markets, and hectares cultivated and bales produced more than doubled between 1915 and 1926. Nevertheless, lack of irrigation, labor, and transportation kept production within

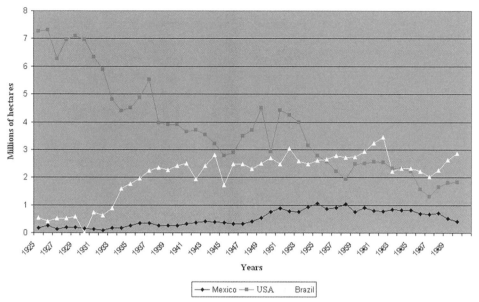

Areas dedicated to cotton: Mexico, USA, Brazil.

the rather narrow spatial limits of the river valleys of the Pacific Coast. Argentina produced almost no cotton in 1915, but in the early 1920s the crop gained importance in the Chaco region, especially in response to the short years of 1923 and 1924. The expansion of Argentine cotton cultivation was limited mostly by the lack of workers to meet the extraordinary labor demands of the crop. Brazil was Latin America's largest producer of cotton for most of the period between 1900 and 1970, and by 1926 the country had a well-integrated cotton marketing system, which included Latin America's only successful cotton exchange in Sao Paolo, which quoted prices based on the markets in Liverpool and New York. Brazil's textile industry, located in and around Sao Paolo, used all the cotton grown in the southern part of the country, and much of the fiber from the northern cotton zone as well. The northern cotton was of a scarcer and more expensive long-fiber length, and found ready buyers in the textile industries of Great Britain and Japan. Between 1915 and 1924 Brazil more than tripled the land dedicated to cotton, from 204,000 hectares to 634,000 hectares. Some of this increase was probably a result of a government initiative to grow cotton with irrigation in the northeastern state of Ceará.[38]

After a series of short years in the early 1920s, world and U.S. cotton production increased, and the amount of cotton left unconsumed when the cotton year ended on July 31 (the "carryover") rose steadily from about 6 million bales in 1924 to about 12 million bales in 1927. High prices and the global promotion of cotton resulted in two large crops in 1925 and 1926. Most of the increase of world production was the result of an increase in U.S. production, especially in 1926. In that year the United States, which had averaged around 13.8 million hectares of cotton land and around

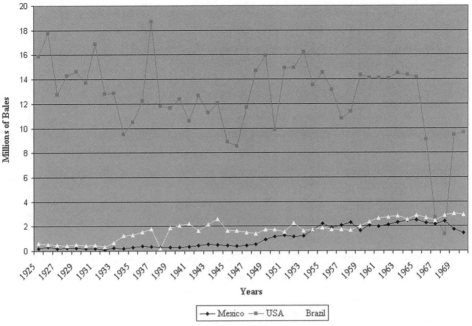

Cotton production: Mexico, USA, Brazil.

12.4 million bales from 1909 to 1913, planted 19 million hectares of cotton and produced about 17 million bales. The price of cotton in the United States fell to 12 cents
a pound; exports from the United States surged and surplus stocks fell. As would be
expected, a sharp dip in production the next year led to 20-cent cotton for 1928, just
before the stock market crash sent cotton prices through the floor.[39]

Irrigated Cotton and the Struggle over the International Rivers

We have followed a commodity—cotton—around the world from 1820 to 1920,
from the markets and textile industries of Europe to the emerging production zones
of the southwestern United States and northern Mexico. To understand the particular shape the global economy of cotton took in particular geopolitical and social
spaces, we have considered the importance of water, land, labor, and capital to processes of cotton production and exchange, and the instability of the regional social
formations that produced the fiber in northern Mexico. By the beginning of the
1920s it was clear to everyone involved in the cotton business that the structure of
world trade favored the consumption of cotton produced outside the old cotton
belt of the southern United States. The obstacle facing Mexico and the United States
in their efforts to take advantage of this trend by opening cotton agriculture in the
borderlands was aridity.

In order to expand cotton production, governments around the world focused
their developmental efforts on irrigation. Cotton was well suited to irrigated

production in hot and dry regions, and the low land values and relative absence of sedentary populations in such regions made them especially attractive to agricultural developers. In Mexico the postrevolutionary government was eager to promote agricultural production in its northern borderlands, and the examples of growth provided by the Laguna and Mexicali regions made cotton an attractive option. However, before any agriculture could be established in the borderlands the government first had to assert control over the waters of the international rivers—the Colorado and Río Bravo/Rio Grande, and the Mexican tributaries of the Río Bravo: the Conchos, Salado, and San Juan. The National Irrigation Commission (Comisión Nacional de Irrigación), founded in 1926, focused its efforts on building irrigation districts on the principal tributaries of the Río Bravo.[40]

By the mid-1920s private and government developers in the United States had been using the waters of the Río Bravo/Rio Grande and Colorado rivers to irrigate agricultural lands in the borderlands for more than twenty-five years. The Colorado River watered the Imperial Valley and Mexicali zone, and claims on that water from the various states of the Southwest were growing more numerous by the year. Mexico had established some rights to the use of the Colorado River water in Mexicali in the late 1880s, in a deal struck between the owner of the Mexicali region, Guillermo Andrade, and the California Development Company (CDC). In 1896 the CDC began building a canal that, because of the region's geography, had to pass through Mexico on its way to the Imperial Valley. Andrade granted permission to use his land for this purpose in exchange for half the water carried by the canal. In 1902 the U.S. federal Reclamation Service was created with the specific mandate to bring water to such arid areas as the Colorado River delta, and by 1904 the Reclamation Service was attempting to take control of the water of the Colorado, arguing that the CDC's irrigation works violated the agreement established between the United States and Mexico in 1848 that no structures would be built on the international rivers that would threaten their navigability. Some advocates of federal control even suggested that the portions of Mexico where the canal was built should be annexed to the United States. In 1919, the Reclamation Service reached an agreement with Imperial Valley landowners, in which the Reclamation Service would build an "All-American" canal entirely through U.S. territory, and the Imperial Valley would participate in a plan to build dams on the river system upstream. The ongoing inability of the CRLC and the Mexican government to secure its access to the waters of the Colorado for the Mexican side of the delta was a major obstacle to realizing the development intentions of both in the region.[41]

Mexico was also in an insecure position regarding the waters of the Río Bravo/ Rio Grande. In 1906, the United States and Mexico signed a convention governing the use of the Río Bravo/Rio Grande between the point where it touched Mexican territory near El Paso/Cd. Juarez, to Fort Quitman downstream. This agreement set each country's quota of water from the soon-to-be-built Elephant Butte dam. Basing its argument in the reigning doctrine of prior use of river water, the United States aimed to build a dam in its territory for the exclusive use of all of the river's water. Seeing little alternative, the Mexican government pressured for its water rights, but was forced to accept a share of the water from that dam, and to retire all complaints and demands on the water downstream.[42]

The postrevolutionary Mexican government made the use of the waters of the international rivers and their tributaries a priority. By the time the generals from the state of Sonora took national power in 1920, all of the water of the Colorado River and the upper Río Bravo/Rio Grande Valley was already, or soon to be, under the control of the U.S. Reclamation Service. While agricultural development projects planned for northern Mexico during the Porfiriato had failed to materialize, to the north of the border colonization and agricultural production were booming, through the control and use of the waters of the international river systems and the labor of Mexican migrant workers. Speaking at the Second National Convention of Engineers held in Monterrey in 1923, engineer Fortunato Dozal voiced the opinion that the three major Mexican tributaries of the Río Bravo/Rio Grande—the Conchos, Salado, and San Juan—should be utilized for the colonization of Mexican migrant workers who were being forced to find work in the U.S. Southwest due to the failure of both the *hacienda* and the *ejido* to provide employment. The *norteño* federal government was eager to emulate the colonization of the U.S. Southwest on its side of the border, to avoid the perceived threat of "foreign infiltrations that periodically provoke secessions of our territory,"[43] or a repetition of the military invasion suffered at the hands of General Pershing and the U.S. Army in 1916. Dozal pointed to the lower Río Bravo/Rio Grande Valley, where the Texas side was rapidly growing into an agricultural emporium while the Tamaulipas side languished, and argued for the need for Mexican state intervention in protecting private property, and providing irrigation, credit, roads, markets, colonization, land reform, and water laws to support agricultural development. The engineer also presented the cotton prosperity of the Laguna region as a model of Mexican development, and contrasted this with the underdevelopment of the rest of the Mexican borderlands.[44]

By using the waters of the Río Bravo for large-scale irrigation projects, the Mexican government hoped to position itself favorably in future negotiations over the international waters of the upper Río Bravo and the Colorado. The only water that Mexico could make a solid claim to, other than that allocated by the 1906 treaty, was that which drained into the Río Bravo/Rio Grande from the tributaries located in its own territory, as well as that carried by the lower Río Bravo/Rio Grande itself. The principal rivers draining into the lower Río Bravo/Rio Grande—the Rio Conchos (Chihuahua), the Rio Salado (Coahuila, Nuevo Leon and Tamaulipas), and the Rio San Juan (Nuevo León and Tamaulipas)—were all in Mexican territory, and were barely used. A binational commission organized to study water use in the lower Río Bravo/Rio Grande Valley found that these Mexican tributaries contributed 70 percent of that water.[45] Furthermore, the growth of agriculture on the Texas bank of the lower Río Bravo/Rio Grande River meant that by 1926 most of this "Mexican" water running in the lower Río Bravo/Rio Grande went to Texans. By planning dams and irrigation zones on the Conchos, Salado, and San Juan rivers, the Mexican government threatened to "dry up" the agriculture in South Texas. This development strategy would position the Mexican government to negotiate a much more favorable treaty with the United States governing the use of the Colorado and upper Río Bravo/Rio Grande rivers, and would secure the water for the development of Mexicali and the Juárez Valley as well as for the tributaries.

Such a water treaty was being discussed at that time. In 1924, as a result of pressure by anxious farmers in the lower Río Bravo/Rio Grande on Congress, the U.S. government began making overtures toward negotiating a treaty with Mexico governing the waters of the Río Bravo/Rio Grande. Three years of fruitless discussions ensued, with Mexico, desperate to secure water for Mexicali, insisting on including the Colorado River in the negotiations. Then, in 1926, when U.S. Secretary of State Charles Evans Hughes took President Hoover's advice and finally agreed to include all three international rivers in the discussion (the small Tijuana River was the other one), resistance by the state of Arizona to enter into a basin-wide dam-building and management scheme for the Colorado River derailed the international negotiations. But regardless of the resistance by Arizonans jealous of their water rights, with the commencement in 1926 of the program by Mexican president Plutarco Elias Calles to build a number of large irrigation systems on the northern rivers, Mexico's position at the bargaining table could only improve.

Conclusion

In the mid-nineteenth century, when the war with the United States ended and the political border was set at the Río Bravo/Rio Grande, the borderlands of northern Mexico was an expanse of arid and semiarid lands with small groups of people clustered around small irrigation systems. Large-scale cotton agriculture, industry, and trade brought deep and lasting changes to society and environment in the region. The trade in the fiber that boomed as a result of the cotton famine of the 1860s was crucial to the formation of capital in northern Mexico, and after the cessation of the Civil War and the cotton famine the Laguna region became a center for the investment of that capital by Monterrey's merchant elite. With the arrival of railroads in the 1880s, irrigated cotton agriculture expanded in the Comarca Lagunera, and factories were built to process the fiber and seed. While the dizzying economic growth of the Laguna was looked upon as a model of development for the rest of northern Mexico, the labor demands of commercial cotton production created new groups of landless migratory workers who played an important role in fighting the Mexican Revolution. The expansion of industry and agriculture was desired; the migrant workers and the revolutionary turmoil to which they contributed were not.

After 1920, trends in the international political economy of cotton favored the expansion of cotton agriculture in the Mexican borderlands, and the leaders of the postrevolutionary state sought to emulate the astounding growth of irrigated cotton zones such as South Texas and the Laguna region, while minimizing the destabilizing social and political effects of such growth. The developmental thought and action generated by government and private-sector leaders during and after the Revolution sought to resolve the contradiction between growth and stability that was inherent to industrial cotton society. These leaders identified aridity and landlessness as key problems, and proposed large-scale irrigated cotton production by smallholding farmers as the path to political stability, economic prosperity, and sustained development. The project to build physical and social infrastructure in the borderlands was made even more urgent by the fact that in the United States private and government agencies were building irrigation works and agricultural zones on the tributaries of the Colorado and Rio Grande rivers. The survival and future development of Mexicali, the Valley of Juárez, Matamoros, and other agricultural zones on the international rivers depended on capturing the waters of the Mexican tributaries and using them for irrigated agriculture.

CHAPTER 3

DEVELOPMENTALISM IN NORTHERN MEXICO, 1910–1934

Cotton agriculture in the borderlands gathered momentum after 1900. The expansion of the Laguna cotton region in the Porfiriato went a long way toward solving a chronic development problem in Mexico by removing the bottleneck in the national cotton fiber supply that had plagued the textile industry since independence. At the same time, however, it created another development problem. Contrary to the enduring ideal of the democratic, productive, rural smallholder society, the Laguna cotton region was characterized by large landholdings and migrant wage labor. The problems that the industrialization and modernization of agriculture was supposed to erase—poverty and social instability, for example—continued and worsened, leading to the decade-long violence of the Mexican Revolution. While there was a great deal of continuity in the practice and process of development before and after the Revolution, there were also significant changes made to confront these problems.

During the period from 1910 to 1934, visions of an agrarian north were adjusted to meet the pressing social issues of land concentration and labor migration made evident by the Revolution. *Norteño* presidents from Madero to Calles made efforts to settle small farmers in irrigation systems: part of a larger plan to lay claim to water from the international rivers, stimulate cotton production, and make the countryside prosperous and peaceful. These were large-scale hydraulic projects, and the ideology of development that underwrote them went through changes even before the Great Depression forced a reevaluation of the dominant neoclassical economic paradigm. During and immediately after the Revolution, Mexican governments were reluctant to invest in development projects because of laissez-faire ideological commitments or lack of financial resources. The government of Francisco Madero provided the private Colorado River Land Company with incentives to irrigate and colonize the Mexicali cotton zone, in the hope that this would stem emigration to the United States and provide political stability to the region. Pres. Alvaro Obregón continued with a strategy that placed the responsibility for development on private investors, until growing U.S. presence in the borderlands, domestic political forces, and conditions presented by the world cotton economy moved him to secure for his government a more active role in the creation of irrigated cotton development projects.

It was during the Calles presidency, however, that the state took the role of directly financing and organizing rural development in northern Mexico through the construction and colonization of irrigated agricultural zones by the newly created Comisión Nacional de Irrigación (CNI). These new irrigation zones were to be settled by *rancheros* who had lost their land during the Porfiriato and the Revolution and had become wage workers, sharecroppers, or migrants. *Rancheros* were thought to be more independent and hard working, and biologically and culturally more European than other Mexicans, which made them especially apt subjects and objects of development. The vision of "integral, regional" development held by CNI engineers and other state actors included racial and cultural as well as economic, social, and geographical elements, and during the Calles administration it guided the creation of the cotton-producing "Don Martín" irrigation system in Coahuila and Nuevo León. The goal of the postrevolutionary government irrigation projects, then, was to recreate the dynamism of irrigated cotton agriculture in areas such as the Laguna, Mexicali, and South Texas in other irrigation zones, but based on stable regional social formations characterized by racially and culturally progressive small property owners rather than large plantations with landless, temporary, and migratory workers.

Development and Developmentalism

What is development? Alan Knight argues that lurking deep within the political projects of Mexico's postrevolutionary leaders was a pervasive "developmentalism"—a modern "current of ideas that stressed the need to develop Mexican society and economy, above all by disciplining, educating and moralizing the degenerate Mexican masses."[1] Knight describes developmentalism as an enduring culture of the state, reflected in the "broader socio-economic ("developmentalist") concerns" of governments before and after the Revolution. The slipperiness of the concept of development is evident in the self-referentiality of Knight's definitions of "developmentalism," and suggests the need for a more precise discussion. As Albert Hirschman has argued, the crisis of the 1930s provided an opening for "development economics" approaches other than the dominant free market ones of the late nineteenth and early twentieth centuries. These new approaches flourished during the cold war, when the desire to maintain consumer power and political stability in the "third world" drove a concerted effort by private and government institutions to jump-start industrial production and generally augment social welfare. However great the expenditure was during those years, by the 1980s global relations had been transformed once again by structural adjustment policies, austerity measures, and the partial abandonment of development for projects such as democratization and human rights.

The decline of development economics coincided with the emergence of the poststructural critique of discourse in the humanities and social sciences, which sank its teeth into the faltering development industry. In the 1990s anthropologists made important analyses of the way the development industry has constructed its object of knowledge, and how this construction leads to certain outcomes and effects.[2] But while these anthropological, cultural analyses of "regimes of representation" of economy, society, peasants, the "third world," and other subjects are nuanced and well evidenced, the representations of developmental social science are sometimes attributed an almost magical power to do things. "Almost by fiat," Arturo Escobar writes, "two-thirds of the world's peoples were transformed into poor subjects in 1948 when the World Bank defined as poor those countries with an annual per capital income below $100."[3] This kind of statement does not sufficiently recognize that intellectual production responds to social processes and events.

Social science is responsive as much as, or more than, it is programmatic: intellectual production is often aimed at ameliorating tensions and conflicts generated by social processes of modern capitalist society such as class formation, migration, urbanization, and the like. The boom in development economics after 1930 was a piecemeal, contested, and fragmented intellectual reaction to economic crisis and social dislocation, more than a manifestation of the inexorable march of modern power. Development agents produce and enact plans in complicated material social fields, and the multitude of actors and the social, economic, and environmental conditions that comprise these fields help to constitute development plans, and are, at the same time, constituted by them. In fact, the objects of development—women, peasants, etc.—learn and tell development "tales" as well as or perhaps even better than the state officials, capitalists, and others who are usually considered to be their authors.[4] This expanded notion of development and developmentalism prompts a search for the specific social determinants of development in the early- to mid-nineteenth-century European context from which it emerged, a context of rapidly growing industrial capitalism with its unprecedented change, social disruption, and human dislocation. Faced with problems of rural-urban migration, poverty, unemployment, and the like, Saint-Simonians and positivists such as Auguste Comte moved away from an earlier notion of development as "that which happens" to development as the means of transforming the present. This new notion of development was a critique of laissez-faire political economists who had relied upon self-interest and competition to provide for the social good. As M. P. Cowen and R. W. Shenton put it, development thinkers in the first half of the nineteenth century saw that "industrial expansion had happened in periods of social disorder precisely because there had been no constructive coincidence between self-interested investment of capital and the need of dislocated populations for employment."[5] Development thinking surges in times of economic and social crisis, in response to unemployed and uncoordinated productive forces of society, especially surplus labor.

Three points about development are particularly useful in understanding the social history of cotton in Mexico during the early twentieth century. First, human dislocation and relative surplus population are among the principal objects of developmental interventions, which often seek to settle migrant workers on land, or manage their movement so as to make them more productive. Second, the concept of development was closely tied to ideas about evolution, and like that related concept included important cultural and racial dimensions. Efforts to promote "integral" development in northern Mexico were directed at the biology and culture of *norteños*, as well as the geography, society, and economy of the region. The third point to be made is that development intervention requires a privileged agent, usually the state, to be responsible for the "external" project of influencing the "internal" process of historical change. The state is the rector of development almost by definition: within capitalist society developmentalism aims to correct for—or "develop"—market forces, which, left to themselves, create problems of overaccumulation, as well as underutilized and socially disruptive relative surplus populations. The agent of development therefore must be distinct from the market or its forces. Developmentalism surged in Mexico around the turn of the century in reaction to the formation of new working classes of mobile and politically volatile workers, and the eruption of revolutionary violence. The dominant developmental goal from 1900 to 1934 was the creation of small farmers who would export commercial crops such as cotton. What changed over this period was the agent held responsible for creating those farmers.

The Development Response to Rebellion: Mexicali

Unlike the Laguna, which had grown into an agricultural emporium by the mid-1890s, Mexicali began to expand in the context of the political turmoil of the 1910–1920 period. The development designs created for Mexicali were meant both to ensure economic growth and to remedy the revolutionary conditions of the borderlands. Almost all of the Mexican side of the Colorado River delta region was owned by the Colorado River Land Company (CRLC), a Mexican company formed by Harrison Grey Otis, Harry Chandler, and a few other California capitalists. In the imagination of the CRLC investors, the delta lands would be sold to hardworking, modern, independent small farmers. However, desires to maximize profits and protect their land from claims by squatters moved the investors to instead maintain corporate ownership of the lands and rent to subdevelopers. In 1910, however, 32,000 acres (12,960 hectares) of prime lands complete with railway stations were sold to a group of investors including Chicago meat-packer John Cudahy with the idea that these investors would build a new community of independent commercial farmers. From the beginning, cotton agriculture and industry were an important part of the plan. The Porfirian government was supportive of foreign investment, as long as such investments or investors did not disrupt regional power relations too greatly. In the case of Mexicali, the relative absence of a regional population and the possibility that the CRLC would secure water rights for the Mexican side of the delta in the process of creating a new pole of development in Mexico's north were strong reasons for the Mexican federal government to partake of the vision of regional development held by Otis, Chandler, and their partners. The Laguna cotton region had proven to be a major source of fiber and other cotton products, and it was hoped that such regional development could be achieved in Mexicali.[6]

Despite its isolation from mainland Mexico, one of the strangest incidents of the Revolution occurred in Mexicali. In January of 1911, Mexican federal forces engaged in a struggle to control the Baja California border area with a multinational army that included followers of the Flores Magón brothers and their anarchist-flavored Partido Liberal Mexicano, socialists, and militants of the Industrial Workers of the World. This poorly equipped and undisciplined group of rebels controlled the town of Mexicali for a brief period, but was defeated by June of 1911. While the *anarquista* threat was quickly subdued, interim president Francisco León de la Barra sent a commission to northern Baja California to study ways of combating such revolutionary effervescence by settling more Mexicans there and connecting the region more strongly to the national center. The rebellion in Baja California reinforced long-standing fears that the borderlands were being lost to filibustering foreigners, and the government sought to reinforce its sovereignty over the region.[7]

As a result of its visit, the commission suggested promoting the development of Mexicali along the lines of the CRLC vision for the Imperial Valley, and a short time later Minister of Fomento Rafael Hernández Madero opened discussions with the CRLC that would continue throughout the Madero presidency. As a result of these talks, the CRLC tentatively agreed to stick to its original plan of subdividing the land and colonizing it with small property owners, but only when a railroad had been built to connect the region to outside markets. While this plan was aimed at securing water rights for Mexico, breaking up a latifundio and taking land out of the hands of foreigners, it was, more important, the means by which the government hoped to create a property-owning rural middle class that, it supposed, would be a force of economic progress and political stability. In other words, the CRLC and the Madero government coincided in the belief that small farmers were agents of development. At the same time, they hoped that this colonization would settle, employ, and demobilize landless and unemployed populations from other parts of Mexico, such as the Laguna.[8]

This plan failed for the same reasons that the CRLC's development vision for Mexicali was not realized. There were few Mexicans who fit the profile of the middle-class colonist farmer among the landless and unemployed, and there was no way for the government to finance the infrastructure or the costs of colonizing smallholders and creating such a group of middle-class farmers. The only way to make such a development vision a reality would be through an exceptional amount of state expenditure, which the Mexican government was neither financially able, nor ideologically willing, to do. Madero's reformism was primarily legal and political; his idea of agrarian reform was limited to technological advances in agricultural production, which he felt would bring greater prosperity to all. So although the creation of an agrarian middle class was certainly a strongly proclaimed goal, there was no agent to make it happen.[9]

Obregón's Tautology: "Evolutionary Development"

... the farmer, like all the other sources of wealth that have served the progress of humanity, achieved an admirable evolution in recent times, an evolution that in other countries has, combined with capital, intelligence and work, enabled the land to produce at its maximum level, with a minimum cost. ... In our country, unfortunately, the majority of the landowners have remained absolutely untouched by the evolution of agriculture ...[10]

ALVARO OBREGÓN, 1920.

President Álvaro Obregón was the second of the series of Sonoran military commanders that ran Mexico for the fourteen years following the Revolution. The Sonoran dynasty set the course for the formation of a postrevolutionary state that remained dedicated to promoting foreign investment and economic growth while incorporating or repressing popular mobilization. Based on his personal experience with irrigated farming in Sonora, Obregón saw the economic future of the country as lying in modern, commercial agricultural production for export, and he was a strong critic of the *hacienda*. Peons lived miserable lives in Mexico and chose to emigrate to the United States, he reasoned, because the *haciendas* compensated for outmoded and inefficient production techniques with tariff protection and low wages. For the most part, however, Obregón inherited the laissez-faire posture of Madero, rejecting an interventionist role for the state in modernizing agriculture through the breakup of large landholdings, and hoping instead that smallholding in rural Mexico would "evolve" with only the limited support of the government. There would be no land reform, Obregón declared, "before the evolutionary development of small agriculture has been achieved."[11]

Obregón's statement defined his position in a debate that had been brewing in the United States and Mexico since the turn of the century over the appropriate roles for the state and private capital in financing irrigation and colonization. The more orthodox stance was that private investment should and would take care of financing these works, as part of larger colonization and development projects. Andrés Molina Enríquez—who had the ear of Madero—maintained that only private investors should get involved in irrigation.[12] In response, Roberto Gayol argued that the experience of the U.S. Reclamation Service showed that the state was the only entity that could amass enough capital to finance such enormous public works as dams, and that direct state investment was much more efficient than subsidies to the private sector.[13] A compromise was struck when in 1908 the state promised to guarantee bonds emitted by a consortium of private banks, which would be used to establish a development bank called the Caja de Préstamos para Obras de Irrigación y Fomento de Agricultura. Although the Caja did in fact provide loans to a few private developers during its short existence, these projects came to nothing.[14] Obregón, whose government was held responsible for the debt of the *Caja,* was well aware of the failure of state investment in irrigated agriculture, and he tended toward the position taken by Molina Enríquez.

Distrust of state intervention existed in uneasy tension with a consciousness that something had to be done to ease the social problems that gave rise to the Revolution. In order for the productive forces of Mexican society to come together efficiently and harmoniously, some developmental agency had to exist. In the thinking of Madero and Obregón, much of this agency was to be found in the dynamic of evolution. An idealized and historically inaccurate understanding of the internal process of development was repositioned as its own external agent of development, and thus the historical process of capitalist expansion was entrusted to change the social problems it had created. Land reform, Obregón thought, would be achieved through the "evolutionary development" of the small proprietor, rather than by state redistribution. Obregón's evolutionary thinking, moreover, lent itself to racialized theories of development. With no actor such as state or capital responsible for the transformation of marginal *mestizo* and indigenous migrant workers into small property owners, the agency of development was relocated to the bodies of those workers. The concept of evolution commonly held in Mexico and the United States at that time was an amalgam of social, economic, cultural, and biological dimensions. For Obregón, the socioeconomic progress and prosperity of the agricultural working class would result from immanent biological and social evolutionary processes.

The laissez-faire posture taken by Molina Enríquez, Madero, Obregón, and others reveals a classic tautology of seeing development as both a process and an end result. In order to settle migrant workers, make them productive, and form them into a prosperous agrarian middle class (the process of development), the Mexican government placed the agency of such development in middle-class farmers themselves (the goal of development). Even if they could be found, these farmers would already be developed, and the problem of development—relative surplus labor, and the failure to coordinate the forces of production—would remain unaddressed. That "middle-class" farmers could not be found was the very problem that development thought intended to address.

Although nineteenth-century evolutionism figured prominently in his thought, Obregón also responded to the new conditions present in Mexican society in the first years after the Revolution, showing concern for the problems of labor migration, low agricultural production, lingering revolutionary tendencies, and the poverty of the Mexican state. The political incorporation of rural activists (*agraristas*), for example, helped the Sonoran leader overcome subsequent attempts to derail his fledgling government, most notably the De la Huerta rebellion of 1923 and 1924. Regarding the agrarian question, however, Obregón's first preoccupation was with increasing a still weak national agricultural production, rather than redistributing land. Despite an extremely limited budget, in 1920 the president began to lay the legal and institutional groundwork within the state for increasing irrigated commercial agricultural production. He created the Dirección de Irrigación, within the Secretaría de Agricultura y Fomento, which oversaw the management and maintenance of existing irrigation works, began collecting basic hydrological information about the nation's rivers, and began studies for building large irrigation systems.[15]

Conjunctural events in the political economy of cotton production in the borderlands prompted the Obregón government to take bolder action. The postwar depression of 1920–1921 brought on a crash in cotton production and a surge in 1922–1923 in the number of unemployed migrant workers crossing the border back into Mexico. To make matters worse, a drought caused the failure of the 1922–1923 cotton crop in the Laguna. The federal government declared its intent to stimulate cotton production in Baja California, Sinaloa, Tamaulipas, and Oaxaca, in order to recuperate production levels and secure a supply of the fiber for national industry. In 1922 Obregón decreed the expropriation of small extensions of land held by the Colorado River Land Company. However, this was mostly a threat aimed at forcing the CRLC to speed up its own efforts at colonizing Mexicali with middle-class Mexican farmers. Obregón imagined that these farmers could be found among the *repatriados* returning from the United States during 1921–1922, and charged governor of Baja California José Lugo with the task of finding and settling them. Of course, these efforts to settle middle-class Mexican farmers in Mexicali were, like all the others made between the creation of the region in 1900 to the Cardenista agrarian reforms of 1937, frustrated by the simple fact that there were no middle-class Mexican farmers to be found. In 1923 the Secretaría de Agricultura y Fomento also sent a team of engineers to study the possibility of colonizing federal lands in Tamaulipas with experienced cotton farmers from the United States or other regions of northern Mexico. Obregón's moves in Mexicali and Tamaulipas failed to produce concrete results.[16]

It could be argued that Obregón's government took the tautological position of entrusting rural development to the process of development itself, because it simply did not have the money that subsequent governments had to support land reform, irrigation, and colonization projects. Obregón received proposals for many such schemes, but consistently responded that the government could not afford to support them financially. However, when the national textile industry was threatened by a scarcity of cotton fiber and unemployed, landless migrant workers began to mass in the agricultural zones of northern Mexico, Obregón actually did come up with money for an irrigated development project. In response to a statement by the government that it would support cotton agriculture, in 1922 a group of sixty farmers from the Laguna region calling itself the "Sociedad Colonizadora de Agricultores de

San Pedro de las Colonias" offered to form a colonization company to help the government split up *latifundios* and cultivate cotton. The group planned to bring along landless cotton workers, to settle them on parcels of 5 hectares each, and to build a town as the project's regional center. By January of 1923 the colonists had re-formed themselves as the "Compañía Colonizadora y de Fomento del Cultivo del Algodón en los Estados de Oaxaca y Guerrero, S.A.," and had identified land on the Oaxaca/Guerrero border owned by American Lewis Lamm. Obregón agreed to provide the group with rail passes, charging them to the Secretaría de Agricultura y Fomento, and Alfonso Madero headed up the first expedition to identify colonization sites in the area. In August the "Sociedad Colonizadora" told Obregón that 700,000 hectares were available, and the 40,000 of these suitable for irrigation could produce 100,000 bales (*pacas*) of cotton yearly. All this land was to cost 695,800 pesos, and would support three to four thousand colonists. One of the landholders planned to set up a cotton ginning business in the region using the money earned from the sale of his land to colonists.[17]

Despite its limited resources, the Obregón government loaned the colonization project 400,000 pesos for the first payments on the lands contracted in Oaxaca. Obregón felt that the Oaxaca development project would "help to resolve the crisis in the Laguna region and open new fields of great promise to the cultivation of that fiber which is so necessary for the development of our industries."[18] He asked Mr. Santa Ana Almada Jr., Gerente of the Comisión Monetaria, to give the colonists good terms on the payment of these loans. These colonists were to be Mexicans repatriated from the United States. While the leaders of the colonization project were in Oaxaca organizing land purchases, a convoy of seven hundred families of Mexicans was traveling south through Texas to Cd. Juárez, Chihuahua. Obregón ordered the Adminstrator of Aduanas in Ciudad Juárez to help the group by making their border crossing easier.[19]

The colonization/development project ultimately ended up a failure. It was far from any railroad, and when the colonists tried to set up an ocean communications link, their boat sank with lives lost. Much of the land was swampy, and the colonists feared disease. Furthermore, political relations between the colonists and the region's inhabitants were strained, and the De la Huerta rebellion of 1923–1924 also disrupted the project. Obregón asked Oaxacan governor Gen. Isaac M. Ibarra to lend his support to the colonists, but it wasn't enough. In April of 1925 the municipal president of Jamiltepec, Oaxaca, wrote to Obregón asking him to intervene in order to renew the funding from the Comisión Monetaria. Obregón said that this was impossible, as the Comisión Monetaria had been replaced by a private company, and was thus outside of his jurisdiction. Graft and corruption on the part of the organizers and an almost total lack of planning doomed the project, and the few colonists who remained in the zone were, after a few years, relocated to other areas.[20]

Although the Oaxaca project failed to produce the results hoped for by both government and colonists, a more successful project was mounted at the same time in Guadalupe, Chihuahua. There the Comisión Monetaria distributed 327,000 pesos to a cooperative of four hundred families in order to cultivate 1500 hectares of cotton. Two thousand bales were produced, easily covering the investment. Gustavo Serrano, an irrigation engineer then serving as the head of the Junta de Aguas Internacionales, lauded the project as an example of a successful development effort, for those families stayed in Mexico "to work and develop the country rather than swelling the number of those living in the United States."[21] In his study of irrigation in the northern borderlands, Serrano warned the federal government that it must bring development efforts to the north before the United States used all the water of the international rivers, and before the migration of Mexicans to the United States crippled Mexico's economy and society. The Guadalupe project, like the Oaxaca project, combined the three elements that came to define subsequent agricultural development projects in northern Mexico in the 1920s and 1930s: repatriation and settlement of migrant labor, irrigation, and cotton production. After 1926, however, development was not entrusted so much to private capital, to the marketplace, or to the evolutionary spirit and bodies of the migrant workers themselves. Instead, the state took over the organizational and financial responsibilities of development.

Calles's "Revolutionary Irrigation"

Obregón's successor, Plutarco Elias Calles, did not let the failures of the Porfirian Caja de Prestamos and Obregón's Oaxaca project stop him from increasing state involvement in irrigation. Building upon on the institutions established by the Obregón government, in 1925 he began to push forward a plan to reshape Mexican agriculture through a sustained program of irrigation, colonization, and financing. Calles and his bureaucracy retained many of the development goals of previous administrations: the repatriation of Mexicans in the United States, the establishment of small and middle-sized farmers with progressive production methods, the creation of irrigated cotton zones as the foundation for industrialization and national progress. He differed, however, from Obregón in a crucial way: although he retained a biologized and evolutionary vision of development, he made the state the principal agent of that development. Calles found in the state-built irrigation zone a way to establish small farmers and settle repatriated migrants without dismantling the industrial-agricultural *latifundios* he and his predecessors felt were of central importance to the nation's prosperity. To put this irrigation politics into effect, Calles's government passed laws and allocated a sizable amount of capital—7.4 percent of the federal budget in 1928.[22]

The first steps were legal. In 1926 two linked laws were passed: the Ley sobre Irrigación con Aguas Federales and the Ley Federal de Colonización. The first created the National Irrigation Commission (Comisión Nacional de Irrigación, or CNI), a government agency devoted to building and managing irrigated agricultural systems. The second law declared irrigable land—private or public—to be of public utility, and made the irrigation of such land compulsory. Ignacio López Bancalari, a long-time friend of Calles who had been advocating state control of irrigation even before the Revolution ended, and who was appointed director general of the new CNI, saw this as the most efficient way to get private land irrigated and colonized. As with the irrigation of these lands, their colonization was to be carried out either by the National Agrarian Credit Bank (the Banco Nacional de Crédito Agrícola, or BNCA) or by private colonization companies and landowners. The latter two nongovernmental entities were required to get the approval of the Agriculture and Development Ministry (Secretaría de Agricultura y Fomento, or SAF) regarding the boundaries of the property and their financial capability to carry through such irrigation and colonization.[23]

The *callista* irrigation engineers identified the state as principal agent for the development of rural Mexico, and, in so doing, made a decisive move away from tautological developmentalism. Calles shifted the bulk of the responsibility for the creation of this modern rural Mexico from "evolutionary development" to the increasingly powerful Mexican state. But despite the increased role of the state, the irrigation and colonization politics written into law in 1926 retained their basis in a profoundly liberal, *norteño* agrarian vision, not much different from that of Madero and Obregón. "In a word," proclaimed the editors of *Irrigación en México,* the mouthpiece for the CNI, "the agricultural development of an irrigation system is not going to be only the work of the Government. . . . The good results that are expected will depend almost exclusively on the will of the colonos."[24] The insistence on individual initiative and the importance of the free market in promoting the "evolutionary development" of Mexican agriculture remained strong. But to even get to the point of colonizing irrigation systems the government had to invest a huge amount of resources in building them.[25]

The *callista* government made a clear distinction between its brand of agrarian reform and the agrarian reforms carried out by previous governments in response to *agrarista* mobilizations. *Agrarismo,* it was argued, was the intellectual and political product of the lower ranks of the *hacienda* workers, who were the least economically or intellectually advanced sector of the rural population.[26] From the CNI's standpoint, there were two related problems with *agrarismo.* First, because it was not aimed at promoting the more "advanced" sectors of the rural population, it would not help to increase agricultural production, nor help create a sustained social and economic development in the country. In the *callista* logic, the repeated revolutions in Mexico were caused by the lack of a Mexican middle class of small property owners or small tenant farmers to buffer the antagonisms of *hacendados* and *peones.* Because they were not comprehensive, and were directed in a piecemeal fashion at placating popular demands, previous agrarian reforms had not been designed to create such a middle class. Rather, land reform directed by the postrevolutionary state followed a well-established precedent in which *haciendas* and colonial governments distributed "*pegujales*" to *campesinos,* parcels that provided *campesinos* with enough food to support themselves, but not enough to free them from working as agricultural laborers.[27]

The second problem that the CNI encountered in *agrarismo* and the *ejido* was that it ignored the very elements that could, if supported by the state, make up such an agrarian middle class: the nation's 410,000 renters (*arrendatarios*), communal landholders (*comuneros*), and sharecroppers (*medieros* and *aparceros*). Athough they recognized them as belonging to the same class as the peons that worked on *haciendas,* the *callistas* viewed these tenants as more independent and progressive, and irrigation was aimed at developing them. In fact, the Ley Federal de Coloni-zación ranked the "sharecroppers or renters of the estate that is colonized" as the first priority for colonization of the irrigation zones. Whereas *agrarismo* was said to reproduce economic stagnation and revolutionary social tensions in rural Mexico, the state-led "irrigation politics" ("*política de riego*") was expected to solve both of these problems by combining state investment with the entrepreneurial essence of the smallholding colonist.[28]

The *callista* irrigation program was a social, agricultural program to cultivate the middle class of economically progressive and politically stable smallholding farmers long desired by Mexican liberals. There was a strong moral, or cultural, component in the project of forming this agrarian middle class through the *política de riego.* The state was in the position of choosing the colonists within its irrigation zones, and it sought healthy, entrepreneurial, landless farmers with some amount of economic resources, and "a cultural level more elevated than that of [the] peons."[29] Once estab-lished on their parcels of land, it was imagined that the process of working toward ownership would reinforce and expand qualities of economic autonomy, a feeling of self-worth, and a moral love of liberty. The success of these *colonos* would serve to teach neighboring *ejidatarios* to aspire to economic improvement, and would pre-vent the landlords from reestablishing their monopoly over the land.[30]

Many of the small renters and sharecroppers described by these irrigation engineers and politicians were previously independent *rancheros,* and the *callista* "*política de riego*" was aimed at "rehabilitating" the *ranchero* society and culture damaged by the privatization of land through geological surveys and fencing, and by revolutionary violence and plunder. Northern Mexico was largely settled in the years during and after the Bourbon reforms, and while *norteños* certainly maintained very insular communities (constructed, in part, through a long and violent encounter with Indians), formal communal landholding was not typical. The *rancheros* and agriculturalists of the Chihuahuan mountains described by Daniel Nugent, for ex-ample, maintained individual possession of parcels of agricultural land, even though their productive use of that land was organized through the community.[31] The image of an agrarian middle class of independent small farmers that guided Calles's irriga-tion program was based in this *ranchero.*

For *rancheros* who managed livestock on the vast unfenced expanses of north-eastern Mexico, possession of the land was not as important as access to its use. In the Lower Río Bravo/Rio Grande Valley, for example, the land was "owned" in the form of *porciones* and *haciendas,* but the regional economic dependence on ranching made its use by all members of the community more important than its possession by individuals. Nevertheless, the political and economic independence central to *ranchero* political culture was certainly linked to the *ranchero's* access to land, and his (for although inheritance and land ownership was not necessarily patrilineal, men were those that managed livestock) control over that piece of land on which he and his family resided. Paradoxically, the goal of the revolutionary irrigation program was to replace the livestock ranching society with an agricultural society by radically changing the ecological, geographical, and productive bases that supposedly generated those qualities of *ranchero* society most desired by the state. The new *rancho* was to produce cotton, not cattle.[32]

The reconstruction of *ranchero* society was presented by the engineers of the CNI as a way to end revolutionary disturbances in northern Mexico. This was the same argument for the creation of the agrarian middle class out of former sharecroppers (*aparceros*) and renters (*arrendatarios*), but the *ranchero* was identified as the revolutionary element in need of "rehabilitation." Irrigation engineer Alejandro Brambila, in his survey of northeastern Mexico, found that many of the region's *rancheros* had, through land surveys and sales, been converted into small, impoverished agricultural producers. "In the zone that I have just finished visiting," he wrote in 1930, "the independent *ranchero* that lives where property has been subdivided, is in an absolutely disastrous condition; in the moral order and in the economic order."[33] Apart from the loss of common grazing lands from surveys, between 1902 and 1923 the *rancheros* of the north lost, according to one estimate, more than 75 percent of their livestock, much of that to finance and feed the armies of the Revolution.[34] Their decline as a class meant trouble for the northern border states, and fearing continued social tumult, the government felt obliged to take on "the rehabilitation of those states of the Federation, giving them new elements for life so that, to the extent possible, they would be protected against the risks of a revolt."[35] Furthermore, the demise of *ranchero* society in Mexico's northeast and the rise of irrigated agriculture in the southwestern United States led to a huge increase in emigration from the rural north between 1900 and 1920. The Mexican government planned to repatriate and settle those migrant ex-*rancheros* on its new borderlands irrigation projects.

At the same time that these ex-*rancheros* of northern Mexico were viewed as a political problem, they were also considered a valuable cultural and racial resource. Race was a key element of the notion held by politicians and irrigation engineers that the population of northern Mexico would be especially responsive to state-led development. Popular beliefs about the European racial-cultural character of northern Mexico found expression in the colonization of *callista* irrigated development projects, which, because a priority of CNI construction efforts was to utilize the waters of the tributaries of the Río Bravo, were located in the north. For example, in the preliminary study for an irrigation project in Santa Gertrudis, in the Valle Bajo del Río Bravo, one engineer reported that "the region's dwellers are similar in every way to those of the rest of the borderlands of the States of Nuevo León and Tamaulipas; they are of Hispanic ancestry, white, bearded, with caucasian features, tall and robust. . . . They eat meat and eggs daily. . . . All wear shoes, pants and jacket as well as hats of palm fronds or felt. . . . It is undoubtable that irrigation will bring them uncountable benefits that they will know how to take advantage of."[36] "As can be seen," another writer for the CNI echoed, "very little of the indigenous race exists in the northern region, for the majority of the inhabitants are *criollos*. . . . They are in general European-looking, intelligent, hard-working, sober, frank, hospitable. . . ."[37]

These descriptions of the *rancheros* and ex-*rancheros* of the borderlands reflect the enduring and widely held idea that northern Mexicans are whiter and more hard-working than their counterparts in the center and the south of the country. Generally speaking, *norteños* are considered to be more European, to live in an arid environment that has taught them to work hard for their livelihoods, and to eat foods that are more European and less indigenous—such as wheat tortillas. The popular concept of the "three Mexicos"—south, center, and north—defines these regions by race and ecology, and ranks them in a unilineal evolutionary hierarchy, the north being the most advanced (or "developed") and the south being the least so. The engineers of the CNI felt that government intervention in the productive geography and infrastructure of northern borderlands would combine with the racial and cultural progressiveness of the region's inhabitants to ensure an integral development of the region. In the discussion of the racial "character" of the north the concept of "evolutionary development" reappears, but as an instrument to be used by the state rather than as its own motor of progress. By making race both a tool and an object of developmental state intervention in the borderlands, the Calles government—like many governments during that time—took the turn to eugenics. Together with the strategic priorities of increasing agricultural production, utilizing the waters of the international rivers, and stabilizing a landless, highly mobile, and politically volatile regional population, the government sought to rescue and rehabilitate the European "character" of northern Mexican *ranchero* society. Racial ideology was one factor, among others, that moved the state to channel resources to the north, thus contributing to the reproduction of uneven development in Mexico and the perpetuation of a particular Mexican racial formation.[38]

"Don Martín"—A *Callista* Development Project

The Don Martín project, located in the states of Coahuila and Nuevo León in northeastern Mexico, was the first big irrigation project built by the state from the ground up, and its history shows how the guiding tenets of the callista "revolutionary irrigation" were put into action. The director of the CNI, Ignacio López Bancalari, called the Don Martín project—officially named the Sistema de Riego Río Salado, or the

Sistema de Riego #4—the "most important" of all the CNI's works planned in the late 1920s, because it was the most ambitious in terms of its physical scale and the scope of the government's development intervention.[39] Perhaps the biggest issue at stake in the engineering of society in the irrigation zones of the CNI was that of land ownership, for it was the pattern of land ownership that would give rise to the structure of social classes in the region. In the Don Martín project the CNI hoped to enact its project to rehabilitate humble *rancheros*, so that, as one engineer put it, "today they would be sharecroppers and tomorrow, property owners."[40] To avoid the monopolization of land, the maximum extension permitted to a single owner by the 1926 Ley Federal de Colonización was 150 hectares, but the CNI set the limit for Don Martín at 100 hectares, and hoped to establish an average property size of just 20 hectares within its jurisdiction. The land was to be cleared, readied for planting, and sold in different sizes according the financial possibilities of the buyers: from a minimum of 8 hectares up to the limit of 100 hectares. The geography of the Don Martín zone was planned to facilitate the movement of labor and products to and from the fields, and all farms lay within 2 kilometers of a road and within 5 kilometers of a train station. The fields were leveled, which made irrigation more efficient and made the products grown in those fields of more uniform quality. Soil types were mapped and classified, and lots were priced according to that classification.[41]

Apart from rehabilitating *rancheros* as small and medium property owners, the CNI planned to create a sizable class of *campesinos* in the Don Martín system, who would be settled in small rural communities of five to ten families. Each of these *campesinos* would purchase a plot of 1 or 2 hectares, which would provide sustenance when he was not employed on the region's cotton *ranchos*. By fixing this agricultural working class on its own properties, the CNI hoped to provide the workers with the means to survive in the case of unemployment, and to avoid problems of landlessness and indigence in the region. These *minifundios* were not unlike the tiny parcels given to *ejidatarios* by agrarian reforms: they were "*pegujales*" that would assure the presence of a peasantry in the region whose labor could be utilized for commercial agriculture. Unlike the *ejidatarios*, however, these *campesinos* were to benefit from all the moral improvements that the ownership of property was thought to entail.

In planning society in the Don Martín, the engineers of the CNI held the ideal of the independent landowning *ranchero* in ambiguous relation to an ideal of cooperativism. As one CNI spokesman put it, "we want to build in the irrigation zones of our Systems strong and consistent groupings of rustic small property owners; in which the individualist sentiment so deeply rooted in that social class continues acting as the best incentive for progress, but conscious that the coordination of the isolated efforts of each member of the colony will lead to its prosperity, and thus to the prosperity of those who comprise it."[42] While the CNI hoped to establish unique relationships with individual colonists through the sale and purchase of land, thereby reinforcing the independent responsibility of each, it also sought to organize the colonists into cooperatives. The engineers of the Don Martín system took as their model the Texas side of the Lower Río Bravo/Rio Grande Valley and called for the creation of strong corporate groups to administer credit, production, consumption, and the commercialization of products. These cooperatives were to serve two main purposes. First, the cooperative would enhance the earnings of the individual producer/consumer by eliminating the cost of maintaining a commercial class. Cooperatives, it was argued, would perform the functions of the merchant, but would work to elevate the price of the products and lower the price of consumer goods for the benefit of all cooperative members, rather than for personal gain. Second, the cooperatives would serve to mediate between the individual and the Mexican government, especially for the purposes of managing credit provided by the Banco Nacional de Crédito Agrícola (BNCA). It was also hoped that these cooperatives would play a leading role in the dissemination of technical knowledge.[43]

The CNI thought its way out of the logical contradiction between individualism and cooperativism by arguing that the very space of the irrigation zone would promote collective sentiments and social relations between individual farmers. "It is a proven fact of 'human geography,'" claimed the CNI, "that the organizations of water users, with the characters of ours, constitute a peculiar geographic space in which all the fruits of the collective ideal bloom."[44] The engineering of social space, then, was the key to integrating the individual and the social in the irrigation districts. But the tension between individualism and cooperativism presented infrastructural difficulties for the region's planners. On the one hand, the supposed love that the small farmer held for his land as well as the constellation of moral qualities that emerged from that relation between producer and means of production all depended on the farmer actually living and working on his parcel. Physical presence on the land was also held out as a preventive against absentee landowning and the emergence of sharecropping or tenancy relations in the irrigation system. However, the CNI also wanted to provide the services of modern society—potable water, electricity, education, sports centers, health care, and "centers of honest fun"—to the region's inhabitants, a project that would be immensely costly if all the region's inhabitants lived on their farms. Dispersed settlements would also make it more difficult to monitor and maintain the health and moral status of the rural population once it was established.[45]

The answer to the problem of providing services and controlling the population was found in urban planning. The inhabitants of the new irrigation districts were grouped into "agricultural cities" and "agricultural towns," where the government could concentrate its subjects, its investment, and effort. Because the new irrigation zones of the 1920s were built in areas with no previous settlements of this magnitude, the planners felt they could make the new agricultural cities modern and efficient, unburdened by the inherited geographies of Mexico's colonial-period cities. To make these cities function as regional centers, they were to be located at the center of the irrigation zones and near to railroads or highways. Smaller towns were to be dotted uniformly across the landscape to make it easier for inhabitants to reach the fields, and located near principal canals so that water could be had at all times. The planning of these urban centers took into account the social classes of inhabitants residing in the town and the costs and technical problems of building the town or city. There were also aesthetic issues to be considered: if possible, the towns and cities were to be located where the inhabitants would be able to enjoy the scenery.[46] By the 1940s Ciudad Anáhuac, the capital of the Don Martín system, was one of four such cities built by the CNI in its irrigation zones.

The engineers of the CNI also concentrated on shaping the domestic space of the irrigation zone's inhabitants. The CNI decided that the success of the entire irrigation system was at risk if the colonists were not provided with housing. It was quite possible that the *colonos* would not be able to afford to build their own houses, especially if they had to buy materials from commercial middlemen. On a cultural level, the CNI argued that by providing the farmer with a house, it would oblige him and his family to live in better conditions. The enjoyment of a more costly and refined domestic space would, it was thought, help generate the cultural and economic benefits of middle-class life, such as increased productivity and political stability. These benefits, however, had to be weighed against the costs of construction, and excessively elaborate and expensive dwellings were ruled out. Alejandro Brambila, the engineer charged with designing the domestic environment of the CNI's *colonos* in the Don Martín system, evaluated the ways that housing was provided to colonists in Australia, New Zealand, and Argentina before coming to the decision that the most efficient and appropriate housing construction was to be found in the very region where the CNI's *sistemas* were located—the northern borderlands. Brambila had done fieldwork in the Don Martín region for the CNI, and had learned about the building techniques and designs popular among the region's inhabitants. These were *jacales* covered with *adobe:* wattle-and-daub structures with a door, a window and a chimney, and a dirt floor. All the materials were to be found locally, and the structure itself provided exceptional insulation against the extremes of temperature common in the north.[47]

The work of anthropologist Manuel Gamio on migration, repatriation, and colonization had some influence on the colonization of the Don Martín system with migrant *rancheros* repatriated from the United States. During the late 1920s and early 1930s Gamio carried out a study of Mexican migrants in the United States, part of a larger effort by the National Research Council and the fledgling Social Science Research Council to confront the problems of race, nation, and sovereignty posed by human migration. The authors of the preliminary study for the Don Martín project had read and probably met with Gamio, and an unpublished text of his is cited at length in the study. It was not enough, the anthropologist argued, to provide repatriated Mexican colonists with irrigation, credit, machinery, and other "economic" tools, if cultural aspects such as education and hygiene were not also attended to.[48]

Gamio believed the Mexican *repatriados* were technologically and culturally progressive, and that this productive culture needed to be harnessed by the state to promote development. Gamio wedded ideas of acculturation that were strong among anthropologists at that time to a Lamarckian social evolutionism and a hierarchical model of "civilization," and argued that the progressive culture of the *repatriados* could be transmitted to other rural Mexicans. He explained that the reimmigration of workers to Mexico could serve as an enormous educational system, in which the *repatriados* would be the "teachers of life in general." The problem with such a model of acculturation, however, was that the opposite was also true: the *repatriados* could also learn the regressive productive culture of rural Mexico. To prevent this, Gamio suggested that the *repatriados* be placed in settlements separated far enough from the rest of the population to protect them from negative cultural influence, but close enough so that their culture would still have a positive effect on their countrymen. He suggested creating "isolated rural centers" to achieve this end.[49]

The "social objective" sought by the CNI in its irrigation zones was to "elevate the material level of the *campesino* as much as the cultural level," and like Gamio, the CNI intellectuals argued that the means to achieve this end was the engineering of social space. Orive Alba, long-time director of the CNI, argued that "the incorporation of the *campesinos* into the highest norms of civilization can only be achieved by making them live grouped in agricultural settlements where it is possible for the cultural action of the State to reach them . . . the cultural, civilizing work of the Government, will only reach the *campesino* if he is grouped in rural settlements that, although very modest, are properly planned to fill the objectives of a more just, healthier, better civic life."[50] This conceptualization of space and development informed the CNI's plan to settle its Don Martín system with *repatriados*. While the *repatriados* were shouldered with the responsibility of educating the "uncultured masses," it was the government's role to ensure that the material culture and social space of the settlements and the households in its new regions encouraged this process of developmental acculturation.

Attempts at social planning often go dramatically awry.[51] Of course, even the most modest of plans must be adjusted to suit new conditions as they arise, and this was certainly true of the Don Martín irrigation zone. When construction began on the irrigation works of the Don Martín system in the late 1920s, only two types of agricultural parcels were contemplated, for two types of inhabitants: the *ranchero* and the agricultural worker. Colonization of the zone began in 1931, and apart from the pamphlets and organizational campaigns of the CNI and activities of the Mexican consuls in the southwestern United States, colonists reported that there were men stationed at the border to inform Mexicans crossing into Mexico of the possibilities of settling in Don Martín. "There they were on the bridge, talking to anyone who would listen about the new irrigation system," recalled one *repatriado* interviewed in 1998. "It was the Depression, there were no jobs in Texas, and so I headed for Anáhuac."[52] By April of that year, 268 property owners and their families had set up temporary camps and had begun the process of building and planting. Thirty percent of these held large plots of between 75 and 100 hectares, but about half of them had less than 25 hectares. The land was sold for between 270 pesos and 300 pesos per hectare, depending on the quality, and the colonist had to pay at least 5 percent at the start, as well as demonstrate that he or she had at least 40 pesos of operating capital for each hectare.[53]

In 1930 the CNI founded Ciudad Anáhuac on the bank of the Río Salado, near an older settlement called Rodríguez. Ciudad Anáhuac was to be the industrial and commercial center of the region—an agricultural city that would group the colonists together so as to facilitate the provision of material services, as well as the "cultural, civilizing work" of the state.[54] Construction on Ciudad Anáhuac really began in 1932, to accommodate the settlers that began to arrive in early 1931. A radial design was used that, according to local inhabitants, was derived from the street plan of Paris. The design was thought to make access to the center of the city easy from all directions. Parks and fountains were planned, as was a central plaza at the hub of the city's street plan. Originally the CNI engineers only contemplated the settlement of colonists, and the installation of an administrative and commercial center around the main plaza of the city. That they did not anticipate the need for homes for industrial workers in a city where cotton industries were sure to spring up is surprising.[55]

The Don Martín system expanded enormously between 1931 and 1935. According to government statistics, 1932 was the first year that more than tiny amounts of cotton were grown in the Don Martín district: 2226 bales of cotton were grown that first year, but by 1934 the number had ballooned to 17,574. As the irrigation district grew and production increased through the early 1930s, agricultural workers flooded in to pick crops. These were mostly workers who included the irrigation zone on their yearly migration circuit, or who were displaced from wage employment, rental, or sharecropping arrangements in rural Texas by the economic crisis and anti-immigrant politics that grew in severity from 1929 to 1932. Many of the repatriated workers who ended up in the Don Martín region traced their roots to nearby *ranchos* and towns such as Sabinas Hidalgo, in northern Coahuila, and were, in a sense, returning home. Some stayed just long enough to pick the cotton crops; others stayed after the crops were picked, hoping to settle down and contribute to the prosperity promised for the region.[56]

According to the information provided by the CNI, none of the agricultural workers that arrived in the region purchased 1- or 2-hectare lots at that time. In the CNI's planned community there was no space assigned to receive this property-less, migrant working class, and they were forced to set up camp in an impromptu village called Nuevo Rodríguez. Others settled across the river from Ciudad Anáhuac in a town called Camarón. In order to better accommodate penniless *repatriados* and to find buyers of land during the Depression, by 1932 the CNI altered its contracts for colonization in the Don Martín system. Individuals willing to settle and work the land themselves or with wage labor could purchase parcels of up to 25 hectares, while those who promised to work as sharecroppers on the government's land until they owned it could purchase up to 100 hectares. In 1934 the CNI responded to the growth of the unplanned settlements by adding a "workers' neighborhood" ("*colonia obrera*") to Ciudad Anáhuac, and by adding a sector to the city layout to accommodate the small farms for agricultural workers whom the CNI originally intended to group together in agricultural towns in the countryside.[57]

Just when the planned growth of the region began to gain strength, crisis struck. The Depression that began in 1929 sent workers streaming back into Mexico looking for work, and by 1935 Ciudad Anáhuac, with ten thousand inhabitants, was the second largest city in the state of Nuevo León, after Monterrey. That year, however, began a period in which the Río Salado failed to provide its expected volume of water to the reservoir of the irrigation system, resulting in an almost total cessation of farming in the region. This drought was the result of the decision made by President Calles years before to build an irrigation zone that depended on a river for which there was only limited information about stream flow. The political struggle to control the water of the international rivers made dam-building on the tributaries of the Río Bravo a priority, but Mexican engineers only had adequate information regarding the flow of water in the Río Bravo itself. To judge the number of hectares the Río Salado could irrigate, the engineers had to infer from data on the flow of the Río Bravo how much water the Río Salado contributed. The Don Martín dam was built to hold enough water to irrigate 65,000 hectares, when the actual flow could support no more than 30,000. Needless to say, after a few years the dam went dry, throwing the region into severe crisis and initiating a vast resettlement program by the federal government. Many of the region's inhabitants were relocated to the Valle Bajo Río Bravo in 1937 and 1938, a movement that will be discussed in subsequent chapters. By 1940, there were only about two thousand inhabitants in Ciudad Anáhuac.[58]

Conclusions

The creation of the Comisión Nacional de Irrigación by Calles in 1926 marked an important change in the way the Mexican state envisioned the development of northern Mexico, and in the manner by which that development was to be secured. The Laguna, while considered a model of regional development, did not produce the liberal agrarian utopia of peaceful and prosperous small farmers. Instead, the Laguna and other zones of intensive, irrigated commercial agriculture such as Mexicali produced a politically volatile class of migratory laborers. The mostly *norteño* leaders of the Mexican government during and after the Revolution were well acquainted with the social problems of northern Mexico, and made their resolution a priority of the development efforts. They sought to emulate the economic growth of the southwestern United States and the Laguna region, while avoiding, and correcting for, the creation of a politically unstable floating population of workers in the region.

The vision of progressively skilled small farmers producing cotton with advanced technology on nationalized lands irrigated by the waters of the international rivers guided their actions.

Before 1926 the Mexican federal government supported development and colonization projects in Mexicali, Oaxaca, and Chihuahua. These, however, were exceptional cases, and federal investment in such projects was extremely limited. With an evolutionary philosophy of development and severe limits in the state's financial resources, governments before that of Calles largely abstained from intervening with agrarian reforms or spending on irrigation works. Calles reformulated the concept of development by creating a government agency—the Comisión Nacional de Irrigación—that was expressly devoted to making profound interventions in the society, economy, and culture of northern Mexico, in an effort to realize those enduring visions of an agrarian northern borderland.

Regardless of its failure to achieve even the most basic expectations of its creators, the CNI's Don Martín system shows how the strategic priorities of the Mexican state led to the formation of a regional society in northern Mexico. It was built to lay a claim to international waters, to take advantage of an expanding market for cotton produced outside of the United States, to rehabilitate the *ranchero* class, to settle emigrant Mexican agricultural workers, and to use these material and cultural resources to drive the economic growth of the country. The CNI's version of social engineering was based on a notion of development that included strong racial and spatial aspects, and the colonization of the irrigation systems with *rancheros* and *repatriados* was backed by the idea—widespread among rulers and ruled alike—that these *norteños* were culturally, economically, and racially more progressive than their compatriots living in the center and the south of the country. The state's effort to engineer regional society reinforced and reproduced what Michael Omi and Howard Winant refer to as a regional "racial formation."[59]

The vision of *norteña* agrarian society coupled with an evolutionary idea of development and acculturation to guide the construction of physical space in the Don Martín irrigation system. Well-bounded irrigated regions such as that one were created by the CNI to house the progressive landowners of the new agrarian north, who were settled in agricultural cities and small towns in order to reinforce their progressive tendencies and facilitate the "integral" actions by the Mexican state to accentuate their development. A few years later these same priorities would guide the creation and colonization of an irrigation system on the Mexican side of the lower Río Bravo/Rio Grande Valley. However, the economic crash of 1929 and the ensuing social crisis dramatically changed the conditions within which the government's effort to develop rural northeast Mexico was mounted. These changes caused alterations to the vision of development guiding the government's actions, and in the specific means used to achieve that development.

PART II

THE RÍO BRAVO/RIO GRANDE DELTA

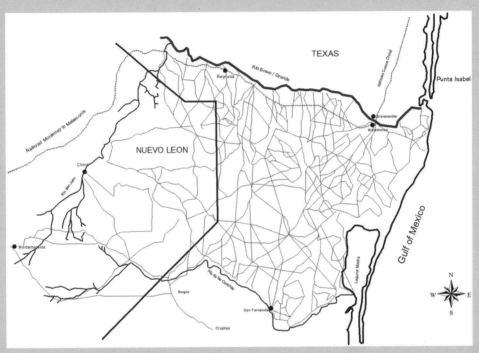

Roads and footpaths of northern Tamaulipas, c. 1900.

CHAPTER 4

THE SOCIAL FIELD OF DEVELOPMENT: LAND AND LABOR IN THE RÍO BRAVO/RIO GRANDE DELTA, 1780–1930

In 1935 Mexican federal government engineers began building a regional irrigated agricultural development project in the southern half of the Río Bravo/Rio Grande delta. Like the Don Martín project before it, the Valle Bajo Río Bravo project was an effort to create a new productive landscape, with irrigation and flood control works, roads, schools and houses, and a regional population of small farmers growing cotton. Despite the dramatic changes made to the landscape and society in the lower Río Bravo/Rio Grande Valley after 1935, this development initiative of the government headed by Pres. Lázaro Cárdenas was not created in a vacuum, and took shape in relation to existing regional geographies and social formations, as well as to previous plans and efforts to develop commercial agriculture on both sides of the delta region. In this chapter I describe the patterns of land tenure and the social classes that formed during the long period from the colonization of the region in the late 1700s until 1930, and how developers sought to transform these at the beginning of the twentieth century. This, together with discussions of the political economy of cotton and state engineering presented in subsequent chapters, give us an understanding of why the Mexican government's project to develop the northern borderlands took the shape that it did, at the moment that it did, in the Valle Bajo Río Bravo.

To incorporate global, national, and local elements into a history of the Valle Bajo Río Bravo project, I describe how land use and tenure formed the basis of an evolving mode of production and social field in the Río Bravo delta between 1780 and 1930. When the Río Bravo/Rio Grande delta region was colonized in the mid-eighteenth century, most of the land along both banks of the river was given to colonists in the form of "*porciones,*" a division that ensured river access to each. A bit further back from the river, enormous land grants were awarded to a small number of Mexico City elites. In what is now northern Tamaulipas, a land grant of nearly one million hectares of arid scrubland constituted the *hacienda* known as "La Sauteña." Throughout the region small groups of *rancheros* established communities based on the shared use of grazing land and water, and the private cultivation of a very limited amount of land for domestic consumption. These *rancheros* most often held the land informally through inheritance or kinship rights to *porciones,* but many could

UNITED STATES

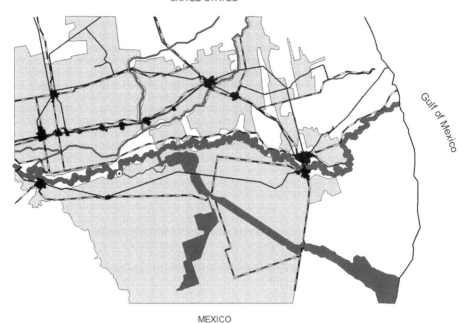

MEXICO

Irrigated lands of the Río Bravo/Rio Grande delta (the "Valle Bajo"), c. 1960.

not make such claims based on legal title or kinship. Many *ranchos* were established on the property of the Sauteña, which was never put to use by its owners. The delta region remained poorly integrated into systems of industrial capitalism through the nineteenth century, except for the brief period of frenzied cotton commerce during the U.S. Civil War (1861–1865).

The pattern of land tenure established in the late colonial period remained largely intact until the twentieth century, when flood control, irrigation, and railroads facilitated the conversion of regional society from one based in ranching and commerce to one based in agriculture and industry. Irrigation and railroads brought commercial agriculture to the Texas side of the Valley around 1900, incorporating Mexicans and Mexican Americans in the region as wage laborers, and adding impetus to plans to develop northern Tamaulipas. Some of the landowners along the Mexican riverbank cleared land and grew cotton, either through rental or sharecropper arrangements, or through the use of agricultural wage laborers. Plans to emulate the growth of the Laguna region by developing and colonizing the huge expanse of the Sauteña were formed as early as the 1880s. But although the Mexican owners of the Sauteña and their U.S. allies raised immense amounts of capital, built a few irrigation works, and settled a small number of colonists in the years before 1910, the Mexican Revolution halted the project. It was to be resurrected by Pres.

Lázaro Cárdenas in 1935, but in the first decades of the twentieth century northern Tamaulipas was still a vast expanse of thorn forest with scattered settlements connected by footpaths and wagon trails. (see map, p.65).

In 1930, just before the economic crisis hit, the Texas side of the delta was already engaged in commercial citrus, vegetable, and cotton production. The Mexican side of the border, on the other hand, was only beginning to move weakly from ranching and the reproduction of wage labor for the Texas side of the river, to commercial cotton. The pattern of land tenure in northern Tamaulipas was changing from an earlier system marked by a somewhat communitarian use of unfenced grazing lands and water sources to one in which private ownership of clearly delineated agricultural land was more important. Immigrants to the Valle Bajo Río Bravo filled the ranks of the sharecroppers, tenants, and agricultural workers who labored in the emergent cotton agriculture on the Mexican side of the river, as well as in the flourishing agriculture of the "Magic Valley" of South Texas. This new class of agricultural laborers remained largely foreign to the region's kin-based social relations and landholding system, and many arrived to the region bearing revolutionary-period concepts of land reform and social justice. In the 1920s conflict erupted in the Valle Bajo Río Bravo between the original class of landowning *rancheros* and the emerging class of sharecroppers and agricultural workers that constituted, and was constituted by, the long-term shift in regional production. These tensions within regional society were ameliorated by a negotiation and realignment of property and power among the principal actors in the region, an arrangement that staved off developmental intervention by "outside" political and economic actors such as U.S. cotton capital and the Mexican federal government until the mid-1930s.

Development and Developmentalism in the Delta, 1860–1930

In 1767 the Bourbon reforms reached the twenty-odd towns established in Nuevo Santander during the colonization of the 1740s and 1750s in the form of a new land regime based in private, individual property. But although the modern, liberal agrarian vision of the freeholding small farmer may have been preferred for the few communities already established at that time, the Bourbon government continued in the colonial custom of awarding most of the rest of the scarcely populated province as enormous land grants (*mercedes*). Most of the southern bank of the Río Bravo was awarded in 1781 to Antonio de Urízar as one enormous latifundio—El Sauto— called "La Sauteña" by the region's inhabitants. The Sauteña was truly gargantuan: 1 million hectares stretching from the Río Bravo south to the Río San Fernando, and from the Gulf of Mexico to the border of Tamaulipas with Nuevo León. The owners lived in Mexico City and made no effort to make the property productive. They were rather more disposed to selling off small portions of the *hacienda* to settlers and colonists in search of lands, and it was by this mechanism that the banks of the Río Bravo from Reynosa to Matamoros were colonized in 1784. The Sauto passed into the hands of the Conde family, which took over the role of absentee landlord, renting lands to cattle ranchers and selling pieces of the *hacienda* to pay taxes.[1]

When the liberals gained power toward the end of the 1860s, they put pressure on the Sauteña to pay land taxes, a measure as much aimed at promoting productive use of land as it was at increasing government income. The owner of the *hacienda* could neither make the holdings productive nor withstand the fiscal pressure of state and local governments, and in the 1880s the Conde family sold its lands to a group of investors. These investors then commissioned a survey (*deslinde*) of the entire region, establishing their property rights over the land. This survey also ratified the pronouncement by the Secretaría de Fomento (Ministry of Development) that, having reviewed the legal records, there were no national lands within the limits of the property, or basis to claims made upon that property by any other than those who had documentation of land transactions with the Conde family.[2]

The *deslinde* and the declarations by Fomento made the lands of the Sauteña potentially alienable, gave legal basis for the new owners' efforts to reclaim the land from regional settlers and squatters, and paved the way for its subdivision and sale to colonists. In the 1880s and 1890s, during the presidency of Porfirio Díaz, a series of concessions and contracts were celebrated between the Sauteña and the Secretaría de Fomento, by which the land company secured water rights on the promise that it would colonize the region and create agricultural ranches, livestock nurseries, and salt works. Díaz and his vice-president Manuel González, a native of Matamoros, had high hopes for attracting capital investment to Mexico, and were especially close to the merchant elite of South Texas with their financial connections in the northeastern United States. As John Mason Hart shows, before Díaz took power in the late 1870s, he cut a deal with those Texas businessmen in which he promised that the Mexican government under his rule would establish order in exchange for money and arms. The simmering conflict in South Texas accompanying the shady transfer of land from Mexican to Anglo hands and the chronic and structural persistence of contraband posed risks to the property and investments of the Texans. The control of independent regional leaders, "bandits" and smugglers such as Juan Cortina, along the Tamaulipas-Texas border was especially important to these financiers, who sought to invest more heavily in the region.[3]

With the *deslinde* and legal regularization of the Sauteña properties, the infusion of capital by the Sauteña's new owners, and the procurement of water rights, many of the conditions necessary for the establishment of modern, capitalist agricultural ranches in northern Tamaualipas were met. Transportation, however, was lacking. Railroads financed by U.S. capital were being built all over the western United States and northern Mexico in the 1880s and 1890s, but the lower Río Bravo/Rio Grande Valley was bypassed in favor of routes farther inland. The owners of the Sauteña were dependent on U.S. railroad builders to connect the Matamoros region to markets, and the railroad builders were strongly influenced by Brownsville elites, who decided to concentrate their construction efforts on a railroad through the border town of Laredo, farther upriver. In 1904, the Saint Louis, Brownsville, & Mexico railroad began bringing "homeseekers" to the Valley, and on Cinco de Mayo of 1905 Díaz inaugurated the building of a new rail connection between Matamoros and Monterrey, which would be completed in 1910 with the opening of a rail bridge between Matamoros and Brownsville.[4]

The railroad connected the Texas Valley to the rest of the United States, but irrigation made commercial agriculture possible. Failed efforts to grow sugar and cotton made it clear that the region's development depended as much on irrigation works as it did on railroads. "I tell you candidly," W. H. Chatfield wrote in letter to a Brownsville newspaper in 1892, "if the people of this section wish to rise with one bound from poverty to wealth, from depression to happiness, with occupation for the poor, banishment of bandits and a glorious future for their progeny, they will say less about a railroad and secure the prime factor for building railroads—development of the lower Rio Grande Country by means of irrigation."[5] The irrigated agricultural society proposed by Chatfield marked a fundamental shift in the imagination of how development would proceed in the lower Río Bravo/Rio Grande. Rather than legal and illegal commerce—the region's traditional mainstay—promoted by its location on an international border, agricultural production would drive the economy. By 1900 the possibilities of irrigated agriculture in the region were evident, and investors began to form small companies to buy land, install pumping plants, build irrigation systems, and settle colonists. Most of the settlers were from the midwestern United States and purchased from 10 to 40 acres.

The Gulf Coast border region is, in general, quite dry and supports what is known as Tamaulipan thorn brush: a low scrub vegetation that includes mesquite, huisache, cactus, yucca, and grasses. Although there were few permanent water sources in the area, the landscape supported grazing animals. Agriculture, on the other hand, was limited both by the difficulty of moving the water out of the river channels onto fields and the poverty of the soil in most of the region. The delta of the Río Bravo/Rio Grande received periodic floodings that watered and enriched the soil with nutrients, and was therefore home to a much more opulent flora and fauna. Along the Río Bravo/Rio Grande extensive stands of sabal palms thrived, and a bit farther from the river the forest was composed of hardwoods such as mesquite and ebony that reached heights of 30 feet. The understory was a dense thicket of thorn bushes that in many places was impenetrable.

To convert these lands to agriculture required a great deal of work. First the brush had to be cleared and burnt, then followed the arduous task of felling hardwoods with axes and saws. Once the trees were felled, burned, and turned into charcoal, the stumps had to be removed. This was a truly grueling task that involved uncovering and chopping enough roots so that the stump could be ripped out of the ground. Then the stumps would be hauled into a pile, burnt, and made into charcoal. Working with a team of draft animals, as was common on the Mexican side of the delta until the 1940s, it could take a man and his family a year or two to clear

10 hectares of land. In the Texas Valley tractors that ran on steam were available, and the arrival of gasoline-powered tractors after 1910 made this work much quicker and easier. Once cleared, the land had to be leveled, so that the irrigation water would not pool and cause salinization of the soil.[6]

Unlike most of the U.S. borderlands areas that received irrigation works from the U.S. federal government after the passage of the 1902 Reclamation Act, the Texas side of the lower Rio Grande/Río Bravo Valley was irrigated by private developers. Instead of a unified irrigation zone under the management of a single authority (the federal government), the Valley was a patchwork of many irrigation systems that drew water from the Rio Grande/Río Bravo through huge pumps. Because the existing international water treaty prohibited both countries from constructing works that obstructed the navigability of the international rivers, a dam on the Rio Grande/Río Bravo was out of the question. For this reason, and the fact that the lower Rio Grande Valley was not publicly owned land, the U.S. Reclamation Service did not enter into the Valley's development. The absence of a dam controlling the entire region's water was paralleled by the absence of a single authority governing the use of the water. As it stood, whoever got to the water first could use it as they pleased.

The Matamoros side of the lower Río Bravo/Rio Grande Valley did not experience the enormous development of the Texas side during the first three decades of the twentieth century, but that was not the result of a lack of planning. In 1904 the railroad finally reached Brownsville, and the following year the line was begun between Monterrey and Matamoros. In 1906 the company that owned the Sauteña signed a contract with the state of Tamaulipas in which it promised to build irrigation works, and to clear and colonize 100,000 hectares of land. This infrastructure required a huge amount of capital, and the Sauteña was reorganized in 1907 in order to raise money through the sale of shares. In 1909 some of the developers who organized the creation of irrigation works and the colonization of settlers in the Texas Valley got involved in this project for the Tamaulipas bank of the Río Bravo.[7]

Apart from private loans and investment, the owners of the Sauteña were also quite successful at generating state funds for the Sauteña cotton development scheme. In February of 1909 the federal government promised to directly fund the Sauteña scheme to the tune of 6 million pesos, and the land company promised to use the money to open up 100,000 hectares to irrigated cultivation. The Secretaría de Fomento also made the Sauteña agree to submit all its specific irrigation and colonization plans and projects for approval, and established time limits for the implementation of the approved plans.[8]

The changes in the productive landscape proposed by these contracts were as massive as the Sauteña itself. A pumping station was to have been built near Camargo at the confluence of the Río San Juan and the Río Bravo, opposite the Texas town of Rio Grande City. Following the example of the Texas side of the Valley, the pumps would lift the water 7 meters out of the Río Bravo and into a canal that would flow southeast into the center of the Sauteña, a route of more than 100 kilometers. Another equally long canal was to run from a dam on the San Juan River near China, Nuevo León (the site of today's "El Cuchillo" dam), into the center of the Sauteña. Furthermore, a railroad spur was planned that would head south from the Ebanos station (later Colombres; now the town of Río Bravo), crossing the entire property to connect with the town of San Fernando. Another spur was to connect this line to the Gulf Coast, where a port was to be established. As in the Texas Valley, colonization was considered essential to the establishment of small farmers, and in 1909 the Sauteña hired a U.S. company to organize the colonization of its land with colonists from the United States and Europe.[9]

John Mason Hart traces the involvement of this U.S. firm in the Sauteña colonization plan to a connection with the Texas Company, a group of investors involved in the oil industry that also played a major role in financing development projects in northern Mexico and Texas. The Texas Company included James Stillman, a prominent New York financier and son of Brownsville founding father Charles Stillman. Porfirio Díaz was close to Stillman, and it was through this connection that he was able to arrange huge loans from the National City Bank and the Speyer Bank of London to fund the Caja de Prestamos. The Sauteña secured a 5 million peso loan from the Caja de Prestamos and a 16.5 million peso stock emission backed by the Banco Central Mexicano.[10]

Cotton was proposed as the principal crop for the Sauteña, on the basis that it would provide a way to pay off the investments in irrigation and colonization. To the Sauteña's developers, cotton represented a promise of prosperity and progress, as it had to the farmers who settled East Texas after the Civil War, to the plantation owners of the Laguna, and to the investors in the Texas half of Río Bravo Delta. Of course, cotton had a long history in the lower Río Bravo/Rio Grande Valley, and the region's inhabitants associated the commodity with the immense prosperity enjoyed during the U.S. Civil War. During the last thirty years of the nineteenth century cotton was grown as a cash crop by the farmers on both banks of the river, and some large ranch owners had set up sharecropping arrangements for the production of the crop. But while by 1906 cotton was a traditional crop in the Valley, it was also viewed as the business of the future. It was also clear that Mexican farmers could not hope to produce perishable food crops such as produce or citrus for U.S. markets, because of trade barriers and tariffs. The Sauteña owners saw both the success of the Laguna region and the domination of cotton in the Texas side of the Valley, and planned the same for Matamoros.[11]

The efforts of the Sauteña to reproduce the growth of the Laguna and the Texas Valley led to legal skirmishes with local *rancheros,* and generated antagonism against the absentee landowners and their local representatives. Beginning with the *deslinde* of 1888, the *rancheros* who had established themselves on the abandoned *hacienda* over the previous century were pressured by the *hacienda* owners to move off the land. Backed by the federal government, the Sauteña won all its legal actions against these *rancheros,* but this only fueled regional antipathy toward the *hacienda.*

With the surge of radical political ideologies such as *magonismo* in the borderlands from 1907 onward, the Sauteña *hacienda* became a target for popular sentiments of nationalist revindication. In 1910 forces loyal to Venustiano Carranza and led by Lucio Blanco and Francisco J. Múgica occupied the headquarters of the Sauteña in the town of Río Bravo, and handed over land titles to sharecroppers. Only a very small part of the Sauteña was divided and redistributed during the Revolution, and this action was more symbolic than substantive. However, the development plans and projects of the Sauteña's development company were abandoned due to the fighting and insecurity. In 1912, when the Banco Central Mexicano signed its contract with the company that owned the Sauteña, 89.5 percent of the company's assets were its unimproved land, and its water concessions amounted to another 9.5 percent. Machinery, works completed, railroad material, and all other investments amounted to a minuscule 1 percent of the company's worth. The massive debt contracted by the Sauteña with the Banco Nacional de México by way of the Caja de Prestamos soon went into default, and, despite a renegotiation, in 1920 the Caja began the legal process of acquiring title to its lands.[12]

After the Revolution ended and the slow process of state formation began in the early 1920s, the business of the Sauteña lurched onward, despite the spectacularly costly failure of its owners to put their development plans into place. The Secretary of the Treasury (Secretaría de Hacienda, or SHCP) made some concessions regarding the accounts of the bankrupt company, and a new company was formed that was owned and managed jointly by the government and the Banco de México. This presence gave the postrevolutionary government power to act upon its pronounced *agrarista* objective of redistributing land, and just like the old company, the new one sought to divide and colonize some 400,000 hectares of the *hacienda*. In 1923, drought in the Laguna provoked a failure of the cotton crop, prompting President Obregón's Secretary of Agriculture and Development (Secretaría de Agricultura y Fomento, or SAF) to seek new sources of cotton fiber. The SAF decided to designate a committee of engineers to study the agricultural situation in Tamaulipas, and to consider bringing in Mexicans from the United States and other regions of Mexico who had experience with the crop. Cotton cultivation experiments were to be made on the Sauteña by these settlers, who would later be offered the chance to acquire those lands. A government-supported cotton cooperative would help convert agricultural laborers into smallholders. Despite continued interest in the region, the government would take no action until it was forced to do so in the 1930s by a set of conditions generated by the global political economy of cotton and the changing regional social formation in the Valle Bajo Río Bravo.[13]

The "Magic Valley" of Texas in 1930

For the first three decades of the twentieth century, Matamoros and its surrounding areas lived in the shadow cast by the splendor of the "Magic Valley" of South Texas. The colonization of the Texas side of the delta by "Anglos"[14] was swift, and by

1910 the crop pattern of vegetables, cotton, and citrus that formed the basis of the huge agricultural boom of subsequent years was established. Because of the high costs of irrigation and land, the business of agriculture was not always as profitable as the new farmers hoped, and many businesses failed. However, when World War I brought high prices for agricultural products, success was ensured. The 1920s saw the high point of this agricultural expansion, in which exorbitant land values and costly irrigation works were compensated for by meager wages to Mexican and Mexican American day workers and high prices in the produce markets of the Midwest and Northeast. The Valley became one of the principal producers of cold-season fruit and vegetables, holding an advantage over Florida and California because its produce matured earliest and reached market when prices were highest. In 1904 the Valley produced a total of $3.7 million of goods. By 1916 this had risen to $16.5 million, and by 1924 it reached $25.3 million. Cotton reached a level of production in 1924 that it would maintain through the 1940s: around 90,000 bales. While cotton continued as king in the region, between 1921 and 1928 rail shipments of citrus had risen from fifteen to more than a thousand. By 1936 the Valley was shipping more than twenty thousand carloads of citrus, and a huge industry had developed around the packing, canning, and processing of fruit and juice.[15]

The growth of the Valley was part of a larger expansion of irrigated agriculture in the southwestern United States during the first few decades of the twentieth century. The spread of cotton into the Southwest was spurred by an effort to reduce production costs, and these new cotton areas were comprised by flat, large farms (often more than 200 acres, or 80 hectares) where tractors and other labor-saving machinery could be used. Wells and pumps watered cotton on relatively cheap, dry land around Abilene, Lubbock, and Amarillo, Texas, where cotton production increased from 9,240 bales in 1909 to 554,000 bales in 1923. The price surge during World War I was another factor in boosting production, and coincided with the building of irrigation zones in Texas, New Mexico, Arizona, and California. Near Ciudad Juárez, cotton production began in the Elephant Butte Reservoir agricultural zone the year after it was completed in 1916, and by 1924 there were some 74,000 acres of the crop. The Salt River Valley of Arizona and the Imperial and San Joaquin valleys of California also produced large amounts of a new variety of long-staple cotton with the help of irrigation. Most of the large irrigation zones were created by the U.S. Bureau of Land Reclamation, and were settled by the Bureau with colonists.[16]

The migration of cotton westward in the first three decades of the twentieth century resulted in another migration: that of agricultural laborers. With the end of slavery, production in the old cotton belt of the United States was largely organized through sharecropping and rental agreements. It was a much more densely settled zone than the southwestern United States, and the extraordinary amount of labor needed to harvest the cotton was provided by families of farmers or local wage laborers. The irrigated agricultural zones of the West were opened in areas with relatively little population, and were often characterized by relatively larger parcels

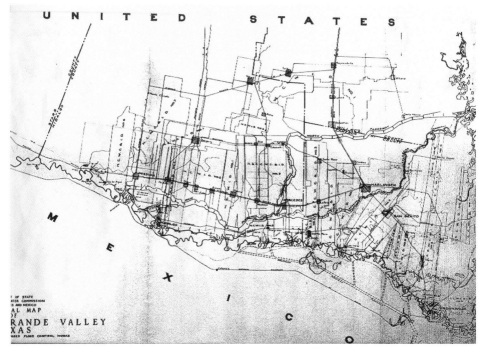

Irrigation districts and proposed works of the Río Bravo/Rio Grande delta, c. 1930.

and mechanized production. These conditions created a demand for a large migrant workforce, especially during the harvest, which was done manually until the 1960s. Despite the presence of African Americans and Anglos, the proximity of Mexico to the Southwest United States as well as planter attitudes toward African American, white, and Mexican workers meant that this labor force was largely made up of Mexicans and Mexican Americans. During the 1900–1930 period complex migration circuits evolved that included the fruit, vegetable, and cotton crops of South Texas, as well as the sugar-beet harvest of the Rocky Mountain states and the Midwest.[17]

Cotton production in the "Magic Valley" included many of the features of southwestern agriculture: colonization, irrigation, mechanization, migrant labor. However, the particular social organization of production that grew up in the Valley was determined by a number of local historical and ecological conditions as well. Unlike many irrigation zones of the western and southwestern United States, the districts in the Valley were privately built, owned, and run, and instead of using water from a dam or reservoir, each took water directly from the river using large pumping stations. Irrigation infrastructure was planned by individual real estate developers to service small, independent tracts, and although there was a good degree of coordination among them, by 1930 there were some one hundred different private irrigation districts in the Valley, and thirty-four pumping stations. These districts irrigated some 600,000 acres (240,000 hectares) of good alluvial soil.[18]

Another distinguishing aspect of the Texas Valley was its location on a national border established by conquest. A sizable labor pool for the agricultural development in the region was provided by Mexican Americans living in the border counties of South Texas, many of them working lands once owned by their ancestors. Equally or more important to the Valley's agricultural production were the workers who came from the interior of Mexico, for the low wages earned by these workers kept production costs at a minimum. Low wages and exploitative rental or sharecropping agreements for Mexicans and Mexican Americans made the Valley one of the few places in the country recognized by the U.S. Chamber of Commerce as being "prosperous" during the Depression of the 1930s. Apart from the labor force residing in the region, the Valley also became the first stop or the departure point for migrant workers traveling a long circuit from South to North or Northwest Texas cotton fields, and then to the sugar-beet regions of Colorado, Montana, and elsewhere.[19]

Commercial agriculture, colonization, and migration wrought dramatic changes in the environment, the patterns of land tenure, and the demography of the region. In South Texas, the huge ranches that characterized the era of cattle grazing and commerce were split up and sold to newcomers as agricultural plots. In Cameron County, for example, the average size of the rural landholdings changed from 770.1 acres (311.9 hectares) in 1910 to 45.6 acres in 1930. Intensive agriculture brought with it a dramatic increase in population, as laborers from Matamoros as well as the interior of Mexico went to work on the farms belonging to recently transplanted midwesterners. Brownsville's population jumped from 6,305 in 1900 to 10,511 in 1910.[20]

The Valle Bajo del Río Bravo in 1930

The arrival of the railroads, irrigated agriculture, and immigration to the binational delta region after 1900 were making their influence felt in Matamoros as a slow transition from a rural economy based on ranching to one based on cotton production and the generation of migrant workers for Texas agriculture.[21] These changes resulted in a complex social formation and a system of landholding arrangements that incorporated both customary and capitalist property relations. To the south of the riverbank agricultural zone the Sauteña remained in possession of a vast territory dedicated almost entirely to cattle grazing, and inhabited by isolated *rancheros* and small communities with only informal claim to their land. Along the river there was a patchwork of large and small parcels of uncleared *monte* and agricultural lands, with the large proprietors often renting lands or contracting sharecroppers. These riverbank properties were originally constituted as large tracts called "*porciones*" in the eighteenth century, and in 1930 much of the land was still owned in common by the descendants of those original grantees. However, immigrants to the binational region swelled the ranks of the sharecroppers, tenants, and agricultural workers. The cotton crop was financed largely by merchants in Matamoros, who in turn did business with the banks and cotton companies in Brownsville.

Ranchero house. *Courtesy of the Archivo General de la Nación, Mexico. Fondo Presidentes, Ramo Lázaro Cárdenas, 503.11/3-1, Caja 564.*

The Sauteña remained largely intact through the nineteenth century, mostly because aridity made its lands almost useless for agriculture without irrigation. Although the population tended to stay close to the Río Bravo and the Río San Fernando, over the course of more than a century of neglect by its owners, people established small *ranchos* on the *hacienda,* which was not fenced and was only patrolled beginning around the 1880s. Generations of families came to think of their corners of the Sauteña to be, *de facto,* their property. The *rancheros* inhabiting this sub-humid scrub forest were few and far between, and did not observe clear limits to their properties.

The same was true for the inhabitants of the riverside *porciones.* While in most cases the individual *porción* remained in the name of the eighteenth-century recipient, over time it came to be inhabited by many people, including the owner's descendants and their in-laws, who often established *ranchos* within the *porciones,* and nonrelatives such as sharecroppers or tenant farmers. Most of these inhabitants held an informal propriety over some land for their house and small agricultural plot, although these parcels were often not formally delineated. This was especially the case of the *rancheros* living on the land farther from the river that was not cleared and remained as *monte,* or scrubland. For those more privileged descendants of the original recipients of the *porciones* who lived near the river, access to the precious water of the Río Bravo was ensured by a social and legal abstraction in which the already narrow and long *porciones* were split into even narrower fragments to ensure all shareholders a piece of the riverfront. These divisions could not be formalized as actual properties, but were practiced through the common use of river water.

The categories of rural landholdings and dwellers, such as *"rancho," "ranchero," "hacienda," "aparcero,"* and *"mediero,"* were flexible and relational. Government officials used a number of such terms to describe settlements, landholdings, and landholders in the Valle Bajo Río Bravo. In 1920 the population of the region was predominantly rural, despite the limits to agriculture imposed by the region's aridity. According to the federal census taken that year, the city of Matamoros was home to 9,215 people, and the rural area of the county (*municipio*) held 11,025.[22] Most of these rural dwellers lived in *ranchos,* of which there were 449 in the *municipio.* "Rancho" is a term that referred to different things at different times, and these significations often overlapped in its usage. In 1930 in Matamoros the category included a social element (a group of people) as well as a geographical or spatial element (a place). On the one hand, the word referred to small settlements or communities who were usually related by close kinship ties. Many of these *ranchos* were simply named after the family that lived there: Los Valadeces, El Longoreño, and so forth. In this sense *rancho* refers more to the people and the grouping of houses than to an extension of land. This concept of *rancho* was more appropriate when describing settlements farther away from the agricultural zone of the riverbank, settlements with uncertain boundaries that were often surrounded by an expanse of uncleared brush. On the other hand, the word refers to an extension of land. Those *ranchos* located in the riverbank zone were more oriented toward agriculture, and were more likely to have defined spatial limits. In this case the word *rancho* had a connotation similar to "farm." *Ranchos* were generally quite small, averaging about thirty people, although there were a dozen or so large ones that counted one or two hundred inhabitants. Two of the larger settlements in the riverside zone—"Las Rucias" and "Los Borregos"—were listed in the census as *haciendas,* in reference to their size, to the commercial rather than domestic type of agriculture practiced on those lands, and to the relationship of tenancy or sharecropping that existed between the landowner and those that lived on his land.[23]

The biggest landowner in the region was, of course, the Sauteña, and many of the *ranchos* were located within its boundaries. Despite repeated legal efforts by the Sauteña to assert its property rights, people continued to settle in the unguarded open range south of the riverbank agricultural zone throughout the late nineteenth and early twentieth centuries. The Sauteña itself created more than a dozen *ranchos* by selling lands to colonists in the first years of the twentieth century. One of the *ranchos* mentioned by a Sauteña employee interviewed in the 1930s—La Llorona Vieja—was located near the Presa La Llorona built by the Sauteña 50 kilometers south of Reynosa. Like the unfinished canals and the crumbling buildings dotting the landscape, this original generation of colonists—such as the fifty-odd families of the Congregación Garza—remained on their lands bought from the *hacienda* long after the Porfirian development vision faded.[24]

About eight hundred people lived in what is now the town of Río Bravo, which grew up around the headquarters of the Sauteña. In response to a petition, in 1924 the federal government awarded 30 hectares of Sauteña agricultural land as an *ejido*. These *ejidatarios* had been sharecroppers (*aparceros*) and wage laborers (*jornaleros*) on the lands of *ranchos* as well as those of the Sauteña. With the creation of *ejido* lands, land tenure in the Río Bravo area was a heterogeneous mix of *latifundio* (Sauteña and other *haciendas*), *pequeñas y medianas propiedades* (small and medium-sized *ranchos*), and *ejido*. The inhabitants of the region fell into the categories of "*colonos, ejidatarios, particulares* and *pequeños propietarios*." Some of the *particulares,* a category that was not defined by a form of land tenure, attended the business of the Compañía, and others worked for the La Titania oil company that was exploring the lower Río Bravo/Rio Grande region in the 1930s.[25]

The variety of kinds of landholdings and the polyvalent meaning of terms such as "*rancho*" suggest that in 1930 land tenure and property relations in the Valle Bajo Río Bravo were based as much in custom as in law. Much of the land not within the bounds of the Sauteña was still owned formally by the descendants of the original recipients of the *porciones* handed out by the Bourbon government in 1785. Some of the landowners had cleared their land for commercial agriculture, and had registered their holdings with the government. Regardless of land titles, groups of *rancheros* and isolated homesteaders dotted the region, some of which could trace some lineage to any number of the original recipients, and some of which could not. There was almost no attention paid to registering these holdings with the government, and little effort made to establish formal property lines. A customary regime of communal and familiar land tenure overlapped one based in individual property rights.

Most of the information about land tenure in the 1930s was generated by state officials intent on regularizing property holding, establishing *ejidos,* and settling colonists. The informal and communitarian possession of land in the lower Río Bravo Valley was a puzzle for federal officials, who were charged with establishing firm property relations so that agrarian development could proceed. As these officials saw it, "since the awarding of *porciones* and the division of the ancient *ejidos* a long series of legal and informal domestic relocations have been made by residents of the region that have given rise to the formation of large, medium and small properties."[26] The numerous small holdings were not backed by any land title, but rather by the hereditary and customary rights asserted by their occupants. There was also a good deal of land that was said by the inhabitants to be the property of the descendants of the original settlers, but that in practice was common land used for firewood, hunting, and grazing.

Agronomists who carried out a study of the Valle Bajo Río Bravo region for the federal government's Agrarian Department (Departmento Agrario) found the supposedly communal social and property relations to derive from the history of occupation and use of these vast and scarcely populated ranchlands since the Bourbon *reparto* of 1785. Some, such as Reynosa native, Tamaulipas governor, and prominent agrarian reformer Marte R. Gómez, looked even farther back, arguing that the communal and customary nature of land tenure in northern Tamaulipas in 1930 were holdovers from the communal form in which the land was originally given by the Conde de la Sierra Gorda, before its partition by the liberal Bourbons. Despite their differences, these viewpoints shared the conviction that customary landholding patterns developed over the course of more than 150 years of livestock ranching in the Valle Bajo Río Bravo were incompatible with commercial agriculture based on individual private property.[27]

Setting aside the question of origins, we can focus instead on the relationship described in these accounts between environment, production, and land tenure in the region. For the ranching society of the Río Bravo/Rio Grande, access to water was paramount, and rigid, fenced property lines were detrimental. Most *rancheros* residing outside of the limited agricultural zone on the riverbank made a living from cattle that roamed freely in the thorn scrub. Personal ownership of this grazing land was unimportant to ranchers, for undeveloped land had very little value. Water, however, was very important, and the Río Bravo/Rio Grande was virtually the only source of water. Thus inherited rights to a place on a *porción* included access to the Río Bravo/Rio Grande, but implied no set territorial ownership beyond the immediate household and community space of the *rancho*. This led to a remarkable situation in which each of the many thousands of legitimate heirs of the original property recipients in the Valley enjoyed, according to the state's logic of inheritance, formal rights to parcels that measured centimeters along the riverfront by kilometers inland. For many of the smallholders in the region, these rights to particular pieces of land could only exist in the abstract. As Marte R. Gómez correctly pointed out, these legal rights mapped an impossible geography of "ridiculous and agriculturally unusable extensions of land."[28] In reality, small *rancheros* exercised ownership over their house compound, which usually included a garden-sized agricultural plot. The primary cash crop during the 1920s and 1930s was cotton, while corn, chile, beans, yams, tomatoes, and melons were always planted for domestic needs.[29] The statement by Gómez is representative of the position of the agrarian reformers and engineers who, viewing a region in transition, saw the earlier mode of production as an obstacle to what they considered rational, progressive development based on irrigated agriculture. Over the course of 150 years of cattle ranching the people who lived in the Bajo Río Bravo had formed a pattern of land tenure that did not fall within the control of a modernizing state.

The government officials concerned with developing commercial agriculture in the Valle Bajo Río Bravo saw that within the unified category of property "in law," there was a variety of forms of land use and ownership "in fact." One source of diversity emerged from a clear difference between the owners of *haciendas* with many thousands of hectares documented in the Public Registry of Property, and those who simply "owned" the land they cleared for their home and agricultural *parcela*. The first group of landowners was formed for the most part by descendants of the region's founders, who continued to hold large amounts of that land, or who had expanded their holdings through purchases. Sometimes these lands were still held by the family, as was the case with "Maximiliano G. Rodriguez, Sucesores," who owned 16,856 hectares divided among fourteen tracts. Gertrudis R. de Montemayor owned 9,381 hectares spread through the *porciones* 6 to 19 that were assigned by the viceroy in 1785, as well as the *rancho* "Santa Gertrudis" of 5,979 hectares.[30] Other large landholders simply bought land as an investment. Some of these, such as the Compañía Mexicana Dunn Kinder, were foreigners. There were many large property owners who owned more modest amounts of land: anywhere from 50 to 1000 hectares. A good number of these large property owners did indeed register their holdings with the municipal governments of Reynosa and Matamoros, but many did not, as by doing so they would be more easily taxed. Many had no precise idea of where their land began and ended, even when it was rented or used by sharecroppers. As Tomasa Guerra said of her 183 hectares on the river 15 kilometers northwest of Matamoros, "there were never lines, boundary markers or indications that would demonstrate the reality of the division."[31]

Lodged between and within these large properties was a much more numerous group of *rancheros* that owned very small parcels of land. Some were descendants of the original families who had simply established themselves somewhere on a *porción* to which they held some familial claim. Others could only claim the land they lived on based on their own continuous occupancy. One example, described by the agronomists of the federal government's Departmento Agrario, was that of the settlement of "Santa Anita," located within the rancho "El Longoreño," some 16 kilometers upriver from Matamoros. The engineers wrote that some of the inhabitants of Santa Anita, who together asked for an *ejido* in 1934, "lack lands, despite the fact that they work in agriculture," and that the land they settled "is found to be in a state of indivision"; that is, communally owned land originally and legally held by kin lineages.[32] At the same time, many of the other inhabitants were legally owners-in-common occupying small parcels that in practice were individual properties. Many in the Valle Bajo Río Bravo could make no such genealogical claim to common ownership, but were able to settle on land that was unused and unguarded. In general, all these very small landholders worked their lands themselves, or made a living from livestock kept on the open ranges south of the inhabited zones of the riverbank. When the government and its local allies launched land reform in the region during the Cárdenas period, this variety of customary claims to and uses of land was the source of much conflict and misunderstanding in the constitution of the *ejidos, colonias,* and *pequeñas propiedades* that were recognized as legitimate forms of landholding by the Mexican government.

The gradual emergence of commercial cotton agriculture in the Valle Bajo Río Bravo region caused a shift from kin- or occupancy-based ownership and communitarian use of land for ranching to a property regime marked by individual owners and well-bounded agricultural plots. It was also a shift from a somewhat pastoralist cultural ecology based in the adaptation to a landscape of forest and brush, to an agricultural one that required the clearing and intensive exploitation of that land. The Mexican side of the Río Bravo/Rio Grande delta did not enjoy the phenomenal growth of the "Magic Valley" of South Texas, although it did produce some amount of cotton yearly between 1900 and 1930. Production statistics for the Matamoros region are available from about 1925 on, when the postrevolutionary government had finally established enough authority and institutionality to begin monitoring, directing, and planning agricultural production. In 1925, a representative year, the government determined that the Matamoros region produced and ginned about 13,000 bales, 9 percent of all Mexican cotton. Despite the relative insignificance of this amount when compared to the Laguna region or the "Magic Valley," it still made the Matamoros region the third largest producer of cotton in Mexico between 1925 and 1934. Although, in 1926, levees were completed that protected agriculture to some degree from flood damage on the Mexican side of the river, cotton production rose only briefly (21,000 bales in 1926 and 1927, due to high international prices) before resuming characteristic levels of 12,000 to 14,000 bales.[33]

In the 1920s and 1930s a rural social formation began to emerge that was based in a regional mode of cotton production that accentuated the differences and divisions between landowners and landless *campesinos*. One reason for this was an increase in the number of immigrants, displaced by revolutionary chaos and attracted by the growth of commercial agriculture on both sides of the Río Bravo. In mid-1928 deportation campaigns began in Texas, and the economic crisis that hit in late 1929 also swelled the numbers of Mexicans returning from the United States. From the information gathered by the censuses of 1920 and 1930, it appears that the population of the Bajo Río Bravo (Matamoros and Reynosa *municipios*) grew 40 percent between 1920 and 1930: from 26,638 to 37,296. The Municipio of Reynosa, with a whopping 93 percent population increase, grew more than the Municipio of Matamoros, at 23 percent. Reynosa's rural sector expanded some 75 percent, while the city grew 129 percent. Matamoros's population grew more slowly, and almost entirely in the countryside, which expanded some 38 percent. All told, the rural population in the lower Río Bravo Valley grew by almost 50 percent, 20 percent more than the urban centers.[34] As landless *campesinos* streamed into the region, those that were already there and had genealogical rights to, or de facto possession of, land took on the structural position of landowners, regardless of their actual conceptualization or documentation of their property rights. Thus many of those new arrivals clearing land and planting crops were involved in a relation of sharecropping (*aparcería*) with the prior owner of that property.[35]

The terms of the sharecropping relation varied throughout the region, depending on whether the producer contributed his own tools or depended wholly on the property owner for materials. While the general term for sharecropper—*aparcero*—usually appears in the archival records, the term *mediero* was sometimes used. As Jane-Dale Lloyd has shown in a discussion of *rancheros* in Chihuahua, the term "*mediero*" was used popularly to describe "a small rural cultivator dedicated to sup-plying family needs."[36] While a *mediero* normally possessed some land and tools, to supplement income he would sharecrop land provided by a more wealthy relative, giving in return half of the crop produced. Although it is likely that at least some of the *medieros* in northern Tamualipas were poor *rancheros* like those of Chihuahua, it is also probable that many were migrants new to the region who had neither land nor tools, and no choice but to sharecrop on the halves. One local historian claimed that sharecropping arrangements were even more onerous, with the landowners receiving three-fourths of the product of the "land they sharecrop," and the share-cropper a mere one-fourth.[37] The parcels cultivated by these sharecroppers were certainly very small, considering the labor requirements of cotton cultivation. Also, most sharecroppers and small *rancheros* could not afford to lose a sizable investment due to the lack of rain or to flooding, both of which were quite common before the flood control and irrigation works were built in the late 1930s and 1940s. Perhaps for these reasons Matamoran merchants reported that in the mid-1930s farmers usually bought only enough cottonseed to plant one-half hectare—about an acre.[38]

While farmers may have produced other food crops, cotton was the only crop produced through sharecropping contracts. And while on the larger, more indus-trially organized plantations these contracts were sometimes quite formal written documents, on smaller *ranchos* more informal, "paternal," or familial productive relations were common. Such was the case with the twenty-six families in the settle-ment of "Villaverde," who worked as sharecroppers on three neighboring *ranchos.* Tomasa Guerra, who owned two of those ranchos, did not let her professed igno-rance of fixed property lines (cited earlier) prevent her from setting up sharecrop-pers on her land.[39] The establishment of cotton sharecropping embodied the transi-tion from a more insular society organized around the kin relations of the original community of families to a more fragmented social formation that included new groups with no genealogical connection to those families.

Not all those farming other people's land were sharecroppers or small produc-ers who used only their own labor or that of their family. With the expansion of cotton agriculture after the Revolution in the Mexican side of the delta, large-scale, industrialized production came to be increasingly important in the region. Stimu-lated both by the example of agriculture on the Texas side of the river and the high prices at the end of World War I, some entrepreneurial farmers rented more sizable plots and produced cotton using day labor. By 1927 many renters hired wage labor-ers to help them bring the crop in.[40]

There were some industrial farming operations in Matamoros that resembled the large industrial cotton plantations of South and East-Central Texas. The *haci-enda* Las Rucias, for example, owned by Juan H. Fernández, was known as one of the older plantation-style *haciendas* operating in the region. According to one source writing in the 1950s, in 1910 "Las Rusias," along with "San Vicente," were the only two large *haciendas* in Matamoros, apart from the Sauteña.[41] Located on the river just upstream from the town of Matamoros, by 1929 Las Rucias had installed what Mexico's CNI deemed "perhaps the only well-installed and modernly arranged" pumping plant in Tamaulipas, which sucked 830 liters of river water per second to irrigate 1,035 hectares of land.[42] The land was worked by sharecroppers who signed formal contracts with the *hacienda*. According to the *hacienda* owners, these *aparcero* families lived in dwellings built and owned by the *hacienda*, in a settlement known as "El Ebanito." A census raised in 1927 by the Departmento Agrario in response to a request for *ejido* lands (*solicitud de dotación de ejido*) showed the settlement to have had 64 families and 328 inhabitants.[43] These sharecroppers and wage laborers of El Ebanito staged a land invasion to support their demand for an *ejido*, an example of the serious tensions in this emergent social formation that will be discussed later in this chapter.

By 1930 many rural communities near Matamoros were established on land that was not owned by them, and both they and the landowners were well aware of this. Reports filed by rural teachers of the Secretaría de Educación Pública working in the Matamoros district in the late 1920s and early 1930s invariably stated that the landlord or *rancho* owner donated the plot of land and sometimes the building for a school, and that the "*vecinos*" or "*comunidad*" of the *rancho* usually built the schoolhouse, implying a categorical separation between the owner of the land and the workers living on that land. For example, in the *ranchería* "El Galaneño," owner D. Crispin Luna gave the parcel of land for the school, while the "community" built the schoolhouse.[44] While the CNI claimed that these ranchlands "belong to everyone and no one, that is to say, they have converted into communal lands," it was often the case that proprietors owned the land farmed by the sharecroppers, the land on which the *rancho* communities were located, and even their houses and school buildings.[45] The awareness by the region's inhabitants of these unequal property relations would be clearly demonstrated when the federal government's Valle Bajo Río Bravo project set about redrawing regional geography and reforming property ownership during the mid- and late 1930s.

The expansion of cotton agriculture in the Valle after 1900 was accompanied by an expansion of the urban merchant and industrial capital that financed the agriculture. Cotton production was organized by Matamoros cotton factors such as Juan B. Cross and his Compañía Algodonera Mexicana, or Fred Donato of J. D. Donato Sucursales, both of families that came to Matamoros in the mid-nineteenth century from New Orleans. These cotton merchants provided seed and credit to farmers in exchange for raw fiber, and from about 1920 onward, both operated gins. Moreover, these merchant capitalist families also owned a good deal of land in the region. Meliton Cross, at least, held the title to 2,664 hectares of land, including the *predios* "La Tijera," "El Seteadero," "El Azafranado," and "Los Barriles" in Matamoros—properties where, not surprisingly, cotton predominated. This was an integrated business operation, in which Cross contracted sharecroppers or rented the lands, supplied the seed, and ginned the cotton produced. *Casas refaccionarias* such as that of Cross often directly contracted renters of small parcels of their lands, sold them seed, and commercialized their cotton.[46]

Another regional cottonman who controlled all aspects of production was Roberto F. García, who was born on the *rancho* Santa Rosalía, on the riverbank outside of Matamoros. His social connections on both sides of the river helped him to get started in commerce, and in financing and supplying cotton production. His prominence in regional society also helped him at that time to begin a long and very successful political career. With his brothers Macedonio and Simon, he founded the M. J. García y Hermanos y Sucesores company, which by 1919 was one of the town's principal merchant houses. Cotton trade was central to the success of the "Casa García," and by 1920 the company owned two cotton gins. In 1924 the García brothers got involved in large-scale cotton production on their *rancho* "El Tejon," which was located about 60 miles southwest of Matamoros near the Río San Fernando. Throughout the 1920s and 1930s Roberto García's 5000-acre (2000-hectare) ranch was known in international cotton circles for its advanced production techniques and large output. His twenty-five tractors helped to produce 3000 of the 21,000 bales produced in the Matamoros region in 1927; bales that he ginned on his ranch. The García outfit was exceptional for its integration of agriculture, industry, and commerce, and because most of the agricultural land in northern Tamaulipas, although held in large ranches, was cultivated by sharecroppers in tiny plots.[47]

The 1920s brought important changes to cotton financing in Matamoros, at the same time that the organization of rural cotton production and social relations were changing. As cotton production grew, it supported the formation of a cotton ginning industry in the region, and generated figures such as Roberto F. García. The expanded and industrialized cotton business required greater amounts of capital, and it attracted the attention of investors from outside Matamoros. For example, Shelby Longoria came to Matamoros in the late 1920s to buy cotton seed for his father's laundry soap factory in Nuevo Laredo. The Longoria family held original land grants from the eighteenth century near Ciudad Camargo, and owned industries and banking operations in Nuevo Laredo, which, because of its location on trade routes, was a more prominent border commercial center than Matamoros. Shelby Longoria and Roberto García established business ties in the early 1920s, for the Longorias supplied soap to the "Casa M. J. García," and Longoria got cottonseed oil from the García ranch to make that soap. Another ginning company, "La Cruz Blanca," was established in the 1920s by other investors from Nuevo Laredo. Shelby Longoria was representative of the new industrial class of cotton capitalists that would come to dominate the Matamoros economy beginning in the 1940s.[48]

Tensions in the Valle Bajo Río Bravo

The rising tide of commercial cotton production in Matamoros over the first few decades of the twentieth century caused an influx of migrants, and an increased importance of sharecroppers and wage laborers in the region. At the same time, the rise of commercial cotton gave basis to the constitution of new players in the regional political-economic elite. The swelling of a rural workforce was accentuated by the growth of commercial agriculture in the Texas valley, the Mexican Revolution, and periodic immigrations of Mexican workers pushed out of the United States by economic downturns such as that of 1920–1921. Because of the influx of a new rural population, and the increased value of land for cotton production, the communitarian aspects of land tenancy and ownership that had developed over the course of 150 years of livestock ranching and low land pressure were placed in question. The growing rural population of cotton producers could not be assimilated into the existing kinship-based tenancy system, despite a continuing abundance of uncleared land. Because they were not integrated into the traditional kin-based web of land tenure and social relations in the region, this new class of sharecroppers and tenants was a potentially radical force in the region.

The social divide that gained importance in the Valle Bajo del Río Bravo fell between those who were from the region and held hereditary claims or legal title to property, and those who were recent migrants and had no such claims or titles. This structural divide led to conflict, as landless sharecroppers and wage laborers began to militate for *ejidos* to be established from the holdings of their *patrones,* or bosses. These *patrones* were most often large landholders, although some *patrones* actually rented the lands that sharecroppers then cultivated. A third social group— apart from the sharecroppers/wage laborers and large landholders—were the small-holding *pequeños propietarios,* who because they held possession of just a small bit of land usually neither had sharecroppers or wage laborers working for them nor worked as sharecroppers or wage laborers themselves. These small property owners often lacked legal title to the lands they held, but were usually from the region and could claim continual use or some genealogical inheritance. When these landless sharecroppers and wage laborers formed political organizations to demand *ejidos,* the sizable group of *pequeños propietarios* generally fell into an alliance with the *patrones* that held large properties. Some, however, joined *ejidos* for fear that because they lacked titles, the *ejido* was the only way to retain the use of "their" lands. The general solidarity between small and large property owners was reinforced through kinship and friendship, as well as the fact that the *pequeños propietarios* saw state-supported *agrarismo* as a threat to their usually informal or customary, rather than legal, ownership of their land.

The rise of commercial cotton agriculture in the Valle Bajo del Río Bravo was accompanied by a surge in revindicatory agrarian ideology (*agrarismo*), which both helped produce, and was reproduced by, the revolutionary social movements of the 1910–1920 period. Matamoros was the site of the first agrarian land redistribution (*reparto*) of the Revolution, that of the *hacienda* "Los Borregos." Whatever *agrarismo* may have been fomented by the 1913 *reparto,* it did not produce any more land reforms in the region during the Revolution, perhaps because landowners such as the Sauteña hired and armed "white guards" to prevent such a threat.[49] However, the reform brought Francisco Múgica to the region and made him aware of the agricultural potential and development plans for the lower Río Bravo Valley. Some twenty years later Múgica would return to oversee the irrigation, land reform, and colonization project in Matamoros from his position as the director of the Secretary of Communications and Public Works (Secretaría de Comunicaciones y Obras Públicas, or SCOP) under Cárdenas.

Worker and peasant radicalism in the Matamoros region was intimately connected with Tamaulipas strongman Emilio Portes Gil, who in 1924 formed the *Partido Socialista Fronterizo* (Border Socialist Party) and ran for governor of Tamaulipas. Most of his popular support came from the *campesinos* of the central part of the state and the workers of the oil and port industries in Tampico, at the southern end of the state. However, on March 18 of that same year, a group of renters in Río Bravo raised a petition for an *ejido* to be given from the lands of the Sauteña owned by the Caja de Préstamos. Portes Gil was elected and assumed the office of governor on February 5 of 1925, and on April 2 the renters of Río Bravo were awarded 8 hectares of land each.[50] In his effort to cement a power base in Tamaulipas, in 1926 Portes Gil founded a statewide *agrarista* organization called the Liga de Comunidades Agrarias y Sindicatos Campesinos, and delivered over 200,000 hectares of land to *campesinos,* mostly in the central area of the state.

Because of the particular combination of paternalistic rural social relations, relative lack of land pressure, and a norteño liberalism that upheld individual possession of the land, *agrarismo* in Matamoros did not gather the same amount of momentum as it did in regions such as Michoacan, the Laguna, or central Tamaulipas. Nevertheless, organized *agrarismo* did find a following among the region's communities of sharecroppers and agricultural workers. Many of the new arrivals that made up the potentially unstable class of sharecroppers and renters in the region hailed from places where *agrarismo* was strong. Regional *campesino* leader Prisciliano Delgado, for example, brought his *agrarismo* with him from Jiménez, in central Tamaulipas.[51]

In 1926 Delgado led sharecroppers from the communities of "El Ebanito" and "San Isidro" in petitioning to form an *ejido* in the lands of the *hacienda* "Las Rucias," owned by Juan H. Fernández. Delgado was the president of the Sociedad Cooperativista Ricardo Flores Magón, and had acquired a bit of institutional power as the official of the municipal government who represented the settlement "El Ebanito" and those around it. Despite this modicum of power, the *agraristas* of Matamoros feared violence from hired guns organized by landowners under the leadership of a contending agrarian leader, Epigmenio García. After presenting a demand for *ejidal* lands, Delgado led a takeover of those lands when the federal Departmento Agrario failed to show up as scheduled on November 29. That same day, "Las Rucias" administrator Emilio Longoria armed seventy men and confronted the *campesinos*. While Delgado was talking with Longoria, shooting erupted between the two groups, and

Delgado's son José was killed. Three others were killed and two wounded in the scuffle, and Prisciliano Delgado was jailed.[52]

Tensions rose as *campesinos* and the landowner/merchant class squared off for combat. At that point, however, cotton entrepreneur and rising political star Roberto F. García stepped in to broker a deal. García had been elected to a lesser office of the municipal government that year, and his company's successes in cotton farming, financing, and brokering had also earned him a leading position in Matamoros' powerful Chamber of Commerce, the Cámara Mercantil y Agrícola de Matamoros. Earlier in 1926 García had used his influence in the municipal government to secure the authorization for his company to open a gin in the town's center, and when violence erupted in the cotton fields of Matamoros, García acted to secure peace and production. The Cámara was, in the words of sociologist Arturo Alvarado, the "collective, concerted expression of the cotton businessmen," and in meetings between the *campesinos* and the Cámara it was agreed that the region's cottonmen would voluntarily hand over 7464 hectares of their own land to the *campesinos,* on the condition that the *agraristas* respect the rest of their holdings. García's actions channeled and defused independent *agrarista* demands in the region, established a paternalistic and regional avenue for the resolution of land issues between landowners and renters, and effectively kept federal and state intervention in rural Matamoros at bay until 1935.

The establishment of *pequeños propietarios* on these lands did not harm the business of the merchants who supplied cottonseed to the region's farmers, even though, as we have seen, many of the merchants were also large landowners. Various companies continued to supply seed, but the Casa García took an increasingly important role in the industrialization of the fiber. M. J. García y Hermanos planned the establishment of the first cotton bale compress in northern Tamaulipas in 1926, and asked the state government to give it exclusive rights to the cottonseed oil pressing business, as well as tax exemptions on cotton. The loss of some land to small cotton producers shifted the capital base of the regional elite slightly from land to commerce and industry, and by 1930, the *casa refaccionadora* M. J. García financed, supplied, and organized 75 percent of the cotton production in Matamoros, while the García cotton farms produced about 14 percent of the fiber.[53] Despite the success of the Matamoros cotton elite at negotiating hegemony during the 1920s, it was unable to control the ongoing processes of immigration, population growth, and the creation of a surplus population in the region, nor effectively prepare itself for the ravages caused by the cycles of the international cotton economy. When the Great Depression hit in the early 1930s, the García cotton enterprise and others went bankrupt, leaving the region without a ready source of investment capital. The economic crisis led to far-reaching changes, as the power vacuum in the region cleared the way for deeper involvement by outside actors, such as national and foreign cotton capital and the Mexican federal government, in the economy and society of Matamoros.

Conclusion

The growth of commercial agriculture in the delta of the Río Bravo/Rio Grande during the first three decades of the twentieth century generated an array of new social actors, from Anglo small farmers to industrialists, sharecroppers, and migrant cotton pickers. In Texas, a complete reworking of the landscape was effected through the clearing of lands and the building of irrigation systems, a process of social and environmental change that only just began to take root on the Mexican side of the river. Along with the physical reshaping of the productive landscape, customary rights to land based in kinship gave way to property rights recognized by the state. Global markets, national government politics, and the social and environmental characteristics of the delta came together to shape an emergent social field of cotton.

In the years from 1920 to 1934, tensions in commercial cotton society and the ideological and political influence of new arrivals to the region led to a number of efforts by landless sharecroppers to establish *ejidos*. Despite these strains and tremors, the kinship-based land tenure system and a lack of concern for property lines and legal titles remained present, hindering the emergence of a strong market for lands in the region. It was not until the Cárdenas presidency that ranching and small-scale agriculture based in customary property relations were displaced through a massive agrarian reform, and the region's social tensions were defused through a reorganization of people and production in the Matamoros countryside. Although transcendent principles such as the nobility of small property, the superiority of whiteness, and the sovereignty of the state guided this reorganization, the development blueprints for the construction of the new irrigated cotton zone of Matamoros were drawn in relation to the specificities of the social field of cotton.

CHAPTER 5
CRISIS AND DEVELOPMENT IN THE RÍO BRAVO DELTA, 1930–1935

The crisis of the 1930s has attracted a great deal of interest from historians and social scientists. Economic historians debate the causes of the economic crash of 1929–1933 in Europe and the United States, and differ over the nature of recovery. The unique experiences of Latin American countries in this process have received close attention, and although not a representative case for Latin America during the 1930s, a number of works discuss Mexico's economy.[1] The crisis served as the catalyst for a long-term transition in the primary sector of the Mexican economy from ranching and mining to commercial agriculture, and the northern borderlands was home to this new agriculture, which was largely focused on cotton.[2] While these studies recognize variation between northern Mexico and the center/south, few focus on this transition in particular regional spaces, landscapes, and societies in the 1930s, and none recognize the central importance of cotton. The history of Matamoros shows how and why the transition was made to a cotton-driven economy and society during this period of crisis.

Social fields such as that constituted by cotton in the borderlands must be understood historically to avoid encountering the problems of stasis that various structuralisms got bogged down in during the 1970s. Antonio Gramsci's dialectical notion of history is useful in understanding this temporal aspect of the social field. "A common error in historico-political analysis," he wrote in his prison notebooks, "consists in an inability to find the correct relation between what is organic and what is conjunctural. This leads to presenting causes as immediately operative which in fact only operate indirectly, or to asserting that the immediate causes are the only effective ones."[3] To understand the history of crises, Gramsci suggested a balanced analysis not only of the various political, economic, social, and cultural actors and elements that comprise a particular social field at a particular moment, but also of the different temporal frames in which these kinds of phenomena present themselves.

The way in which the lower Río Bravo/Rio Grande Valley experienced the crisis of the 1930s was determined by the organic and conjunctural histories of cotton, class, water, and development ideology that congealed in that place at that moment, catalyzing the transition from cattle ranching to commercial agriculture. During the 1920s, cotton production became increasingly costly in the old cotton belt of the United States and relatively cheaper in the southwestern United States and in other countries, resulting in a dramatic increase in production in the latter areas. In 1929 the New York stock market crashed, exacerbating these structural tendencies in the political economy of cotton, yet Mexico's borderlands cotton zones were dependent on U.S. capital, which hindered their ability to increase production. Although the expansion of cotton westward and southward was accentuated after 1933 with the U.S. government's programs of cotton acreage reductions and price supports, Mexican production continued to be limited by aridity and the lack of new irrigated lands in northern Mexico.

The mixture of "organic" and "conjunctural" conditions—a world market increasingly favorable to cotton production in Mexico; aridity; problems of flooding and unemployment in the delta region—shaped the social field in the Valle Bajo Río Bravo, as well as the development project the Cárdenas government mounted to address the crisis in that part of the borderlands. In the early 1930s, the decapitalization of cotton agriculture in Matamoros was accompanied by a massive return migration of Mexicans to the region, provoked by a fall in agricultural and industrial production and deportation campaigns in the United States. This unemployed, unsettled population encountered extreme hardships as a result of a series of floods that struck the Mexican side of the delta region of the Río Bravo/Rio Grande during those years. Directing his actions toward the sharecroppers, renters, and rural workers generated by the incipient transition to cotton agriculture during the first three decades of the twentieth century, and toward the thousands of Mexicans repatriated during the Depression, Cárdenas backed agrarian reforms and the establishment of *ejidos* and *colonias agrícolas* in the region. The president expanded his support base in the region by allying with the *portesgilista* political leaders who had been displaced from municipal power a few years earlier. By supporting both *campesinos* and elements of the cotton elite, he laid the foundations for a regional political bloc that would back the project to irrigate and colonize the Matamoros region. Despite the fact that this project was based on abeyant plans to create an agricultural emporium in the Sauteña, it took shape as a result of a discussion between various dependencies of the Mexican government, the personal initiative of the director of the public works project, Eduardo Chávez, and the actions and ideas of the thousands of inhabitants of the region. Specific proposals for flood control and irrigation works changed significantly during this period, but a number of factors remained steady: the language of development used by all the actors involved to describe the future of the region, the goal of settling the region with Mexicans repatriated from the United States, and the plan to dedicate the entire region to cotton production.

Cotton and the Great Depression

As the stock markets weakened and the prices of agricultural commodities fell in the summer of 1929, the U.S. government began to expand its efforts to support cotton agriculture. The Farm Board, whose original mission was to organize cooperatives, switched to bolstering prices. Cotton prices plummeted after the stock market crash in October, and in mid-1930 the Farm Board created the Cotton Stabilization Corporation (CSC), with the goal of purchasing cotton and keeping it off the market to brake the slide. The CSC bought a total of 3.3 million bales of cotton between 1929 and 1931, a move that may have detained the fall of cotton prices a bit, but at the cost of swelling the surplus. The prediction of an extraordinarily large crop for the 1931–1932 season, and thus even more surplus, resulted in prices falling to 5 cents a pound, placing the entire southern economy in a truly desperate situation. Aggregate earning of U.S. cotton farmers dropped from $1389 million in 1929 to $751 million in 1930, and $528 million in 1931. Although between 1929 and 1932 fewer hectares were dedicated to the crop each year, high yields meant that production did not decrease in response to poor prices.[4]

The consumption of U.S. cotton by industries outside the United States had been falling since World War I, and the events of 1929–1933 exaggerated the trend. The United States stopped lending dollars to overseas buyers in 1930, and would accept only gold as payment. This move had the effect of inflating the dollar in relation to other currencies, which in turn made cotton exported from the United States even more costly. Naturally, European industry turned to the emerging cotton agriculture of its colonies or of "new countries,"[5] where scarce dollars bought more, cheaper cotton, or where it could trade in European currencies. Also, crisis-era currency devaluations in non-U.S. cotton-producing countries made their fiber even less costly in relation to that of the United States. So while world consumption of U.S. cotton dropped from 15.1 million bales in 1928–1929 to 10.9 million in 1930–1931, consumption of cotton produced outside the United States *increased*: from 10.8 million bales in 1928–1929 to 12.2 million in 1929–1930; and to 11.6 million in 1930–1931. In 1930–1931, for the first time since the cotton famine of the U.S. Civil War, more non-U.S. cotton was consumed than U.S. cotton. Not counting the glut year of 1926, U.S. cotton production only increased 7 percent between the 1909–1913 period and the 1926–1930 period, while production outside the United States increased a whopping 49 percent.[6]

In the first years after the stock market crash, cotton agriculture in Mexico fell sharply, despite the improved position and increased production of countries outside the United States. From 203,000 hectares and 60,000 bales in 1928, in 1932 cultivation decreased to 78,000 hectares on which 22,000 bales were produced. This fall in production was due primarily to the crisis in financing in the border zones that were closely connected to the U.S. cotton industry. Because Matamoros and

Mexicali were largely oriented toward exports, were integrated into U.S. cotton markets, and were dependent on U.S. capital, production there fell off more than the Laguna region, which produced for Mexico's textile industry. The amount of hectares planted with cotton indicates the change in investment in the different regions. For the period between 1925 and 1929, Mexicali and Matamoros together accounted for 43 percent of the nation's acreage, while the Laguna made up 46 percent. By 1933 the border zones only accounted for 29 percent of the cotton acreage, while the Laguna had 52 percent.[7]

Matamoros was hard hit by the crash in agricultural prices and land values on the Texas side of the Valley, which led to a rash of bank closures in 1932. In March of that year the Mexican Consul in Brownsville reported that the Merchants National Bank had closed its doors, severely affecting the wealthy men of Matamoros who held their money in Brownsville banks. The regional capitalists who had supported production in Matamoros suffered greatly, and cotton cultivation in Matamoros was cut by half between 1930 and 1932. For example, the Casa García in Matamoros, which by 1930 controlled 75 percent of the Matamoros production, went bankrupt from the crash in cotton prices in 1930. Matamoros's Cross family, also hit hard by the crisis, sold its cotton gins to the Anderson Clayton Company that same year.[8]

Mexicali also suffered a crisis in financing which led to the sale of regional cotton industries to the Anderson Clayton Company. In 1925 Juan F. Brittingham, an industrialist and banker from the Laguna with a long history in the cotton business, established the Jabonera del Pacifico cotton gin and seed oil plant to finance and process the crop produced by the colonists of the Colorado River Land Company (CRLC). Faced with disastrous prices in 1929 and 1930, Brittingham sold the Jabonera to Anderson Clayton, which already controlled the compression and transportation of Mexicali and Imperial Valley fiber through its port facilities in Los Angeles.[9] Colonists and sharecroppers working for the Colorado River Land Company in Mexicali planted 61,340 hectares in 1928, but by 1931 investment had fallen to the point that only about 28,800 hectares were planted.[10] In early 1932 the Anderson Clayton Company announced that it would not finance any cotton production that year in Mexicali, and other regional cotton businesses followed suit. With *repatriados* swelling the ranks of the region's landless workers, Baja California Governor Olachea organized a plan to rescue the region. Two "land companies" provided land and tools, while the government of Baja California (a territory under federal jurisdiction) provided the funds for 1500 *colonos* to grow cotton. Contracts were signed by which the territorial government agreed to finance the production, and Anderson Clayton's Jabonera del Pacifico would gin the product for a fee. Only 11,000 hectares were brought into cultivation through this deal, but in 1933 an identical deal was struck that increased the plantings to about 22,000 hectares.[11] In effect, the federal government took the role of an agricultural development bank, financing sharecroppers on private land. Despite this intervention by the government, Brittingham predicted that by 1931 the Anderson Clayton Company would "get absolute control of both cotton agriculture and the industrial end in Mexico."[12]

The drop in cotton production in Mexico was a problem for the country's industries, which needed raw materials but wanted to avoid purchasing cotton and cottonseed in the United States due to the unfavorable terms of trade. The textile industry had been struggling since 1928, and was running far below capacity when the crisis struck in late 1929. According to a U.S. Department of Commerce report from early 1932, it was "the announced policy of the Mexican Government to encourage the cotton industry in every possible way."[13] Aside from tariff measures facilitating imports of raw materials, the Mexican government formulated plans for opening up new lands to the crop. Fifty thousand hectares in the Don Martín irrigation system were to be put into production, and cotton acreage was to be "greatly increased" in the other river valleys of the north and the Pacific coast. But the greatest increase in cotton production was planned for the Matamoros region, where several hundred thousand acres of land were to be cleared and converted to agriculture using large pumping plants on the Río Bravo/Rio Grande. This was another version of the development vision held out for the Sauteña, which, like the many prior iterations, never went much beyond the planning stage. Nevertheless, because of a conjuncture of international conditions—struggles to control the waters of the international rivers, favorable cotton markets, the development problem of surplus labor—and the rise to power of Lázaro Cárdenas, within a few years the Mexican government would indeed move forward with a plan to greatly expand national cotton production through the development of an irrigation system in the Bajo Río Bravo.

The New Deal for Cotton

In 1933 cotton production outside the United States was even further stimulated by new crop reduction and price-stabilizing measures of the U.S. government's Agricultural Adjustment Administration (AAA) and Commodity Credit Corporation (CCC). By the spring of 1933 the situation of the U.S. cotton economy was absolutely desperate. Prices were extremely low, and in August of 1932 the world cotton supply had increased to an all-time high of 17 million bales, all of which was due to unconsumed U.S. cotton. In March of 1933 Franklin Delano Roosevelt entered the presidency, and immediately took drastic steps to alleviate the national farm crisis. On May 12 of 1933 the Agricultural Administration Act was passed, giving the federal government the power to balance production and consumption so as to elevate and maintain the purchasing power of farmers at pre–World War I levels. Despite the fact that a million farmers participated in a program of the Secretary of Agriculture, and withdrew 10.4 million acres from production, the amount of cotton produced did not diminish. Congress then approved the Bankhead Act, which established compulsory production limits through the mechanism of a steep tax on the ginning of all cotton that exceeded the quota allowed to each individual farmer. When the acreage reduction plan failed to reduce unused stocks of cotton, prices were bolstered by federal loan programs administered by the CCC, which was established in October of 1933. The CCC loaned money to farmers against their cotton crop, which was then held off the market by the government as collateral.[14]

Because of the increase in production outside the United States, by 1930 non-U.S. cotton began to play an important role in the demand for, and price of, U.S. fiber, and vice-versa. Because other countries produced about half of the world's crop, the goal of the AAA and CCC cotton programs—to increase the purchasing power of the farmers in the United States by creating scarcity in the world market—could only be achieved if foreign countries also reduced production. The production restriction and price supports in the United States had the exact opposite effect, however, as cotton businessmen, producers, and governments outside the United States scrambled to take advantage of artificially high world-cotton prices bolstered by U.S. domestic policy. Egypt responded by increasing the production of cotton in the fiber lengths of U.S. upland varieties by 32 percent, displacing the long-fiber varieties that were traditionally the bulk of that country's exports. Brazil expanded cotton production an incredible 300 percent between 1933 and 1935, due to government actions such as the legal restriction on planting coffee trees, and the active promotion of cotton cultivation by domestic and foreign capital. Japan sought to locate sources in southern China, and the Soviet Union planned a 70 percent increase in cotton production to drive the industrialization plotted in the five-year plan of 1933–1937. With their noses to the winds of change, "certain American financial interests" were, Secretary of Agriculture Henry Wallace reported, "active in furnishing capital to promote the expansion of the cotton business in several parts of the world" in 1934.[15] The Anderson Clayton Company was one of these interests, for its subsidiaries financed and handled cotton throughout Latin America.[16]

Mexico exported whatever cotton was left over after national industry fulfilled its needs from a total production that varied significantly year to year according to environmental and financial conditions. Although industrial demand fell about 20 percent from 1928 to 1931, national consumption over the five-year span between 1928 and 1932 was almost exactly the same as for the previous five-year period. Despite stable consumption, imports of cotton remained quite limited, and the fall in production was compensated for by a decrease in exports. After 1933, with the intervention of the U.S. federal government in the world cotton markets, prices recovered somewhat and financing picked up, leading to greater production in Mexico, and a resurgence in exports. The domestic/export market dynamic had strong regional dimensions. While the Laguna provided the cotton for the industries of central Mexico, the border zone of Mexicali exported all its fiber. Matamoros cotton found its way to both domestic and export markets, in ratios that depended largely on the ability of the more centrally located Laguna to fill the orders of Mexico's industries.[17]

Unlike cotton-producing countries such as Brazil and India, Mexico did not—could not—respond quickly to the changing conditions of world cotton trade by

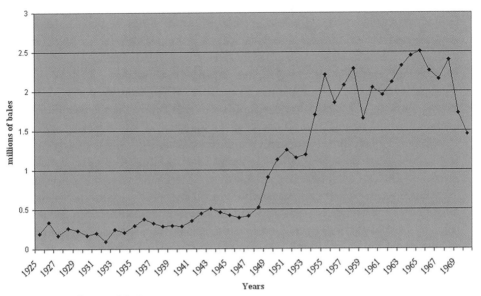

Cotton production: Mexico.

increasing exports. First, cotton for export was financed with and sold for dollars,
and thus the only advantage in production costs was the lower price of labor on
the Mexican side of the border. Second, production of the fiber could not rapidly
overcome the environmental constraint of aridity. The Mexican government simply
could not expand cotton production beyond the actual territorial limits of the existing irrigation projects, and new projects required many years and huge amounts of
money to complete. In contrast, because of an abundance of rain-fed agricultural
land that could be converted immediately to cotton, Brazil's government was able
to increase production three-fold between 1929 and 1934.[18] Third, the areas where
cotton could be produced without irrigation (Veracruz, Oaxaca, and Guerrero, for
example) lacked the credit sources, technical knowledge, and marketing systems
required for modern industrial production (see pp. 38, 39, and 97).

Events of 1929 to 1934 gave further impetus to the production of cotton outside
the United States, but the Mexican government could not, due to a variety of factors, increase exports to take advantage of the situation. To make matters worse, the
Don Martín irrigation system—the CNI's most celebrated and ambitious effort to
create a modern cotton region from the ground up—was left dry by an unplanned
and chronic shortage of water in the reservoir. The events of the early 1930s clearly
demonstrated the federal government's inability to implement a program to increase
cotton production, and revealed a continuing lack of control over its rural economy.
When the government of Lázaro Cárdenas outlined its development program in
the Six-Year Plan of 1934, it included the goal of overcoming the social, economic,
environmental, and cultural factors that limited the expansion of cotton exports.
This revamped cotton politics (*política algodonera*) lay at the heart of the federal

government's regional development project in the Valle Bajo Río Bravo, begun in earnest in 1935.

Matamoros Faces the Crisis—Relative Surplus Population

In early 1929 the future looked bright for the political and economic elite of Matamoros, although commercial cotton production and a changing social panorama provided constant challenges. Cotton prices in Matamoros had fallen steeply when the record-breaking 1926–1927 U.S. crop of 16.1 million bales sent world production up to 27.8 million bales. Simultaneously, *agraristas* had raised the specter of land takeovers and expropriation by state and federal forces. Nevertheless, these agrarian disturbances of 1926 were largely resolved through an agreement negotiated between the *campesinos* and the *portesgilista* group installed in the Chamber of Commerce, the Casa García, and the municipal government, and from 1927 to 1929 cotton production and prices stabilized a bit.[19] Soon, however, the cotton crisis brought on by the Great Depression would bring the regional economy to its knees, and send thousands of Mexicans streaming back from the United States into the lower Río Bravo/Rio Grande Valley of Mexico.

Cotton production on the Texas side of the Valley varied from year to year, but apart from the slump of 1927, the area produced about 90,000 to 100,000 bales a year. At least fourteen thousand laborers worked two months to harvest the crop.[20] The rapidly growing population in the Río Bravo/Rio Grande delta meant that no shortage of labor would hinder the success of plantation-style mechanized cotton agriculture on both sides of the river, nor would the smallholders constituted by the 1926 *arreglo* have trouble finding cotton pickers. This reserve army of laborers free to enter into wage or sharecropping relations was exactly what the region's merchant/industrial bourgeoisie needed to provide cotton to the waiting markets. When cotton production evaporated in the early 1930s, however, the region's laborers became superfluous, and problematic.

The repatriation of Mexicans from the United States and efforts by both governments to manage and benefit from this movement actually started before the crisis of 1929 and the 1930s. Already in the summer of 1928, some six months before the stock market crashed and four years after the 1924 immigration law established immigration quotas and created the U.S. Border Patrol to enforce them, the Immigration and Naturalization Service (INS) began a concerted effort to deport Mexicans working in the lower Río Bravo/Rio Grande Valley. By late April of 1929 the Immigration Office in Brownsville reported that 2600 Mexicans had been deported and hundreds more were held in detention. Many Mexicans working in Texas agriculture were sent back to Mexico by this deportation campaign carried out between mid-1928 and 1931; many more headed back on their own, fearing harassment or deportation by the Immigration Service.[21]

Angry reactions to this deportation campaign came from two directions. First, the Valley's businessmen and especially its farmers cried out in May of 1928 against the deportation of the agricultural labor force to their representative in Congress, John Garner, who then brought the issue to the INS in Washington. At the same time, the Mexican consul in San Antonio ordered Brownsville consul López Montero to monitor the legal cases of Mexicans held for violation of immigration laws, and to protest any infringement of their rights. López wrote that despite rumors to the contrary, "there have been no cases reported, at least that I know about, of deported Mexicans having suffered damages and prejudices from abandoning their interests and properties," and that the federal immigration officer in charge of the campaign was "a tested and honest functionary, who has a lot of consideration for our nationals."[22] The INS's Border Patrol was not held in such high esteem, however, and in September of 1929, López Montero published an open letter in the *Brownsville Herald* complaining of abuses against Mexican nationals in the Texas Valley.[23] In one case, the Border Patrol rounded up Mexicans waiting for papers outside of the Mexican Consulate and deported them before they had a chance to pack their bags. The climate of persecution grew, and even before the Depression hit in late 1929, Mexicans and Mexican Americans were seeking ways to emigrate from Texas to Mexico.

The Mexican government responded to the harassment of Mexican workers by reiterating and publicizing its desire to accommodate repatriated workers in its irrigation zones. The colonization and irrigation laws of 1926 gave priority to new settlers repatriated from the United States, but the sharp drop in cotton production in 1927 in both Mexico and the United States accentuated the difficulties of settling and employing idle migrant agricultural laborers.[24] Then, in the summer of 1928 the well-publicized deportation campaign waged in Texas by the INS spurred the Mexican government into action. Anticipating the completion of some of its new irrigation projects in 1929 (including, most notably, the "Don Martín" system), in November of 1928 the CNI published an elaborate bulletin that included both information about the irrigation zones being built in the country and a lengthy application form to be filled out by prospective colonists.[25]

In response to the deportation campaign in the Texas Valley, in May of 1929 Brownsville consul López Montero met with Mexicans in the towns of Río Hondo, Harlingen, and San Benito to promote the efforts of the CNI to settle repatriated Mexicans as colonists in the new *Sistemas de Riego*. López Montero had read various CNI circulars about colonization and repatriation, and, in his own words, he "inculcated the idea [among Mexicans in South Texas] . . . that they should think seriously about a return to the homeland, with the goal of colonizing lands that our Government has prepared for cultivation by building grand irrigation works."[26] Shortly thereafter, the CNI's parent organization—the Secretaría de Agricultura y Fomento (SAF)—sent engineer Enrique de Silva to the Texas Valley to investigate the effects the deportation campaign had on Mexican workers, and to "listen to the petitions of all those that are ready to return to Mexico in the status of agricultural colonists."[27] In June, meetings with de Silva were organized by Mexican and Mexican American voluntary societies in Río Hondo, Harlingen, San Benito, and Raymondville, and local committees were set up to organize this repatriation. Two months later the consul reported that these committees were working busily at organizing groups for repatriation, and asked the SAF for more specific information about colonization in the President Calles and Don Martín irrigation systems.

Despite the SRE and SAF's interest in repatriating the Mexicans living in the Valley in the summer of 1929, little advance was made, and in 1930 Consulate Inspector E. A. González wrote in his report about the Matamoros district that the large number of agricultural workers ready to return to Mexico still lacked detailed information from the SAF about the process of acquiring lands. Consul López Montero personally wrote the Sauteña owners to ask about the possibility of settling repatriates on the *hacienda,* and received a firm negative response. The empty lands of the Sauteña were an attractive lure to sixty families in Río Hondo Texas, however, who, energized by the advice of Consul López Montero and armed with the knowledge that the Sauteña was property of a Mexican government bank, established themselves on *hacienda* property near the town of Río Bravo.[28]

As the Depression took hold of cotton production in 1930, the movement of people from the United States to the Mexican side of the border increased. Many of those thrown out of work in Texas settled on lands in Matamoros, including a good number of Mexican Americans.[29] Even before the crash of 1929 the CNI was not able to live up to its optimistic plans to settle Mexico's émigrés on irrigated lands. And when the economy fell apart in 1930, the flood of repatriates overwhelmed state repatriation efforts.

Matamoros Faces the Crisis—Flooding

If bad cotton prices, the bankruptcy of regional capital, unemployment, and the influx of *repatriados* were not enough to constitute a crisis, in 1932, 1933, and 1935 Matamoros was pounded by tropical storms. The delta region of the Río Bravo/Río Grande had always experienced periodic flooding, and the agriculture of the region depended on those floods to bring nutrients to the soil as well as water. However, since the first decade of the century developers of the agricultural zone on the Texas side of the river had raised levees on the river to protect their lands. Floodwaters that previously covered both banks of the river channel now headed south into Mexico, where the levees were lower.

The Mexican government was waiting for a resolution of the conflict over rights to international waters before investing in flood control on the lower Río Bravo/Río Grande. By the 1930s both the U.S. and the Mexican governments knew that the best remedy for flooding and drought in the lower Río Bravo/Río Grande Valley was a system of dams on the international river. The existing treaty, however, forbade such constructions, and a new treaty was not in sight. A plan for floodwater diversion works had been proposed even before 1930 by the Ministry of Communications and Public Works (SCOP), but while the governments of the delta counties in Texas had been able to finance an impressive system of levees and flood channels on their side, the Mexican side remained relatively unprotected.[30] The flooding of 1932 underscored the need for a regional, binational flood control system, and the International Water Commission (Comisión Internacional de Aguas) drew up a preliminary project to create such a system, pending funding and approval by the governments of Mexico and the United States.

In April of 1933, the U.S. federal government took over responsibility for the flood control works from the counties of the lower Rio Grande Valley in Texas, and hired unemployed U.S. citizens to reinforce the levees. Despite the improvements, on September 4 another tropical storm caused major flooding on both sides of the river. On the Mexican side water extended well south of the railroad tracks, leaving the town of Matamoros as an island. Faustino Saldaña, the rural teacher of the federal school in *rancho* "El Moquete," reported that the cyclone flooded the community and sent its inhabitants fleeing to a nearby dry spot, where they were stranded by water that reached "two or three meters deep for a radius of 5 leagues in every direction."[31] After the storm clouds passed, clouds of mosquitoes bred in the waters left standing, and much of the population fell ill with malaria. Saldaña, left without possessions and most of his clothes by the raging flood, caught the disease while administering medicines from his schoolhouse first aid kit to more than three hundred people. The railroad connection between Matamoros and Monterrey was cut by the flood, as were all normal forms of transportation within the region. Saldaña had to hire a boat to take him to Matamoros.[32]

After the floods of September 1933 it was clear to the Mexican government that it had to make a major investment in flood control works. At the same time, the farmers of the Texas Valley stepped up pressure for a water treaty, to allow dams to be built on the river. Although Roosevelt brought the "good neighbor policy" with him to the oval office in the spring of 1933, and droughts and floods continued to imperil the Río Bravo/Rio Grande delta, a comprehensive binational flood control plan remained at an impasse when Lázaro Cárdenas took office in December of 1934.

Cardenismo in the Bajo Río Bravo: Agrarian Reform

When, in mid-1934, the Partido Nacional Revolucionario produced its Six Year Plan (*Plan Sexenal*) for the 1935–1940 presidency, all the elements for the development of an irrigated agricultural zone in the Matamoros region were contemplated. In a discussion of irrigation, the party of the state pledged to finally move forward with the ancient plan to irrigate the Sauteña, as well as a dam project for the Río San Juan, which fed into the Río Bravo/Rio Grande just above Reynosa. Government-owned lands such as those of the Sauteña held by the Banco de México and Banco Nacional de Crédito Agrícola were made a priority for redistribution. Cárdenas and his advisors directed this land reform toward the "establishment of agricultural colonies of repatriates . . . preferably in scarcely populated areas; but sufficiently close to centers of population to provoke, on the one hand, the reincorporation of the recently arrived, and, on the other hand, the assimilation of their useful knowledge by the regional inhabitants."[33] This was the vision of "agricultural cities" that the CNI implemented in designing the Don Martín system, and it reflects the developmentalist, anthropological ideas of acculturation held by its author, Manuel Gamio. Gamio was part of a group of intellectuals charged with drawing up the sections of the *Plan Sexenal* that dealt with population, colonization, repatriation and demographic policy.[34]

Repatriation was a main topic of the *Plan Sexenal,* and during his preelection tour of the border Cárdenas focused on that issue. In a campaign visit to Matamoros, the presidential candidate called upon Mexicans living abroad to return to Mexico, and told audiences that if he received their vote all the problems of flooding and unemployment that beset the Valle Bajo del Río Bravo would be taken care of. During his travels he sought to identify regions adequate for the repatriation and settlement of *colonos,* and "reviewed with special detail the projects for the amplification of the Valle de Matamoros, in Tamaulipas, next to the border; projects that involve works of flood control, of colonization and of agriculture, to increase the cultivable surface area from twenty thousand hectares today to the hundred thousand that are possible, with a capacity to accommodate fifteen thousand repatriated families."[35] The projects reviewed by Cárdenas were the old colonization and irrigation plans of the Sauteña and the regional flood control plans formulated by the Comisión Internacional de Aguas in response to the flooding of 1932. Responding to the problem of a large surplus population of unemployed workers returning from the United States during the crisis of the early 1930s, Cárdenas made the settlement of those *repatriados* the objective of the plans to colonize the Sauteña.[36]

By the time of Cárdenas's visit to Matamoros in June 1934, the social tensions in the Valle Bajo del Río Bravo quelled by the *arreglo* of 1926 were resurfacing. The influx of *repatriados,* the crisis of the cotton economy, and the destruction and health problems caused by flooding generated misery among the inhabitants of the countryside. As a measure of the success of the 1926 *arreglo* in protecting the land of the region's property owners, before 1935 only one *ejido* was established, despite numerous formal requests. The Sauteña was also shielded from land reform, but by the federal government, which owned the debt of the *hacienda* and guarded hopes that its land would be successfully divided, sold, and colonized through private initiative. Furthermore, from 1933 to 1935 Tamaulipas had a governor, Rafael Villarreal, who was very much anti-*agrarista* in his politics, and actively stymied agrarian movements. But despite the absence of open conflict or land reform, the property regime in Matamoros became an increasingly serious obstacle to the peaceful social integration of the region's rapidly expanding classes of rural dwellers.[37]

The moment that Cárdenas took office on December 1, 1934, militants for agrarian reform (*agraristas*) in Matamoros went on the offensive. On December 5, *agraristas* from "El Ramireño" wrote Cárdenas asking for an engineer to be sent to give them possession of the lands. Without waiting for support from the federal government, sharecroppers throughout the agricultural zone of Matamoros and Reynosa laid claim to and occupied lands, declaring them *ejidos*. The landowners responded by calling for support from municipal and state authorities, and the police. Forty *agraristas* were apprehended in the *hacienda* Las Rucias, and eight more in El Soliseño. *Agrarista* leaders, well versed in the language of social justice, complained to Cárdenas of harassment, and asked that the federal government "put an end to the misconducts and crimes that are being committed against the workers and *agraristas* of the region." *Ejido* president and *agrarista* leader Tomás Benavides of El Soliseño reiterated the need for a federal engineer to legitimize the land takeover in the region, but said that the *agraristas* would defend their lands with or without government help.[38]

To negotiate a solution to the confrontation, Cárdenas sent Graciano Sánchez, chief of the General Office of Complaints of the Departamento Agrario, to Matamoros along with a brigade of engineers. Sánchez met with the *agrarista* committees of each locality and the landowners, and despite initial resistance by the landowners, on December 24 representatives of the two groups signed an accord by which the *campesinos* agreed to the unconditional return of those small properties that were worked personally by their owners. At the same time, the large landowners agreed to rent half of their agricultural land to *campesinos* through sharecropping agreements, but only for the upcoming season, and in accordance with Tamaulipas' Sharecropping Law. By the terms of this new *arreglo*, landowners were forced to enter into legally protected sharecropping relations rather than more exploitative wage-labor contracts, and were simultaneously prevented from retaliating against the *agraristas* by leaving them without land or work. Furthermore, all the imprisoned *agraristas* were released, and the engineers of the Departamento began the protracted process of allocating *ejidos* by mapping property lines and raising censuses of the petitioning communities.

As an immediate gesture of support to the region's *agraristas*, 1144 hectares of the *hacienda* Las Rucias were expropriated by Tamaulipas's agrarian authorities, and handed over in a formal ceremony attended by four thousand people. Las Rucias was owned by the heirs of an American citizen, Juan Fernández, who broke Mexican laws prohibiting foreign ownership of lands on the border, and whose ownership conveniently rankled the nationalist sentiment on which the federal government was establishing its common political ground with regional *campesinos*. The expropriation of Las Rucias thus conserved the landholdings of Matamoros's native elite while placating *agrarista* demands for land. Two more conclusions can be made about the *arreglo* of 1934. First, this popular action by Matamoros *campesinos* did not fit comfortably into the blueprints for development contemplated by the federal government, and Cárdenas moved to reach a temporary compromise between *agraristas* and landowners that would leave room for a more definite resolution of the land tenure problem in the future. Second, the small property owners, especially those with no clear title to their lands, were ready allies of the large landowners in their struggle to quell *agrarista* land reform. This alliance was forged from kinship and social bonds, as well as the fear of having their small, undocumented holdings taken from them.[39]

Cardenismo in the Bajo Río Bravo: A New Political Bloc

At the end of June 1935, Cárdenas made a decisive break with the political machine he inherited from his predecessor, Plutarco Elias Calles, by removing many of Calles's followers from national-level positions of power. The move to the left made by Cárdenas through this purge had repercussions on the state and local levels as well, as *portesgilista* groups displaced by backers of Governor Villarreal in 1932 allied themselves with the Cárdenas government in a bid to reclaim power. In 1934 Portes Gil reactivated his political organization in Tamaulipas in support of the new president. Spurred by the schism between the *callistas* and Cárdenas, in July of 1935 *campesinos* throughout Tamaulipas demonstrated against *callista* Governor Villarreal. The statewide political movement to dislodge Villarreal and reinstall the *portesgilistas* coincided exactly with the flooding in Matamoros, and local *campesino* leaders wrote to the president with accusations that the *callista* municipal authorities were making a business out of the "misery of the people."[40]

Taking charge of the rural unrest in Matamoros, former *portesgilista* mayor Roberto F. García joined with *agrarista* leader Prisciliano Delgado to lead a group of 2500 *campesinos* in demanding the resignation of Municipal President Munguía and Governor Villarreal. García, a central figure in the region's cotton elite, was removed from the mayor's office in 1932 amid political controversy when Villarreal, backed by Calles, took the governorship from Portes Gil. The Villarreal power bloc had effectively stymied agrarian reform across the state from 1932 to 1935, and in Matamoros the anti-*agrarista* position of the municipal government was backed up by the activities of paramilitary "white guards" organized by landowners. Although he was no *agrarista,* García exercised a great deal of power as a mediating figure between *campesinos* and landowners in the region, and was the primary local representative of a Tamaulipan political structure (*portesgilismo*) that was based in organizations of *campesinos* and workers. Accordingly, during this uprising against Munguia and Villarreal, García was named representative of the *agrarista/portesgilista/cardenista* group in negotiations with the city's government, and was poised to regain the mayor's office if the Villarreal group ceded power.[41]

García was the key figure in negotiating the 1926 compromise between *agraristas* and landowners, and he enjoyed a great deal of confidence among all social classes in the region. One of the issues of the July disturbances—the state cotton tax—reflects this regional interclass alliance between cotton capital and *campesinos.* One of the speakers (probably García himself) at the first *campesino* demonstration in the town square on July 21 asked "where is the money from the cotton tax?; Matamoros has enough money for the flood control works."[42] The tax levied by the Villarreal government on cotton was a sore point for all those involved in the region's cotton economy, although it was García who made the statement to the *Brownsville Herald* that the tax was "the principal complaint of the peasants."[43] In speaking for the peasants, García was articulating a regional political position, and producing and reproducing an interclass regional sense of identity among the popular groups that organized in opposition to the Villarreal state government. At the same time, however, García was utilizing a much more complex social movement to further the particular interest of the region's cotton capitalists in fighting the cotton tax. From the late 1930s to the early 1960s the Matamoros cotton elite would continue to speak for the region in struggles against federal and state government efforts to control or impinge upon the region's cotton production.

The municipal government refused to resign, and the demonstrators threatened to march on the municipal palace. Before they could do so the army intervened, disarming the police, taking over the city, and declaring martial law. The *campesinos* retired to the outskirts of the city and waited. The army sent a train full of soldiers and President Cárdenas took the stance of maintaining order and following the political process. Cárdenas sent his Subsecretary of the Interior, Silvano Barba Gonzáles, to Tampico for a conference with Villarreal on August 24, after which Barba Gonzáles telegraphed Roberto García to tell him that the protesters could return to their homes in the knowledge that the situation would be resolved in four days. The conflict ended with Villarreal stepping down from the governorship of Tamaulipas after having been requested to do so by the Cárdenas government. Munguia was replaced by García on November 1, completing the transition of political regimes in the region.[44]

Cardenismo in the Bajo Río Bravo—Public Works

The *arreglo* of 1934 and the return to power of the *portesgilistas* established a regional political bloc with strong *cardenista* allegiances. Cárdenas sought to further reduce social tensions caused by the destruction of floodwaters, and to obtain the allegiance of Matamoros's cotton elite in the process, by promising federal support for the abeyant project to develop the Valle Bajo del Río Bravo through the building of hydraulic infrastructure. During his trip to Matamoros as a candidate in July 1934, Cárdenas reviewed detailed plans for works of flood control, colonization, and agricultural expansion, and in late February of 1935, Municipal President Rafael Munguía Cavazos together with former municipal president and PNR president Guillermo Shears met with Cárdenas in Monterrey to further discuss such plans. The SCOP was to funnel 6 million pesos to its Lower Río Bravo Flood Control Works (Obras de Defensa del Bajo Río Bravo) to condition some 200,000 hectares of Sauteña lands owned by the Banco de México and the BNCA. The plan involved expanding existing flood control works so that they would channel floodwaters over unsettled grazing lands south of Matamoros, converting them into agricultural lands through the deposit of "*calza,*" or silt. Despite the ancient pattern of allowing floodwaters to improve and irrigate land, since the 1880s agricultural development in northern Tamaulipas sought to mimic the pump-irrigation systems built on the Texas side of the Valley, rather than the flood/gravity method of irrigation practiced in the Laguna. However, because levee construction in Texas promised increasingly severe flooding in Matamoros, and because pumps were extremely costly to install, operate, and maintain, flood irrigation appeared as a viable option.[45]

With the process of *ejidal* reform under way in Valle Bajo del Río Bravo, and with concrete plans under consideration for conditioning, irrigating, and colonizing Sauteña land, on April 16 Cárdenas ordered the Departamento Agrario and the SRE to study ways of utilizing international waters to support *ejidos.* To head off the total expropriation of its Sauteña lands, the Compañía Explotadora y Fraccionadora del Valle Bajo Río Bravo (CEFVBRB) offered a development plan in which irrigation would be provided for a clearly delimited "*ejido* zone," free of charge, on the condition that the rest of the irrigated zone be declared formally protected from expropriation. The *Compañía* planned the creation of an "urban agricultural center," and the land was slated for cotton because its relatively high prices would allow colonists to pay their mortgages and water fees.[46]

Before any major progress was made on flood control in the Bajo Río Bravo, another disastrous flood struck. Legislation designed to facilitate an international water treaty was being debated in the U.S. Congress when, on May 22, the river rose to 17.6 feet above normal and streamed through breaks in the levees on the southern bank. Four days later another rise in the river barreled through the delta region, flooding into the Mexican side despite the efforts of six hundred workers conscripted to reinforce the levees. The continued failure of the SCOP's Obras de Defensa del Bajo Río Bravo and the great damage caused to the cotton crop prompted Cárdenas to step up actions in the region. In the first week of June, Rodolfo Elías Calles, who was the minister of the SCOP and son of former president Plutarco, was sent by Cárdenas to the region to survey the situation and meet with the ruling class of Matamoros. The flood control works he proposed followed the designs drawn up by the binational International Water Commission, and included levees with floodgates, and a channel to divert excess waters southward to the ocean. The maintenance of the works would be financed by appropriating a percentage of the state tax on the region's future cotton crops. The works would ensure the safety and productivity of the agricultural zone, and the expanded cultivation of cotton would generate funds for maintenance. While the SCOP was preparing to inaugurate the Obras de Defensa, the CNI was beginning the dam project on the Río San Juan that it had contemplated building since 1926. The retention of the waters of the Río San Juan would help to control flooding in the lower Río Bravo/Rio Grande Valley as well. In late September of 1935 the CNI's chief engineer Adolfo Orive Alba visited the border, telling the press that the San Juan dam, irrigation works, and agricultural zone would be ready for colonization and cotton production in about five years.[47]

By 1935 plans for hydraulic works in the Valle Bajo del Río Bravo were coming from three directions. Since 1926 the CNI had proposed an irrigation system to water the lands near the confluence of the Río San Juan and the Río Bravo, just upriver from the headquarters of the Sauteña in the town of Río Bravo. Also, Mexico's representatives to the Comisión Internacional de Aguas y Limites (which answered to the SRE) were working with the engineers of the SCOP on designing flood control works for the Ciudad Juárez/El Paso corridor as well as for the delta. At the same time, the company that managed the Sauteña was negotiating the shape of an irrigation and colonization project with the Cárdenas government that, responding to *agrarista* activity in rural Matamoros, sought to expropriate the lands of the *hacienda* in order to settle repatriates from the United States. With the appointment of Eduardo Chávez as director of the Obras de Defensa of the SCOP, irrigation, colonization, repatriation, and flood control would be fused into one mammoth plan to establish an irrigated cotton-producing region in the Río Bravo/Rio Grande delta.

Although in September of 1935 the specific shape of the project to develop the Río Bravo/Rio Grande delta was still far from set, it was already decided that the region would produce cotton. There was a long tradition of cotton growing in the region, but the decision to grow cotton was made for the immediate economic purpose of paying for the construction of the works. Subsecretary Vicente Cortez Herrera of the SCOP was sent by Cárdenas to Matamoros on August 20 with news of the immanent construction of a gigantic irrigation and flood control system, to protect a region that would soon be "much richer in cotton production than the Laguna region and the others in northern Mexico."[48] The planned cost was 1.8 million pesos, which was to be split evenly between the federal government and the region's cotton growers. Cárdenas had already approved one-third of the government's share—300,000 pesos—for spending. To pay the cotton producers' share of the works, a 1 centavo/kilo tax on unginned cotton was to be collected at harvest time by the municipal government. Organizations of *ejidatarios* and private property owners (*agricultores*) met with Cortez Herrera and pledged their cooperation.[49]

Another element that came together with agrarian reform and hydraulic works to lay the basis for development in Matamoros was the construction of a deep-water port in Brownsville. As production grew in the Texas Valley, the region's leading business leaders and politicians began pressing for the construction of the port, but it was not until 1933 that work commenced. Even before the Port of Brownsville and its shipping canal were completed, the businessmen in Brownsville and Matamoros who handled cotton production in the Bajo Río Bravo arranged to export the entire Mexican crop in 1935—some 15,000 to 20,000 bales—through Brownsville. The cotton passed through Brownsville without paying import taxes, was ginned and compressed in Harlingen, and moved by rail to Port Isabel, Houston, or Galveston for shipment to foreign countries. Maurice Brulay, a Brownsville businessman, cooperated with Milton West, the Valley's congressman, to have a bill passed by the

U.S. Congress to make the Port of Brownsville a "free trade zone." The bill stipulated that goods from Mexico could enter the Port of Brownsville, undergo industrial processing, and be held there for two years without entering U.S. customs.[50]

The Mexican federal government was aware of the possibilities of exporting Mexican goods through the Port of Brownsville as early as 1933. In April of that year the consul in Brownsville told the SRE that the Port would make Matamoros the single most important point of departure for exports in northeastern Mexico. In 1935, SCOP secretary Francisco Múgica told the press, that "the port that the federal government is building near Brownsville . . . will be of great benefit for the whole region, for there will be more commercial exchange . . . with the entire northern part of Mexico.[51] Múgica toured the Port construction site, together with the governor of Tamaulipas and the engineers of the SCOP.

The success of the Cárdenas government in dissipating political tensions and reinstalling the *portesgilistas* in Matamoros set the terms for a close relationship between the regional hegemonic bloc of *campesinos* and cotton capitalists, and the agencies of the federal government. With Múgica at the helm of the SCOP, and the SCOP in charge of the works, Cárdenas felt assured that his vision of agrarian development would be implemented in the Valle Bajo Río Bravo, and not that of the *callistas*. The alliance forged between Matamoros's García-led political elite and the region's *campesinos* cleared a path for the massive state-organized agrarian reform and colonization implicit in the development project. Having delivered the region to Portes Gil and Cárdenas, the new regional power bloc held high expectations that the state and federal governments would deliver on their promises of development. Major irrigation works and the colonization of newly conditioned agricultural lands were planned, and the Port of Brownsville provided the transportation needed to turn the Matamoros region into a major cotton-exporting region.

Eduardo Chávez, International Water, and the Toma de Retamál

On the day of the inauguration of the Obras de Defensa, Francisco Múgica arrived to Matamoros with Eduardo Chávez, who had been abruptly selected to replace José María Ramírez as director of the project. Chávez oversaw the construction and colonization of the Bajo Río Bravo project until 1942, and played a mediating role between the region and the national government. His job was to put state development visions into practice, and he had to negotiate a constant balance between the priorities of the state and the ecological, political, and cultural constraints of the regional social field in Matamoros. While plans for developing the Bajo Río Bravo had a long history, the specific shape of the SCOP project begun in 1935 was never clear before or even after the works commenced. Descriptions of the project alternated between a levee project like that proposed by the International Water Commission in 1930, which would divert floodwaters through the Matamoros region in channels that led to the Gulf of Mexico, and an irrigation and colonization project like that proposed by the Sauteña. Sometimes these two visions were combined, and

the levee system was expected to condition and irrigate the lands south of Matamoros with floodwaters.

This project continued to change and expand after Chávez took control. In mid-
December Matamoros mayor and cotton entrepreneur Roberto García was in Mexico City to meet with federal officials, and he returned to Matamoros with news of
a plan to increase the spending on flood control in the region to 10 million pesos,
and to embark on a 5-million-peso irrigation project for the Matamoros region. The
CNI's Río San Juan project was to receive 26 million pesos, and a highway was to
be built between Matamoros and Ciudad Victoria for 5 million pesos. Furthermore,
because the rail connection between Monterrey and Matamoros would receive a
huge increase of traffic through the new Port of Brownsville, the federal government
planned to rebuild the line with 5 million pesos.[52]

Chávez undoubtedly played an important part in the decision to enlarge the
flood control project in the Bajo Río Bravo to include irrigation. He was, since 1933,
the foreman of the flood control works in Ciudad Juárez and Matamoros, and it was
his responsibility to oversee the design of the Obras de Defensa. Since his first studies of the region, Chávez had identified the possibility of irrigation using a canal to
take water directly from the Río Bravo/Rio Grande at a place called "El Retamal."
Whether or not he was involved in the initial survey made in June 1935 by CNI engineers Vázquez del Mercado and Gustavo Serrano, he would have at least reviewed
the plans before arriving in Matamoros to take charge of the construction.[53]

Chávez's idea for a gravity-fed irrigation scheme at the Retamal had anteced-
ents in the flood control plans formulated by the International Water Commission
(IWC). The 1931 report by the U.S. section of the IWC stated that "large quantities of
flood water escape through Culebrón Lakes and other low places further upstream
and flow through a natural depression to the lakes situated west of Matamoros."[54]
The Mexican flood control works proposed in that year consisted of a levee along
the river with gates through which water could enter a floodway to the south. The
floodway was to carry the waters by force of gravity, passing through the "Culebrón
Lake" (Vaso de Culebrón) on the way to the Arroyo del Tigre, and then to the Gulf
of Mexico. The gate farthest upriver from Matamoros was located precisely at El
Retamál. Other floodgates were also built by Chávez, following the plans laid out in
the 1931 report, and these were also designed to be used for both flood control and
irrigation (see map, p. 76).

The federal government had a number of reasons to want an irrigation scheme
built immediately in the Matamoros region. First, the serious problem of repatriation demanded that colonization be initiated as soon as possible, and irrigation was
essential for the colonization of the Sauteña lands. While the Sauteña had long been
the object of such plans, by September 8 of 1935, a month before the official inauguration of the Obras de Defensa, Múgica had already told Cárdenas that there were
600,000 hectares of land available for colonization in the Matamoros region, and
Cárdenas' cabinet had agreed to cooperate in formulating inter-secretarial plans

for dealing with problems of agriculture and transportation infrastructure in the region. Second, the mobilization of *agrarismo* in Matamoros implied a reciprocal commitment by Cárdenas to support the *ejidatarios* and *campesinos* of the region. Once flood control works stopped the periodic inundation of the agricultural lands, irrigation would be essential for the productivity of these small farmers. Third, irrigation would ensure the expansion of export cotton production, a major goal of the development project outlined in meetings between federal officials and Matamoros mayor Roberto García in December of 1935, and a goal that would become even more important with the expropriation of cotton lands in Mexicali and the Laguna in 1936 and 1937. The fourth reason for building the Retamal/Culebrón irrigation project at that time was to stake a larger claim to the waters of the Río Bravo/Rio Grande, without waiting for the CNI's Río San Juan project to be completed in the 1940s. Talks with the Roosevelt government concerning a water treaty had resumed in August of 1935, and in September the CNI began its dam project on the Río San Juan. By October the CNI's Adolfo Orive Alba told the press in Brownsville that he expected a water treaty to be signed "within a year."[55] By taking water straight from the Río Bravo through the floodgates of the levees, the Mexican government was placing the agriculture on the Texas side of the Valley in peril, and improving its position at the bargaining table for this international water treaty.[56]

In February of 1936 Cárdenas met in Monterrey with Roberto García and Prisciliano Delgado, who reported on the unavailability of credit for *agraristas* and *ejidatarios* in Matamoros and other issues. Then he traveled to the Don Martín irrigation system, where he dictated a measure to redistribute lands. The Don Martín system had suffered serious social dislocations with the influx of *repatriados,* the desiccation of the reservoir, and the resulting unemployment among rural workers. In August of 1935 thirteen thousand cotton pickers went on strike for higher wages, and soldiers were ordered to patrol the streets of the regional urban centers of Anáhuac, Rodríguez, and Camarón to maintain order. In response to renewed activism in early 1936, Cárdenas ordered that *ejidos* be established to settle unemployed and landless workers. Those that did not receive lands in Don Martín were to be moved to Matamoros and el Mante (in southern Tamaulipas), where there were lands available. Because the Don Martín lands were distributed to those inhabitants registered in the 1930 census, most of those moved to Matamoros were *repatriados* who had arrived more recently.[57]

Eduardo Chávez telegraphed Cárdenas when he was in Monterrey, to tell him that there was a problem that Cárdenas needed to resolve. Apparently Cárdenas had also been briefed on the developments in the Matamoros region by García and Delgado, for he told the press that he would make "a complete survey of flood control, irrigation, sanitation and highway projects" in the Valle Bajo del Río Bravo.[58] When Cárdenas arrived in Reynosa on February 16, he went directly to inspect the Retamal intake that Chávez was building. After meeting with Chávez, Cárdenas backed the project to divert waters directly from the Río Bravo/Rio Grande, and gave the engineer the power to spend money as he saw fit. Cárdenas said he would return to inaugurate the canal on May 1 of 1936.[59]

Conclusion

By the spring of 1936 all the pieces of the Valle Bajo Río Bravo development project were in place. A conjuncture of elements emerging from the economic crisis of the early 1930s had gelled the federal government's developmental commitment to promoting cotton agriculture by ending flooding, reforming the system of land tenure, and making unemployed, surplus workers productive by settling them as small farmers on irrigated land in the region. Alliances had been forged between Cárdenas's federal government, the state government, the municipal government, and the *agraristas* and cotton businessmen of Matamoros. Land reform was in process, flood control works were under construction, and a system of irrigation was being built that would both open new agricultural lands to colonize *repatriados* and pressure the U.S. government into signing a water treaty favorable to Mexican interests in Mexicali and the Río Bravo delta.

The planned expansion of the Bajo Río Bravo agricultural zone would mean a huge increase in cotton production in the region, and by 1936 the Banco Nacional de Credito Ejidal had established its role in financing the cotton of the emerging *ejido* sector. Cotton production on large farms was on the rise, and the region's cotton-seed brokers reported that smallholders had increased their plantings by 400 or 500 percent.[60] The cottonmen of the Texas side of the delta, many allied with the giant Anderson Clayton Company, anticipated increased cotton production and were carrying through legislation to make the Port of Brownsville a "duty-free" zone to facilitate Matamoros's cotton exports. The Cárdenas government promised funding for a new highway from Matamoros to Ciudad Victoria, as well as the reconstruction of the rail line between Monterrey and Matamoros, to bear the increased traffic from the region to the Port of Brownsville.

With Chávez directing the Obras, Múgica at the helm of the SCOP, and Marte R. Gómez in the governor's office in Ciudad Victoria, the development project was under the guidance of a group of people who shared *cardenista* principles. The unity and conviction of the leadership was reflected in a fair degree of coherence in the planning of the project. However, as we shall see, the building of the development project was more complicated than drawing the blueprints, as unforeseen financial problems and political pressures inside and outside the region forced constant modifications of the original plans. In particular, the massive expropriation of lands in the Laguna and Mexicali placed the federal government in control of financing, organizing, and marketing half of the country's cotton production by 1937. With the focus of the federal government now squarely on managing the cotton economy, the Matamoros development planners intensified their focus on the efficient and economical production of cotton, and discarded some of the social aspects of the development project, most notably that of collectivization.

CHAPTER 6

CARDENISTA ENGINEERING, THE ANDERSON CLAYTON COMPANY, AND RURAL UNREST IN THE RÍO BRAVO DELTA, 1935–1939

This chapter examines the importance of *cardenista* development ideology in the realization of the Bajo Río Bravo project. *Cardenista* visions of collectivized agriculture were generated in, and adjusted to respond to, the particular historical conditions present in the mid- to late 1930s. The most important of these conjunctural factors was the expropriation, in 1936 and 1937, of the cotton lands of the Laguna and Mexicali regions, which in the span of six months placed the Mexican government in control of the financing, production, and marketing of more than 50 percent of the nation's cotton. This new position of the state in the political economy of cotton coincided with a national budgetary crisis in 1937, and led to an agreement between Cárdenas, the Banco de México, the Secretary of the Treasury (Secretaría de Hacienda y Credito Publico or SHCP), and the Anderson Clayton Company by which the American cotton leviathan capitalized and marketed the cotton financed by the government's agrarian banks. Cárdenas sought to increase national cotton exports tenfold, in order to balance the nation's books and drive industrial development in the country. This government project to increase cotton production—Cárdenas's *política algodonera*—was undertaken primarily in northern Tamaulipas, where land was available and irrigation systems were under construction. The long-standing goals of settling surplus workers and using the waters of the international rivers were still important, but producing cotton for export became the overarching development priority after 1936. As cotton production for export took precedence, and the state struggled to implement its development design within the existing social field of the Bajo Río Bravo region, the vision of collective production gave way to one based on the individual property-owning farmer.

The government of Lázaro Cárdenas, its policies and practices—known generally as *cardenismo*—have been a focal point of sociological and historical research since the president reached office in December of 1934. The most notable actions of Cárdenas and his government were the expropriation and nationalization of the oil industry in Mexico, and the wholesale distributions of *ejidos* to peasants. At the time they were considered dramatic and powerful socialist measures by those who supported them as well as those who criticized them.[1] In the years since, his acts of economic nationalism have been interpreted by some as the achievement of the popular demands of the Revolution. This has been labeled "populist" history, for it meshes easily with the version of its own rise to power propagated by the Institutional Revolutionary Party (Partido Revolucionario Institucional, or PRI), which ruled Mexico for more than seventy years.

In the last thirty years critical voices have risen against this "populist" historical-political understanding of *cardenismo*. This "revisionism" either argues that *cardenismo* marked a consolidation and continuity of capitalist development, or that the period marks the final triumph of the state over the forces of revolution.[2] For example, Marjorie Becker sees Cárdenas as the architect of a "hegemonic state" that "monopolized violence and the means of production and that . . . persuaded a recalcitrant peasantry to negotiate with him. . . ."[3] Writing against such totalizing portrayals of *cardenista* state power, another strain of revisionist thought seeks to recover the unique character and radicalness of *cardenismo*, arguing against continuity.[4]

Research on *cardenismo* in the Río Bravo delta allows us to make two important contributions to this discussion. First, the close relationship between Cárdenas and the Anderson Clayton Company calls into question the assumed radicalism of agrarian reforms in Mexicali, the Laguna, Matamoros, and elsewhere in northern Mexico. Cárdenas redistributed land to rural workers and peasants, at the same time handing financing, organization, and a good deal of the profits from the newly constituted *ejido* cotton sector over to U.S. cotton capital. Second, ethnographic and archival research shows us that the Bajo Río Bravo agricultural development project had deep and long-standing effects. As we shall see in this chapter and the next, the Cárdenas government reshaped regional productive geography, instituted new forms of land tenure, and fomented new social groups, relations, and identities. But rather that view this as the imposition and domination of the federal government over and against a distinct regional society, I show that *cardenista* state power was built in and through a regional social field. *Cardenismo* and state power in the Valle Bajo Río Bravo was constructed through an ongoing developmental relationship between the government and various regional social actors.[5]

In this chapter I evaluate the tension within the *cardenista* "*política algodonera*" between collectivist development blueprints and two kinds of necessity presented by the political economy of cotton in the 1930s. The first necessity was to maintain the allegiance and passivity of Mexico's borderland communities and migrant workers. *Cardenista* visions of cotton development forged in the crucible of the Laguna encountered a very different social field in Matamoros. The *campesinos* of the region lacked the Laguneros's revolutionary history and their experience with radical organizations on the left such as the Partido Liberal Mexicano and the Communist Party, and were not at all disposed to collectivization.[6] In fact, the *cardenista* planners in the lower Río Bravo Valley had to contend with insurrection by anticommunist *Dorados,* a quasi-fascist group led by Nicolás Rodríguez that found sympathy among the small property owners threatened by agrarian reform.

The second necessity that guided the shape of development in the Bajo Río Bravo was that of successfully financing and managing the *política algodonera* within a global cotton market. The decision by the *cardenistas* to colonize Matamoros with private smallholding farmers rather than impose collectivization not only reduced the financial and organizational commitment of the already overextended federal government in the region, but ensured that the engine of national economic development—cotton production—would be entrusted to skilled, private landholders. As we shall see in later chapters, these necessities proved to be virtuous indeed, as they paved the way for the explosive economic growth and prosperity of postwar Mexico. Seen in this light, *cardenismo* was never as radical as many have assumed, nor was the conservative turn of the Cárdenas government after the oil expropriation of 1938 really that much of a novelty.

The developmental process of social engineering is an engagement of many actors within a structured social field. The important question is not only, as James Scott asked it in a recent book, "how certain schemes to improve the human condition have failed."[7] Nor is it only, as Victoria Bernal finds in her research on cotton in Sudan, how such government schemes successfully "establish authority, encode morality and order social relations."[8] Framed in terms of the success or failure of state projects to impose conditions on society, these questions tend to make the state blueprints divorced from and anterior to the social process, and to equate the envisioning and proclamation of development schemes with their construction and implementation, whether successful or not. Starting with the notion that the actors within a social field are engaged in what Antonio Gramsci called a "war of position," we see that the planning and construction of development projects is the product of a process involving the development agent, or "trustee," and an array of socioeconomic actors.[9] Rather than figuring out if the blueprints of the state are successful or not in establishing "discipline" or "hegemony," the question is to understand the material and ideological negotiation of power that is itself "disciplined" and "hegemonic"—the complex, multilayered, structured process through which the blueprint, the development project, and the encompassing social field are produced and reproduced.

Cardenista Blueprints

Upon taking office Cárdenas carried out measures to change the land tenure and social structure created by Calles in the national irrigation systems. To facilitate agrarian reform in the *callista* irrigation zones, Cárdenas turned over their management and organization to the Banco Nacional de Crédito Agrícola (BNCA) in December of 1935, effectively reducing the influence of the CNI engineers who strongly believed that national development would be led by agricultural entrepre neurs. The BNCA was home to a number of agronomists (*agrónomos*) who shared the *agrarista* and *cardenista* conviction that the new irrigated societies should be composed of genuinely small *ejidal* parcels. Influenced by what James Scott describes as a "soviet-American fetish" for the rationalization and industrialization of agriculture, the *agrónomos* were convinced that collectively organized small producers employing modern methods would work even more efficiently than the wage laborers and sharecroppers who occupied the *callista* irrigated landscape.[10]

When the Don Martín irrigation system went dry in early 1936, Cárdenas decided to move its recently repatriated colonists to Matamoros. The president went to the Don Martín region to resolve a conflict between landless agricultural workers and *repatriados,* on the one side, and large landholders established under the *callista* regimes, on the other. Thirteen thousand cotton pickers in Don Martín had organized a strike in July of 1935, and despite the presence of soldiers, disturbances continued into 1936. The government promised to resolve the issue, and six months later distributed 3000 hectares of irrigable land to long-time residents in the form of *ejidos.* Those who had arrived to the region after 1930 were promised lands in Matamoros and El Mante. To ensure that the new *ejidos* would continue to receive support, the president placed the system under the charge of the BNCA, and increased its budget by 5 million pesos. Despite these measures, the situation in the Don Martín region would grow steadily worse through the 1930s, causing an ongoing need to relocate the inhabitants.[11]

Regardless of the limits of Cárdenas's actions in the Don Martín system, the National Revolutionary Party (Partido Nacional Revolucionario, or PNR; forerunner of the PRI) was quick to publish a pamphlet extolling the achievements of the president, and highlighting the ideological bases for his actions. The pamphlet described the *cardenista* agrarian reform efforts as a frontal assault on the concept of property and productive relations employed in the *callista* irrigation.[12] In early 1936 the *cardenistas* viewed the border development project under construction by the SCOP in the delta of the Río Bravo as an opportunity to build an irrigated society from the ground up based on their principles, without having to confront the inertia of the CNI and the *colonos* already established by the *callista* governments. Irrigated with the waters of the Río Bravo, the Matamoros region was the setting for a *cardenista* vision of rural utopia consisting of "flourishing *ejidos,* collectively organized; rewards based on effort; elimination of exploiters and social parasites; regulated circulation of the wealth produced."[13] The builders and beneficiaries of this "economic emporium" were to be repatriated Mexican colonists moved from the Don Martín system and others brought directly from the United States. As a first step, President Cárdenas ordered that lands be given to the new repatriate community for two hundred houses.[14]

In this early phase of the Valle Bajo Río Bravo project, the "blueprint" for the engineering of regional society mandated the establishment of *ejidos* worked collectively by repatriated colonists. The director of the SCOP, Francisco J. Múgica, was Cárdenas's closest ally in government during the first half of his presidency, and he shared Cárdenas's social vision of development for the region. The hydraulic works were completely changing the productive landscape, and with it the relations between *ejidos* and private property. Settlers to the region, Múgica said, could be found among the Mexicans who would otherwise work in the agriculture of the United States. Like Gamio and the *callistas,* Múgica considered the *repatriados* to be bearers of a progressive culture, and sought both to reinforce that progressiveness and utilize it for the development of the nation. And like Gamio and the CNI engineers, Múgica argued for an integrated, regional development plan that would address aspects of health, productivity, education, communications, credit, domestic space, and geography. Múgica imagined the collective *ejido* as the central social and economic institution of the Valle Bajo Río Bravo—the most efficient way to organize production and to promote a sense of solidarity among *repatriados* who had absorbed the individualism of the United States.[15]

Múgica proposed to Cárdenas a three-step plan that would produce a wholesale geographical and social reorganization of the delta region. The first step was to expropriate all the lands included within the area protected by the Obras de Defensa. Second, he suggested that the map of the region be redrawn according to a "rigid order," with the land divided into sections inhabited by at least one hundred families with communal machinery. The third step of the plan was to establish state-controlled industries in the region to process cotton and cottonseed. The general envisioned a cotton region liberated from the inefficiencies and political problems generated by the existing land system and social formation—a cotton region grander than the Laguna.[16]

There is always a significant distance between the blueprints of social engineering and their materialization. For example, Cárdenas's measures in the Don Martín system were taken to alleviate acute social tensions that arose in a region that was engineered by the *callista* CNI to be a cradle of progressive, productive social harmony. There is also often great room between the reasons for governments to take action and the reasons given for such actions. Cárdenas's Don Martín agrarian reform sought a resolution to a particular social conflict, but was at the same time considered and explained as emanating from a political philosophy of humanistic socialism. Furthermore, action within a social field is shaped by long-term, "organic" historical and cultural processes, such as those that influenced *cardenista* development in the Bajo Río Bravo: the importance of developmentalist thought in Mexico, the status of the properties of the Sauteña, the strategic effort to control international waters, the problem of relative surplus population in the borderlands, and the dynamic of international cotton markets over the previous twenty years.

While there is always slippage between blueprints and their realization, the history of development in the Valle Bajo Río Bravo shows that blueprints themselves are produced through a material, political process. Over the next few years, the vision of collectivization that guided Cárdenas's and Múgica's 1936 plans for the

Río Bravo delta encountered and were reshaped by two main forces: the opportunities and constraints presented by the national and international political economy of cotton and those presented by the existing regional social field. The central role played by the Anderson Clayton Company in financing Mexican cotton production turned the government away from insisting upon state-led collective production in Matamoros, thus reshaping the development blueprints for the Valle Bajo Río Bravo project. The *cardenista* development blueprints were also shaped by the regional social field. The large *ranchero* class and regional tradition of individual smallholding were especially important in turning the federal government away from collectivization. These factors strongly influenced the way that *cardenista* development visions were formed, and how they took material form in the Valle Bajo Río Bravo.

Anderson Clayton and the *Política Algodonera* of Cárdenas

> *I am confident in what I stated before, that in permitting you to amplify the commercial activities of your firm in the country, it will allow us to develop in the future a vigorous program to increase cotton production in Mexico, with all the advantages and benefits that such a program will bring to the farmers, to your firm, and the to country's economy.*
>
> LÁZARO CÁRDENAS TO WILLIAM CLAYTON[17]

> *I am lucky to be a piece of the hand which distributes the many and great benefits born in the heart of President Cárdenas, and made possible by the virtue of his administration. Despite having liberated the country from the yoke of the world's greatest capitalists; despite having defeated their powerful resources, with the millions they have available to strangle those that oppose them and to buy accomplices: he has known how to reduce the enormous force of capitalism that used to control the consciousness of the authorities and buy them off, and in so doing has made the workers powerful, as much in the countryside as in the city.*
>
> EDUARDO CHÁVEZ TO THE *CAMPESINOS* OF MATAMOROS[18]

Land reform in the major cotton regions of northern Mexico placed the federal government in control of more than half of the nation's cotton production by 1937. The Laguna region was characterized by large cotton plantations worked by wage laborers, and this highly mobile and politically volatile agricultural working class maintained a high level of militancy throughout the 1920s and 1930s. Labor conflicts and *agrarista* activity dogged the region's cotton growers, and in 1935 a convention was held by government and industry in Mexico City to discuss the problems. Cotton workers continued to strike throughout 1936, demanding higher wages, and even parcels of land and wells for water. On October 6 of that year, Cárdenas decreed a massive redistribution of the irrigated cotton lands of the Laguna, and the formation of collective *ejidos*. Six months later, in response to similar *agrarista* movements in Mexicali, Cárdenas expropriated rich cotton lands of the Colorado River Land Company and formed *ejidos*.[19]

With the creation of *ejidos* in Matamoros, Mexicali, and the Laguna, the Mexican government was faced with the immense job of financing, coordinating, and commercializing the cotton crop. The Anderson Clayton Company—the world's largest cotton factor—had been active in Mexico since 1921, and by the early 1930s it was financing virtually the entire Mexicali crop, and large parts of the Laguna and Matamoros crops. Cárdenas, wary of possible production declines in this highly capitalized, highly mechanized and industrialized sector of the nation's agriculture, and recognizing that his government lacked the organizational infrastructure to assume the task, sought the continued cooperation of the Anderson Clayton Company in managing Mexico's cotton production. William Clayton, president of the Anderson Clayton Company, agreed to channel his company's financing and marketing activities through the government's agricultural banks.[20]

On March 8 of 1937, just one week before the Mexicali reform, William Clayton met in Mexico City with the president of the Banco de México, Luis Montes de Oca, and representatives of the SHCP and various Laguna region banks, to sign an accord by which the Mexican government promised to compensate losses incurred to the Anderson Clayton Company in the process of expropriation in the Laguna. Montes de Oca and Clayton also discussed the topic of increasing Mexican cotton production and exports at that time, and the banker asked Clayton for "any suggestions which might occur to [Clayton] as to how Mexico can increase its cotton production to a point where there will be a substantial surplus for export."[21]

Montes de Oca was a seasoned government functionary who served as secretary of finance (Secretario de Hacienda) under presidents Calles, Portes Gil, and Ortíz Rubio, and enjoyed close working relationships with bankers in New York who financed Mexico's debt. He had watched governments and their political programs come and go, and his priority was continuity and stability in Mexico's economy. In 1937 Montes de Oca was keenly interested in promoting exports to correct for an imbalance in international payments. The global Depression of the early 1930s created conditions of import substitution industrialization that resulted in a thriving industrial sector in Mexico and a resulting overvaluation of the peso by 1937. With exports diminishing as a result of the overheated currency, and foreign capital wary of *cardenista* "socialism" leaving the country, the government's agrarian reform and other social programs put a strain on the treasury, and in 1937 the Banco de México loaned the federal government almost 90 million pesos more than legally allowed. The climate of financial insecurity was aggravated by rumors of a peso devaluation, and of the immanent withdrawal of the oil companies from the country due to labor conflicts. Montes de Oca and Cárdenas hoped that cotton exports would enable the government to pay back its loans to the Banco de México, and provide the export income to balance trade. For its part, the Anderson Clayton Company was at that time seeking to increase its role in foreign countries to compensate for production cutbacks imposed by New Deal legislation for cotton that ensured that prices for fiber financed by the Anderson Clayton Company would remain strong despite economic conditions adverse to the export of other commodities.[22]

In meetings with William Clayton on March 8 and 9 of 1937, the Mexican government established a clearly cooperative relationship with the cotton magnate, and the Matamoros region was chosen as the focus of joint plans to increase cotton production for export. This suited the Banco de México, which still owned most of the property of the Sauteña. After the meeting Clayton flew to Matamoros on his way back to Houston, where he told the press that Latin American countries were eager to expand cotton production "because of the advantage which the exportation of cotton offers in the settlement of international balances."[23] A few weeks later Clayton wrote a long letter to Montes de Oca elaborating upon the issues discussed in the March 9 meeting, saying that Mexico's national development efforts created a "need to export," and that "in this connection, it should be remembered that cotton is perhaps second only to gold as a means of settling international balances."[24] Matamoros, Clayton continued, was the best area to promote increased production, for it comprised "the largest tract of undeveloped land in Mexico suitable for cotton growing." The Anderson Clayton Company handled the bulk of the exports through the just-opened Port of Brownsville in 1936, and Clayton expressed optimism about the future development of the region south of the Río Bravo.[25]

The Mexican government was careful to ensure that its agrarian reforms in Mexicali did not alienate the Anderson Clayton Company. The accord that dictated the process of that land reform in Mexicali was signed five days after the meetings with Clayton, and it stipulated that the cotton already planted on the expropriated land would continue to be the property of the Anderson Clayton Company until it was harvested. When the expropriation was declared, the Anderson Clayton Company's affiliate in Mexicali, the enormous Jabonera del Pacifico, sought and obtained Cárdenas's further assurance that its investment would not be lost. As the 1937 cotton season unfolded in Mexicali, the Cárdenas administration continued to give assurances that it would safeguard the interests of the Anderson Clayton Company against the actions of Mexicali *agraristas*. Often it was Montes de Oca who, fearing the economic consequences of a withdrawal by the Jabonera from financing the region's cotton, pressed Cárdenas to make these promises.[26]

In the process of promoting the irrigated development of the Matamoros region and enacting agrarian reform in the Laguna and Mexicali, Cárdenas shaped and implemented a larger *política algodonera*. Some aspects of this cotton program—irrigation and repatriation, for example—were inherited from previous administrations and given new shape. Cárdenas, however, increased the state's role in the organization of land and labor, while depending on the Anderson Clayton Company to continue to finance and market the crop. He also sought to increase exports tenfold. To do this, the government aimed to maintain the production levels in the *ejidos* of Mexicali and the Laguna, and vastly increase production for export in the emerging Matamoros area. The Anderson Clayton Company would provide the financial, infrastructural, logistical, and technical support for Mexico's new cotton agriculture.

On their way to overseeing the expropriation of *hacienda* lands and a sugar mill in Zacatepec, Morelos, in March of 1937, Montes de Oca and Cárdenas discussed the details of expanding cotton production in the Matamoros region, where lands were being cleared for settlement. Cárdenas had just received a report from the Tamaulipas governor, Marte R. Gómez, on the progress of the Valle Bajo Río Bravo development project in which the *agrarista* from Reynosa suggested a dramatic reaccommodation of the region's inhabitants in order to rationalize settlement and facilitate production. Cárdenas asked Montes de Oca to visit Matamoros with Treasury Minister Eduardo Suárez in order to investigate the possibility of producing enough cotton in the region to "export a million bales a year."[27]

On the first of April, 1937, Suárez and Montes de Oca arrived in Matamoros along with some of the most important figures in Mexican agriculture and finance: Eduardo Villaseñor (president of the BNCA), Roberto López (legal consultant to the Banco de México, director of the Almacenes Nacionales de Depósito, and, by late 1937, director of the newly created Banco de Comercio Exterior),[28] and Vicente Cortez Herrera (subsecretary of SCOP). Cortez Herrera told the press that the group was inspecting the hydraulic works with the intention of proposing mutually beneficial changes to the international water treaties that governed the use of the water of the Río Bravo/Rio Grande. After touring the region by airplane, members of the group told the press that "if our plans go through, by 1940 Northern Mexico will be a limitless expanse of cotton."[29] The officials were met in Brownsville by a partner of the Anderson Clayton Company, D. B. Cannafax, and together they traveled on to Houston to confer with executives at the company's headquarters and visit its installations on the Houston shipping channel.[30]

William Clayton was back in Mexico City at the end of May 1937 to continue discussing the issue of financing Mexican cotton with Montes de Oca and Cárdenas. Clayton reiterated his desire that his company play an active part in financing the program to greatly expand cotton exports, and Cárdenas asked if the Anderson Clayton Company would consider financing this aspect of the development project in Matamoros. Clayton said he would not get his company directly involved in colonization or building infrastructure, but was happy to support cotton farming. The two parties agreed that if the Anderson Clayton Company expanded its financing of the region's cotton farmers, the government would take care of colonization and road-building.[31]

Clayton was asked by Eduardo Suárez to suggest how the Mexican government should market its portion of the 1937 cotton crop (55 percent of the total; about 170,000 bales) while obtaining for Mexican farmers a higher price than that offered on the world market. Clayton suggested that subsidizing agriculture with a tax on industry was a better idea than a government monopoly on the marketing of the crop. Most important, Clayton stressed, was that the existing facilities, organization, companies, and procedures for financing and marketing cotton be conserved. It would prove impossible for the government to organize a substitute for private enterprise on such short notice (the harvest was a month away), and doing so would prove inefficient. Instead, Clayton suggested that the government agricultural banks (the BNCE and BNCA) limit their commercial activity to establishing a few centralized marketplaces for their cotton, where private merchants could purchase fiber. Clayton offered the services of the Anderson Clayton Company in hammering out the details of such a mixed plan, and reassured Cárdenas that its vast marketing system in Europe and Asia placed it "in position to sell Mexican cotton surpluses in the best markets; surpluses which will no doubt increase each year."[32] In response to the offer by Clayton to involve the Anderson Clayton Company in Mexico's fledgling mixed cotton economy, Cárdenas asked the cotton magnate to invest directly in the financing of the nation's *ejidatarios* through the Banco Nacional de Crédito Ejidal, assuring that the recuperation of the cotton company's investment would take priority over that of the government's *ejidal* bank (the BNCE).[33]

After the May 1937 talks, business between the Anderson Clayton Company and the Mexican government grew quickly. BNCE manager Julián Rodríguez Adame went to Mexicali to negotiate with the Jabonera, and by the end of July the company had signed a deal with the BNCE to finance Mexicali's *ejidatarios* for 1938, and was organizing a loan to the BNCE and BNCA for the Laguna region. BNCA President Eduardo Villaseñor traveled to Houston to sign these contracts with the Anderson Clayton company. The Anderson Clayton Company borrowed money from banks in Houston and New York, which it then channeled into its financing operations in Mexico. A loan to the Secretary of Agriculture and Development for buying cottonseed was pending, and loans to the CNI were discussed. To finance small property owners in Mexicali, Montes de Oca and Eduardo Suárez negotiated with the National City and the Chase Manhattan Banks to secure loans against the cotton produced by the farmers.[34]

The role of the Anderson Clayton Company in financing and profiting from the cotton production managed by the official banks met with some criticism by Mexico's cottonmen. Prices slumped in 1937, but the division established between national and export production meant that Mexico's industries could not take advantage of the lower prices by stockpiling cotton, because the surplus was already in control of the exporters. One cottonman suggested the formation of a consortium of private Mexican cotton banks to finance production that would exclude cotton merchants, especially foreign ones.[35] This suggestion would reappear throughout the next thirty years of Mexico's cotton boom, but control over Mexican cotton production by Mexican capital would never be achieved.

While the oil expropriation of March 18, 1938, increased the general uncertainty among foreign investors about the safety of their investments in Mexico, and caused a great deal of diplomatic friction between the United States and Mexico, the

Anderson Clayton Company continued to plow money into, and enjoy profits from, Mexican cotton. Another meeting was held between the two presidents on February 9 of 1939, to discuss the details of that year's financing. Clayton planned to invest 10 million pesos in Mexican cotton that year, which included 3 million pesos for the Laguna's *ejidatarios,* and 5 million to Mexicali. Cárdenas inquired about Matamoros, and Clayton responded that although they had long supplied small farmers with credit, 1938 was the first year that Anderson Clayton dealt with the BNCE in Matamoros, and it only gave 250,000 pesos. Clayton was pleased with the results and promised to continue loaning to *ejidatarios* and private farmers in that region.[36]

While both Cardenas and Clayton benefited from their business relationship, neither was entirely comfortable with it, and both took pains to hide their dealings from public scrutiny. Clayton was a staunch free-trader critical of government intervention in the economy, and a vociferous opponent of New Deal cotton legislation. His relationship to Mexico's cotton *ejidos* was pragmatic and functional, but the cottonman would have preferred to directly finance private property owners without the mediation of the Mexican state. When interviewed by a Brownsville reporter in 1937, Clayton made no mention of the agreements concerning Anderson Clayton investments in Mexicali and the Laguna, nor even that the meetings had occurred. Clayton made a point of telling Cárdenas that he didn't want any news of the February 1939 meeting in Mexico City leaked out, and the cotton tycoon maintained a "no statement" response to inquiries from the press. The magnate sought to protect himself from criticisms from U.S. cotton growers, who were angry that his firm was buying cotton abroad at a time when U.S. farmers were broke and stocks were dangerously high. Despite the efforts at hushing the news, it was common knowledge in the cotton trade, and the *New York Times* published an article insinuating that the cotton broker was helping to export Mexico's fiber to fascist Italy and Nazi Germany.[37]

Cárdenas also sought to conceal the role of the Anderson Clayton Company in financing and marketing Mexican cotton. The Mexican government knew that public knowledge of the collaboration with U.S. capital did not fit well with the rhetoric of economic nationalism it deployed to describe the agrarian reform program in the cotton zones of the north. In a pamphlet produced by Cárdenas in October of 1937 to quiet rumors of a peso devaluation, the president stated that the cotton financing was generated and organized by the Banco de Mexico, eliminating all mention of the U.S. cotton company or U.S. banks.[38] No mention is made of the close relationship developed between the Anderson Clayton Company and the Banco de México during that time, or the role of Anderson Clayton in financing Mexican cotton. That the deal was uncomfortable for the Cárdenas administration is also shown in the fact that the archive created by Cárdenas' presidential office contains no documents related to the negotiations with the Anderson-Clayton Company.

The Anderson Clayton Company would play a central role in the development of the Matamoros region. Cárdenas planned to maintain the financial and organizational responsibilities for the northern cotton zones in the hands of Anderson Clayton, and dedicate scarce government funds to the *ejidos* of the central and southern parts of the country, where private capital was not likely to invest.[39] Large *ejido* sectors were created in 1937 in the Laguna and Mexicali, and although these were financed by the Anderson Clayton Company, they remained nominally under control of the government's BNCE. The Matamoros region, however, was only just being cleared and settled at the time that Clayton, Montes de Oca, and Cárdenas forged their pact. With the support of Anderson Clayton, the Mexican government moved forward with an ambitious plan to expand cotton exports by 1000 percent, and, as we shall see, expanded a flood control project in the Valle Bajo Río Bravo into a massive irrigated cotton scheme.

Private cotton capital had much more direct control in Matamoros than in the Laguna or Mexicali. While the official banks financed 55 percent of Mexican cotton in 1938, they were only responsible for 14 percent of the Matamoros crop.[40] Since it bought the gins of the Cross and Garcia families in 1930, the Anderson Clayton Company had been financing and ginning most of the rest. Beginning in 1938 and 1939 the government expanded cotton production by clearing and colonizing the vast undeveloped and sparsely populated lands of the Sauteña, and Cárdenas and Montes de Oca reached an agreement with the Anderson Clayton Company that it would finance the crop grown on these lands. An early desire to create collective *ejidos* in Matamoros under the control of the government gave way to an effort to establish small property holders as *pequeños propietarios* or members of *colonias agrícolas*. The *colonos* were originally financed through the BNCA, but before long much of their credit was organized directly by the subsidiaries of the Anderson Clayton Company and other cotton companies, with no mediation from the official banks. With the expansion of the irrigation zone in the 1940s and 1950s, the *cardenista* "blueprint" of collectivized cotton production was largely forgotten, and the region came to be defined by small and large private properties. Private, often foreign, capital retained power over cotton production in Matamoros as the *política algodonera* reached fruition over the next twenty years.

Building the Bajo Río Bravo

While Clayton and Cárdenas were orchestrating their enormous cotton deal, Eduardo Chávez oversaw the building of the irrigation and flood control works in Matamoros: the Obras de Defensa del Valle Bajo Río Bravo. The objectives sought by these leaders found material expression in the Matamoros region, although not as they originally imagined. In the Matamoros region the struggle between landowners and landless *campesinos* to control the land gave *cardenismo* its particular shape. The national, state, and local governments consistently acted to reduce the class tensions in the region, which at first were manifested as a struggle between local social groups, including the class of sharecroppers and workers that was swelling from the continuous arrival of repatriates. As word of the Valle Bajo Río Bravo project spread, the region attracted increasing numbers of surplus workers from the United States and other places in Mexico. These newcomers sought jobs and land, further antagonizing the landowners, who responded with violence and intimidation. The government tried to reduce tensions and accelerate the construction of the agricultural zone by putting these new immigrants to work clearing land and building levees and canals.

Collective cotton farms like those inscribed in mid-1930s development "blueprints" for the Laguna and Mexicali were also planned for the Valle Bajo Río Bravo. But by 1939 these were forgotten, and the government was actively recruiting skilled cotton farmers from Texas, in order to colonize them as smallholders in the new irrigation zone. Part of this decision to establish smallholders responded to the conditions of the *política algodonera*. The government had ample private capital available from the Anderson Clayton Company, which had adjusted to the creation of *ejidos* by working through the state agricultural banks, but which preferred to finance private cotton farms. A more important factor, however, was the regional social field of the Valle Bajo Río Bravo. The truce negotiated between *agraristas* and the Matamoros elite in the *arreglo* of January 1935 opened the process of *ejidal* reform in the Bajo Río Bravo, and the number of *ejidos* in the region increased from seven in 1935 to eighty-six in 1940. While the *ejidal* sector claimed barely 4400 hectares in 1935, by 1940 that amount had skyrocketed to more than 88,000.[41]

The *arreglo* of January 1935 reduced class tensions in the region for a while, and the region's *campesinos* and political elite collaborated in a *cardenista* bloc that seized the municipal government from the *callistas*. By the end of the year three thousand of the region's unemployed and landless *campesinos*—more than 5 percent of the entire population of Reynosa and Matamoros *municipios* and perhaps 20 percent of the adult male workforce—had found work in the new Obras de Defensa del Valle Bajo Río Bravo under the direction of Ingeniero Eduardo Chávez.[42] The money funneled by the SCOP into the region made life in the flood-ravaged countryside less precarious, and the plans for developing the region into a cotton emporium revealed by government officials generated a sense of developmentalist optimism reflected in the region's newspapers.

Despite the promise of new horizons for the region's *campesinos* offered by land reform and public works, when the cotton season began in late 1935 and early 1936 they faced an immediate problem securing credit. Many of the new communities that had formed to solicit *ejidos* had not yet received the recognition by the state that they were *ejidos,* and were thus not formally eligible for financing from the BNCE. Private cotton capital was unwilling to provide seed or credit to *agraristas* who did not hold title to land, and many were forced to rent their newly acquired lands back to the former owners, who, because of long-standing social ties, did indeed have the confidence of the merchants. This resulted in the strange situation in which the former owners were renting lands they considered theirs from the *agraristas,* and hiring those *agraristas* as laborers to work the land which they, too, felt was theirs. Despite the oddness of the arrangement, it enabled the region's cotton production system to expand greatly in the 1935–1936 cycle.[43]

Cottonmen on both sides of the border anticipated a bumper crop nurtured by the flood-irrigated soils and protected from damage by the flood control system under construction. By mid-January some 800 tons of cottonseed had been imported from Brownsville to Matamoros by private cotton factors, enough to plant 16,000 hectares. Small farmers increased their plantings 400 to 500 percent, and large producers like the García brothers also increased their production. Matamoros mayor (and cottonman) Roberto F. García and *agrarista* leader Prisciliano Delgado informed Cárdenas of the credit problem, and in early February Cárdenas ordered Carlos Peralta of the BNCE to channel money to the region's *ejidatarios*. Peralta quickly created *ejidal* credit societies for those that had only been provisionally awarded lands, and moved 70,000 pesos of BNCE money into the region. Cárdenas himself confirmed this promise to provide credit to an assembly of *agraristas* in Matamoros's Teatro de la Reforma on February 17.[44]

With the credit problem, the *arreglo* of 1935 showed its weaknesses. During his early-February tour of the region, Cárdenas was asked to deal with a conflict between his *agrarista* supporters and small property holders who complained that their parcels had been taken from them to form *ejidos* during a wave of land take-overs unleashed with the new presidency in early 1935. As was discussed earlier, the lands cleared and held by these small farmers were most often formally owned in common by the descendants of the original recipients of land grants in the region. Confronted by the wave of *agrarista* organizing, some of the region's small farmers joined sharecroppers in asking for *ejido* lands, mostly to assure that they would retain the lands they already worked. However, both the sharecroppers and small-holders who sought *ejido* lands wanted to maintain what they felt was the individual control they enjoyed over the productive process and the land.

Múgica spoke with the *campesinos* about collectivization, and told Cárdenas that they wanted *ejidos,* but "they had a lot of reservation in respect to common use."[45] Other smallholders did not join *ejidos,* but rather defended their holdings tenaciously, forcing Cárdenas to recognize these small farmers as *pequeños propietarios* despite their lack of clear title to the land, and to protect their holdings against *agrarista* land invasions. The director of the Departamento Agrario spoke before the various groups of *campesinos* in the Theater of the Reforma in Matamoros, announcing to them that because they were all "class brothers" the property of the small-holders would be recognized, and they would be supplied with credit, machinery, and other help.[46] This measure reduced resistance among small farmers to federal *agrarismo,* and to keep the *agraristas* at bay Cárdenas paid them to clear and settle new lands. The *campesinos* soliciting lands thus became wage laborers working for the government, which provided them with an income until they could begin farming their new lands. While Cárdenas claimed that the negotiations with local actors and the adjustments to plans for agrarian reform in the region were "extraordinary,"

The Toma de Retamal floodgate. *Courtesy of the Archivo General de la Nación, Mexico. Fondo Presidentes, Ramo Lázaro Cárdenas, 503.11/3-1, Caja 564.*

they are more accurately seen as the commonplace dynamics of development. The vision of collectivization that guided Cárdenas and Múgica ran afoul of the particularities of the already-existing regional social field from the moment social engineering began in the Bajo Río Bravo.

The cycle of cotton cultivation and the on-again, off-again rhythm of federal funding for the Obras were important to the ebb and flow of social tensions in the region. In the planting season of late 1936 and early 1937, when the demand for agricultural credit was at its peak, regional cotton factors generally refused to finance *ejidatarios* or *agraristas* waiting for rulings on their *ejido* requests, and hesitated to finance small property owners who could not demonstrate clear title to their land. Seeking his backing, the *ejidatarios* of the region argued to the president that by increasing BNCE credit the government would undermine the exploitative control of the cotton houses in the region. Cárdenas ordered the BNCE to facilitate credit and cottonseed to *ejidatarios,* as well as to those *agraristas* awaiting *ejidos.* Meanwhile, medium- and small-property-owning *rancheros* began to organize themselves to counter what they felt were abuses by the Agrarian Department, *agraristas,* and *ejidatarios,* citing the promise by Cárdenas that genuine small property owners' lands would be respected by the agrarian reform.[47]

The Obras proceeded rapidly during the first half of 1936. The levees on the river only needed to be enlarged and reinforced, and 3000 SCOP workers with 2250 scrapers and 5000 mules were able to recondition 24 kilometers of these levees between October and December. Chávez began directing work on the Toma de Retamal

Inauguration of the Toma de Retamal. *Courtesy of the Archivo General de la Nación, Mexico. Fondo Presidentes, Ramo Lázaro Cárdenas, 503.11/3-1, Caja 564.*

floodgate in January, Cárdenas visited the project in February, and the structure was inaugurated on April 25, with SCOP Secretary Múgica in attendance. Because the irrigation system's canals were not completed, as soon as the river water began trickling through the canal Múgica ordered it shut off. Chávez had a limited budget for the project, and by April he had spent much of the money that was allotted for flood control on the Retamal project instead. Construction on irrigation works was then suspended until the following October, leaving two thousand men idle, and earning loud protests from regional leaders worried about the consequences of unemployment.[48]

With construction halted during the summer of 1936, conflict between *agraristas* and landowners flared again in the region. The agrarian reform was proceeding, and a growing number of *ejidos* were being created by sharecroppers on the agricultural lands between the river and the railroad tracks. Further land reforms and relocations were made necessary by the building of levees and flood control channels, which cut through existing *ejidos* and private holdings. Furthermore, the workers idled by the cessation of work in May turned their attention to securing lands through the agrarian reform process. A dozen *campesinos* in "La Retama" who filed paperwork to form an *ejido* were chased from the lands on which they had been living by the property owners. *Ejidatarios* in Río Bravo threatened to make colonists settled by the Sauteña in 1925 pay rent to the *ejido,* or remove them from their lands. Small *rancheros* in San Vicente de la Mesa complained that members of the *ejido* "Buena Vista" were forcing them at gunpoint to pay for running cattle on uncolonized and uncultivated ranchlands. Ironically, in this case it was the *ejido* who militated against the communal use of land that prevailed among the *rancheros* of the region.[49]

In a study of rural Matamoros made in early 1936, Tamaulipas governor Marte R. Gómez described how the inability to establish land titles resulted in the various *arreglos* negotiated periodically between *agraristas* and landowners since the 1920s, rather than a decisive, comprehensive, or systematic agrarian reform. This, in turn, produced problematic situations in which smallholders owned land within *ejidal* boundaries, or entered *ejidos* but maintained their properties as if they were private. Smallholders protested that they were forced to abandon their tiny parcels and enter *ejidos,* and viewed the *ejidatarios* as enemies. The *ejidatarios* waiting for lands viewed the smallholders the same way, although they held the same amount of land, lived in the same communities, and were sometimes linked by family ties. Faced with this confusion, and anxious to prevent violent encounters between *ejidatarios* and smallholders, authorities of the agrarian reform moved extremely slowly in the resolution of *ejidal* petitions. Forty-three petitions were being processed when Gómez wrote his report, and because of their indeterminate status these potential *ejidatarios* found themselves unable to secure credit from both the BNCE and the private cotton financiers.[50]

Although Gómez was a dedicated *agrarista,* he was from the region and had a much deeper understanding of the people and their traditions than some of the other government officials. Whereas Múgica displayed a seemingly willful ignorance of the regional social field and the resistance of the *campesinos* to agrarian reform, Gómez was well aware of the intricacies of the social field that befouled the state's efforts to achieve its plans. Apart from the problems that derived from very old land use patterns, Gómez described the problems associated with the introduction of the irrigation zone into the area already dedicated to small property and *ejidos.* Many of the *ejidos* had been awarded grazing land that subsequently fell within the planned irrigation zone, placing those *ejidatarios* in control of 50 or 100 hectares of pasture that was soon to be prime irrigated land divided into 10-hectare parcels. Other *ejidos* fell outside the area protected by flood control or serviced by the planned irrigation, or even fell within the floodways.[51]

Chávez and Múgica responded to the disorder and social conflict of mid-1936 by sending increasingly urgent messages to Cárdenas requesting the funding and freedom needed to enact a truly comprehensive regional reorganization. After five months of inactivity, work restarted on the Retamal irrigation works in late October of 1936, and Múgica asked Cárdenas to authorize the implementation of a three-stage collectivization plan. Cárdenas responded to Múgica's initiative by authorizing the SCOP chief to study and organize the division of lands outside of the old agricultural zone on the riverbank that had already been the object of agrarian reform. In February of 1937 the engineer outlined a plan for ten collective *ejidos* based on the experimental farm run by the SCOP in its headquarters and work camp, named

"Control." Lots of 600 hectares would be occupied by groups of twenty families and a total of fifty working men. After setting aside land for houses, roads, canals, schools, and other social uses, 400 irrigated hectares would be farmed. Social organization and the material improvements were to make the *campesinos* "more refined intellectually and socially."[52]

By 1937 it seemed that the Valle Bajo Río Bravo project was generating more problems than it was resolving. Like Múgica and Chávez, Gómez argued for a total reorganization of the political and productive geography of the region: "we've got to start everything over from scratch," he told Cárdenas.[53] He suggested a collaborative process between the SCOP, the Departamento Agrario, and the state of Tamaulipas, in which *ejidos* in various stages of constitution and property owners large and small could all register their current lands and receive, in exchange, irrigated land within a reorganized landscape. Property owners would be given irrigated lands of equal value up to the limit allowed by law. In the case of the *ejidos,* enough land would be given to satisfy the needs of all the *ejidatarios.* Whatever lands were left over after these two groups were reestablished within the irrigation zone would be used to colonize Mexicans repatriated from the United States. Money would be provided to *ejidos* for the complete clearing of their lands. Once all were given land, Gómez predicted, the conflict between *ejidatarios* and *pequeños propietarios* would disappear, and the smallholders would slowly be converted into *ejidatarios* by the attractive terms of credit offered by the BNCE. This, of course, would entail a parallel elimination of the region's cotton factors as the region slowly became incorporated into the BNCE's credit system.

To provide lands south of Matamoros for the expansion of the irrigation zone and the colonization of *repatriados,* Gómez worked to expropriate the Sauteña. The Sauteña was still, in 1937, managed as a set of private companies, despite the fact that it was owned by the Banco de México and BNCA. At the same time that he made his report to Cárdenas on the agrarian situation in Matamoros, Gómez dictated a pair of measures canceling the tax breaks given by the state of Tamaulipas in 1931 to the companies of the Sauteña, who, with little capital and no advance made on colonization, had absolutely no hope of paying their taxes. Three months later, the governor dictated a decree establishing the legal bases for expropriating the lands of the *hacienda.*[54]

Even as the government was making efforts to establish a comprehensive development blueprint that incorporated the various elements of rural society, news of the development project brought migrants to the region in search of work and land, forcing Chávez and the Departamento Agrario to begin settling people on uncleared lands. Farmers and agricultural workers arrived from the Laguna and the Don Martín irrigation system, as well as organized groups of Mexicans from Texas lured to the region by news of a repatriation program in Matamoros. Chávez saw the haphazard settlement of these immigrants as a grave threat to political stability, and felt that it would create problems difficult to eradicate in the future. He recognized that the process of regional development was generating social conditions that the government had not envisioned, and was unable to control. The project was actually reproducing and augmenting the development problem of an unsettled mass of rural workers, rather than solving that problem. Faced with this unanticipated influx, Chávez placed the immigrants in *ejidos* on uncleared land. He asked the BNCE to pay the immigrants to clear the land, but a request for 100,000 pesos was denied.[55]

The year of 1937 was an exceptionally difficult one for the national treasury, and the SCOP project in Matamoros suffered a funding cut of 280,000 pesos. Plans to increase cotton production for export in Matamoros could only produce results over the long term, while Chávez was faced with the immediate problem of simultaneously finishing the works and opening up more lands to production, with less money to pay for it. Chávez eventually ended up paying for land clearing (*desmontes*) with funds earmarked for the Obras de Defensa, while he continued to seek the support of the official agrarian banks and the Departamento Agrario. He gambled that the wholesale opening of lands would result in a greatly increased cotton crop, which would both reduce social tensions in the region by putting money in the pockets of the *campesinos* and demonstrate to the federal government the financial soundness of his *desmonte* and colonization strategy. With his limited budget, however, he had to divert money away from the completion of the irrigation works in order to pay for the *desmontes,* leaving the works unfinished. Chávez and Múgica hoped the increased cotton production would convince Cárdenas to allocate the funds needed to complete the unfinished irrigation works. However, in mid-October of 1937 the money ran out, and most of the work on the Obras was suspended once again. This was an especially bad moment for work to stop, because the cotton harvest ended in September, and from October to January there was little labor required in fields. Nevertheless, the lapse allowed the Departamento Agrario to create a new wave of *ejidos*.[56]

The arrival of so many migrants to the region and the strategy of settling these new arrivals on untilled lands initiated an environmental transformation of the region that would continue until the 1970s, as new arrivals continued to expand the agricultural frontier. Until the 1930s much of northern Tamaulipas was owned by the absentee landlords of the Sauteña, who never got around to clearing the original subhumid hardwood forest on their lands, and tried to stop others from doing so. There was also little incentive to clear land for grazing, when the sheer vastness of the ranchlands in northern Tamaulipas allowed for extensive exploitation by livestock rather than an intensive pattern. So until Chávez began work on the irrigation and flood control system, only a relatively narrow margin of land along the river and around the city of Matamoros had been cleared and put to agricultural use. When the settlers arrived to the woodlands south of the railroad tracks, the first task was to cut down the trees. They made charcoal from this wood, by leaving it to dry, piling it up, setting it afire, and covering it with dirt. The demise of northeastern Mexico's hardwood forests gave rise, some say, to the popularity of mesquite charcoal in the United States during the twentieth century. This charcoal industry was a major source of income for settlers in the 1930s during the period before the irrigation system was completed and before their land was cleared and ready for agricultural use.[57]

The fauna of the region was also an important resource for the settlers. People who arrived in these early days recall catching and eating a wide variety of animals: hares, snakes, deer, wild boar, wild turkey, pheasant, quail, and dove. There was never a shortage of game to eat, settlers recall. The wild long-horn cattle that roamed freely across the Sauteña's lands were also hunted, although sometimes branded cattle were also sacrificed for food. All of these species declined as their habitat was turned into fields of cotton. The ocelot—or *tigrillo* in local parlance—was common in the region although rarely seen. One woman remembered that as a child she saw a *tigrillo* hiding from dogs in a tree in the windbreak next to her farm. "It was beautiful," she said, "I wanted to take it home."[58] With settlers cutting down the scrub forest and cutting off access to water sources, the ocelot has been virtually eradicated.[59]

With work stopped and *ejidatarios* occupying and clearing their newly awarded lands, agrarian conflict broke out immediately, following the chronic social fault line between *agrarista* sharecroppers and workers, and *rancheros*. A telling example is that of the sharecroppers working the lands of Santiago and Matías Longoria, who on October 16 of 1937 were awarded the *ejido* "El Longoreño." Many small *rancheros* held pieces of those same lands, some with legal titles and others without. Those with titles were not threatened by the *ejido* that was to be formed around them. Those without titles were in danger of having their lands taken from them, and either joined the group soliciting *ejidos* or obstinately defended their parcels.[60]

In response to this and similar conflicts over new *ejidos,* some two thousand *rancheros* organized themselves into an Asociación de Pequeños y Medianos Agricultores (APMA) and petitioned Cárdenas to investigate "numberless" cases in which property owners were dispossessed of their holdings. These formal political measures were complemented with violence. An *ejidatario* was shot leaving a meeting on the *ejido* "La Barranca" on October 17. The leader of a law-enforcement body created by *ejidatarios* of the "La Sierrita" near Río Rico was killed on October 26. By the end of October, five *agraristas* and *ejidatarios* had been killed in the conflict, and *agraristas* asked Cárdenas for permission to arm themselves in self-defense. The conflict between *agraristas/ejidatarios* and *pequeños propietarios* grew stronger as the year closed. Idle *campesinos* worked through the established institutions, but found a source of leadership in rural teacher and Communist Party organizer Guadalupe Galván. The APMA, the head of the Departamento Agrario in Matamoros, and Governor Gómez unsuccessfully sought to have Galván transferred for inciting the *campesinos* to ignore Cárdenas's declaration of protection for private properties. The flood of popular agrarian mobilization in the region threatened to surge over the institutional levees of the state.[61]

The situation reached a climax in December and January 1938, when it came time to finance the cotton crop. Despite the activity of the Anderson Clayton Company, government credit was short throughout Mexico, and during November and December the BNCE decided to suspend its loans to *ejidatarios,* and to those soliciting *ejidos.* The region's private cotton houses, reluctant to invest in land that might be expropriated for *ejidos,* refused credit to the *pequeños propietarios.* Chávez's use of the SCOP budget to fund *desmontes* rather than the hydraulic infrastructure of the Obras brought criticism from his superiors, and the SCOP cut off funding for the project in January. Múgica reported to Cárdenas that Chávez had gone against his orders in funding the *desmontes,* but quickly got behind the decision of the engineer to funnel a small amount of money to 1500 destitute migrant families. The migrants, wrote Gómez, "eat sautéed cactus and consider it a feast when they come across rabbits, snakes and mice while clearing their lands."[62] With no money to continue the Obras, Chávez drove to Mexico City to hand in his resignation, which Múgica refused to accept. Both Múgica and Gómez pleaded to the president that spending resume immediately to alleviate the plight of the immigrants, and to stave off social conflict in the region.[63]

At precisely that moment bands of armed men appeared in the Matamoros zone, engaging in combat with the police and with *agraristas.* On January 28, 1938, fighting erupted in Ramírez, El Soliseño, and La Rosita, with reports reaching Matamoros that thousands of shots had been fired and dozens of men killed. Marte R. Gómez inspected the region, and blamed the violence on the "Dorados," or "Gold-shirts": followers of radical right-wing exile Nicolas Rodríguez. Two weeks later twenty-five members of the APMA were charged with "rebellion," although they denied belonging to the Dorados. Rumors of a border-wide revolt against Cárdenas orchestrated in Texas motivated the army to send troops and planes to patrol the region.[64]

The severity of this round of conflict, and the threat to the sovereignty of the government that it posed, prompted a quick and decisive developmental reaction. The federal and state governments increased spending in order to ameliorate the problem of unemployed workers in the region. While in Matamoros, Marte R. Gómez met with regional cotton businessmen and *ejidatarios* to arrange for the immediate distribution of the cottonseed that the *ejido* sector lacked. Cárdenas then sent Agriculture Secretary Jose Parres, Finance Secretary Eduardo Suárez, and Suárez's director of credit, Pascual Gutiérrez, to Matamoros to confer with Matamoros cottonmen and municipal authorities about a plan to supply small farmers and *ejidatarios* with credit. Convinced by the armed conflict that the situation described by Chávez, Gómez, and Múgica demanded swift action, Cárdenas approved money for Chávez to employ all available men on the flood control and irrigation works. By completing the works, the president reasoned, agricultural development would be stimulated, unemployment reduced, and the threat to his government defused.[65]

The land pressure generated by immigrants and *agraristas* was only temporarily eased by the job program, and demonstrations and bursts of violence erupted periodically throughout 1938. In late February and early March the chronic regional conflict between smallholders and *ejidatarios* once again flared into open violence, as Chávez and the Departamento Agrario began another round of *ejido* reforms. Conflicts in the Rancho "La Bartolina" raised the specter of renewed "Dorado" activity, and *ejidatarios* claimed that the landowners had the backing of all the region's landlords and merchants in promoting a rebellion against the agrarian reform. The APMA staged another demonstration, rallying a crowd of two hundred smallholding *rancheros* to occupy the central plaza in Matamoros, and demanding of President Cárdenas that their property rights be assured and secure credit lines be established with the regional cotton financiers.[66]

Marte R. Gómez made a trip to the Matamoros to deal with the situation on March 16, and shortly thereafter another round of land reforms was made by Eduardo Chávez, to accommodate new arrivals to the region in the *ejidos* "Revolución," "Villa Cárdenas," "La Tijera," and "Los Arados." This was followed in April by a measure dictated by Cárdenas himself, which promised that a resolution of the La Bartolina conflict would be reached in which both *ejidos* and *pequeñas propiedades* would be respected. According to this resolution, the president promised to carry forward a regional reaccommodation in which all the smallholders without titles would have their boundaries surveyed and their properties legalized, putting an end to the land conflicts. Despite this accord signed by the president, by August of 1938 the president's office was receiving more complaints by *pequeños propietarios* of infringements upon their property rights by Chávez and the Departamento Agrario. The head of the Departamento Agrario in Matamoros worried that the mobilization of the smallholders could have "ruinous consequences."[67]

Frustrated by what they saw as illegal invasions of their land, at the end of October the APMA organized another, much larger demonstration in Matamoros. Some two thousand members of the Asociación marched into town accompanied by six hundred members on horseback, and took over the main plaza in front of the municipal palace. The president of the Asociación, Pedro Garza Sánchez, was a former police chief in Matamoros, and he painted the group as "law-abiding, hard working farmers and land owners" suffering "plunders and illegal invasions" by the engineers of the Departamento Agrario.[68] In early December, after their petition was rejected outright, a wave of killings claimed the lives of eight *campesinos*. Despite the obvious need for political intervention of some kind, the government refused to bend to the demands of a group that it believed was being manipulated by anti-*cardenistas* such as Nicolás Rodríguez and the region's landowners.[69]

Despite—and because of—agrarian reforms and public works spending, immigration to the region and the political mobilization of rural workers continued to generate pressure on the land tenure and production system, and continued to influence the shape of development in the region. The government "blueprints" for collectivization had not been made a reality, in part because of insurrectionary resistance from *rancheros* in Matamoros, in part because shortages of money slowed construction of the public works, and in part because the government's priority turned to increasing cotton production in the easiest way possible. By the end of 1938 the *cardenista política algodonera* was up and running, and the federal government shifted attention away from the problem of dividing the existing land in the "old" riverside agricultural zone among the region's *campesinos* and the new arrivals, toward the opening of lands south of that zone held by the *hacienda* La Sauteña and its various successor companies. The flood control works were being completed, and the next phase—irrigation—was beginning. With the construction of irrigation works the lands of the Sauteña would be opened up, establishing small-property-holding farmers repatriated from the United States. These farmers would be established as *colonos* rather than *ejidatarios*.

Conclusion

For much of the 1935 to 1940 period, development efforts in the Valle Bajo Río Bravo took form primarily in relation to the region's class dynamics and the demands of the international political economy of cotton, rather than strictly following the designs of the blueprints laid out by Gómez, Chávez, and Múgica. More accurately, development was the ongoing negotiation of those blueprints between the various actors who constituted and connected with the social field in the Valle Bajo Río Bravo. That Chávez, Múgica, and Cárdenas continued to draw and publish those blueprints was not entirely disingenuous, although Cárdenas's conscious obscurantism regarding the role of the Anderson Clayton Company in the *política algodonera* certainly was. More important, the continuous publication and pronunciation of blueprints was part of the process of social engineering: it formed part of and obscured the social relations of *cardenismo*.

During the Depression of the 1930s, cotton workers and farmers from Texas, the Laguna, and Don Martín streamed into the Matamoros region, entering into conflict with property owners in the region and motivating the government to open new lands and increase cotton cultivation. The force of this immigration would continue to shape the growth of the Matamoros cotton zone through 1940, and the federal government embarked on a renewed initiative to organize the immigration and settlement of small farmers in the region in late 1938 and 1939. This was the repatriation and colonization project that led to the creation of the Anáhuac and 18 de Marzo agricultural colonies, and the formation of what is today the municipality of Valle Hermoso.

CHAPTER 7
REPATRIATION IN THE RÍO BRAVO DELTA, 1935-1940

Beginning in the 1920s, U.S. intellectuals and social workers focused on the question of migration with new interest, and the social issues involving Mexican migrants were well represented in this literature.[1] The politics of immigration restriction, emblemized in the passing of the immigration law of 1924 and in the repatriation movements of the 1930s, generated a good deal of research among social scientists.[2] The Social Science Research Council was formed to study migration, and supported research by Manuel Gamio and Paul Taylor on Mexican migration and repatriation.[3] Memories of forced and voluntary repatriation remained strong in the Mexican American community, and with the florescence of Chicano history in the 1970s the importance of this repatriation was stressed.[4] In the 1980s and 1990s scholars investigated the way repatriation transpired in different regions, and how the events of the 1930s played a part in a longer story of migration and community formation in the southwestern United States.[5] In their book, Francisco Balderrama and Raymond Rodríguez enlarged the scope of research to include both the United States and Mexico, and included a chapter surveying Mexican programs to settle *repatriados* on land.[6] With the consolidation of the *cardenista* cotton policy between 1936 and 1939, the Valle Bajo Río Bravo development project became central to the drive to greatly increase cotton exports, and when irrigation works were reaching completion in 1939, the government set about recruiting Mexican cotton farmers in Texas to colonize the lands of the Sauteña. While the politics of repatriation in the United States have received much attention, very little is known about the fate of the *repatriados* in Mexico, or the larger context of irrigated cotton development that influenced the Mexican government's repatriation efforts.

From Collective *Ejidos* to Repatriated Small Farmers

In this chapter I examine the history of repatriation of Mexicans from Texas to the Valle Bajo Río Bravo (VBRB) project in 1939, and the formation of the Colonias Anáhuac, 18 de Marzo, and Magueyes. Two main arguments weave through the chapter. First, I show how the process of colonization exhibited the development dialectic that characterized the construction and settlement of the VBRB project since 1935. That is, rather than being the result of a radically proactive state project, the repatriation of Mexicans and their settlement in the Matamoros region was an already-existing social process that the government sought to control and improve through the uneven enactment of a haphazardly assembled development plan. For this reason the history of repatriation and colonization found in these pages is much more detailed, much more complicated, and much messier than those usually told. This dialectic of development was negotiated in an idiom of historical progress and regional community shared by both state actors and repatriated colonists, a language of regional development that defined political culture in Matamoros throughout the cotton boom years (1940–1960), and is still strong today.[7]

The second argument I make is that the vision of agrarian northern Mexico guiding the reconstruction of regional society changed significantly from 1936 to 1939, as the *cardenista* state abandoned the model of the collective *ejido* in favor of the model of the *colonia* constituted by small property owners. Repatriation was a cornerstone of efforts by governments since Calles to establish progressive agricultural societies in northern Mexico, and although the shape of development blueprints changed, the *repatriado* continued to occupy a privileged position within them. The *callista* vision of development posited a rural society divided into a class of small and medium property owners, on the one hand, and a class of agricultural workers on the other. Manuel Gamio, who helped to formalize thinking about repatriation and the incorporation of *repatriados* in the irrigation projects of the CNI, argued that Mexicans who had worked in the United States were valuable for their advanced production techniques and their "high cultural level." With the advent of *cardenismo,* the privileged position afforded the repatriated property-owning farmer in earlier visions of national agricultural development was occupied by a new social actor: the collectively organized *ejidatario.* The *ejidatario* on the industrial cotton farm was still considered a progressive, even middle-class social element, but because of his collective relations of production rather than his individual ownership of land. In the irrigation zones of the CNI, this transition in development blueprints was especially marked. During 1936 and 1937, Múgica, Gómez, and Chávez proposed a wholesale reorganization of the *campesinos* in the Río Bravo delta into collective *ejidos,* much like those established in the Laguna. The *repatriados* flowing into the region were grouped into provisional *ejidos* by Chávez, and set to the task of clearing land.

Chávez received his professional training in the *callista* CNI, and as a result of this formation as well as a career spent working in liberal, individualist, *ranchero* northern Mexico, he did not completely share the socialist agrarian vision of Cárdenas and Múgica. Nevertheless, in early 1937 he created a model collective *ejido* for *repatriados* near the headquarters of the Valle Bajo Río Bravo project in Campamento C1K9, also known as "Control." Chávez offered three options for settlement that provided different amounts of land depending on the amount of resources the repatriate could contribute. The engineer did not get very far with this project, for he encountered some difficulty in finding appropriate colonists, and the funding provided to clear lands was cut by the SCOP. Nevertheless, Chávez considered this SCOP experimental farm to be the template for the future colonies of repatriated Mexicans.[8]

By 1939, the government was settling *repatriados* on small private properties. One reason for the shift was that although government officials such as Cárdenas and Múgica took the Laguna region as the model for creating a regional cotton society, there was strong popular resistance to collectivization in Matamoros among the *rancheros,* even those who joined *ejidos* out of political exigency. Most *repatriados* from Texas were originally from *ranchos* in northeast Mexico, where smallholding was the norm and liberal individualism was a deeply rooted cultural formation. These Mexicans had often spent as many as fifteen years living in the United States, an experience that further solidified a predilection for individual, private property ownership. Furthermore, radical political traditions and organizations that supported collectivization in the Laguna—such as the Partido Liberal Mexicano and the Partido Comunista Mexicano—had much less organizational presence in northeastern Mexico. The government sought to demobilize and settle these migrants on land, but as small farmers rather than collectively organized *ejidatarios.*

Another important reason for the abandonment of the goal of collectivization in Matamoros had to do with the role that region played in the national *política algodonera* developed from late 1936 to 1939. Government investment in cotton production in the north supported a large *ejidal* sector, and had loudly proclaimed social goals. Nevertheless, the masters of the national economy were mostly interested in cotton agriculture for its role in maintaining a healthy balance of payments. This was especially true after the 1937 monetary crisis and the March 1938 petroleum expropriation, which greatly reduced government income. Put simply, to ensure that its heavy investments in cotton production generated needed financial returns, the government sought experienced cotton farmers for its Valle Bajo Río Bravo district. Mexicans repatriated from the Texas cotton fields would provide the experienced, skilled labor power for cotton production, but to recruit them they would need to be given something in return—land. It would have been impossible to recruit the kind of relatively well-to-do farmers the government wanted by offering them positions in collective *ejidos.* While the government may have made pronouncements about settling large numbers of repatriates, repatriation as it actually transpired was aimed at securing a very limited number of skilled farmers in order to produce cotton for Cárdenas's project to increase exports of that crop by a factor of ten. Although it didn't settle more than a thousand families, the creation of the Colonia "18 de Marzo" successfully accomplished this goal, although not without the political conflicts and negotiations that constituted the social relations of *cardenismo.*

The Colonia "Anáhuac"

Plans were proposed throughout 1937 and 1938 to repatriate large numbers of Mexicans to farms in northern Mexico, but lack of funds prevented the government from moving ahead with these plans.[9] Even if there had been money, however, there really were no lands suitable for farming available, and only the slow process of building irrigation systems could provide such lands. Flood control works in the Valle Bajo Río Bravo were reaching completion toward the end of 1938, and Chávez was shifting the resources of the SCOP to irrigation. He was prohibited from actually spending money on irrigation before the flood control works were completed, but by October 1938 he was able to organize the construction of three floodgates and canals using the unpaid labor of *ejidatarios* whose land these irrigation works would benefit. By December he sought money to complete the irrigation works proposed in the blueprints for the region. Most important of these was the "*Corte de Retamal,*" a canal that connected the *Toma de Retamál* floodgate on the Río Bravo with the *Vaso de Culebrón,* a shallow lake where the water was stored for irrigation. Secondary canals were also needed to bring the water to the fields.

Although repatriation plans for the Matamoros region were not undertaken in grand scale until 1939, in late 1937 and early 1938 some of the lands south of the railroad tracks were settled by colonists from the Don Martín system. Throughout 1936 and 1937 residents of the Don Martín zone forced to leave by the desiccation of the reservoir arrived in the Matamoros region looking for work or land to farm. Others writing on behalf of the "Sindicato Unico de Trabajadores Agrícolas del Sistema Nacional de Riego #4" and the "Unión Nacional de Veteranos de la Revolución" asked Cárdenas to fulfill his promise to provide them with lands in the Bajo Río Bravo.[10] According to the written testimonies of the founders of the Anáhuac colony, two men arrived at the Campamento C1K9 on November 11, 1937, to ask Eduardo Chávez for lands to settle eighty families from the Don Martín system. Don Fausto, an early immigrant from Don Martín, recalled that they made the long trip to Matamoros in a wagon hauled by horses. At that time Chávez was only creating *ejidos,* and could only offer them parcels of 10 hectares of *ejidal* land. The refugees told Chávez they were not interested in being *ejidatarios,* hoping instead to be given land as *colonos,* as had been common in the Don Martín district. Chávez asked them "are you real men?; are you up to the task?" Chávez gained permission from his superiors to settle these *campesinos* as *colonos,* for he authorized the creation of a *colonia* (rather than an *ejido*) for the Don Martín refugees, baptized the Colonia Anáhuac on November 27. The men returned to the Don Martín system carrying with them, one colonist remembered, sacks of rich delta soil to show the rest of the group the quality of the land.[11]

Once the land was dedicated, each family was given 20 hectares, a quantity that reflected the pattern of colonization in the Don Martín system rather than the 10-hectare parcels given to *ejidatarios* in the Bajo Río Bravo. The living conditions in the new *colonia* were abysmal. There was no land cleared to plant food crops, and the nearest water was located at the *rancho* "Santa Rosalía," some 5 kilometers away. The colonists made tents out of blankets, and slept in their wagons. "One morning I woke up with a big lump under the mattress," one man recalled: "it was a rattlesnake!"[12] To support themselves while they labored to clear the land, the *colonos* formed themselves into the Sociedad de Crédito "Acción" in order to secure BNCA funding. In the meantime, Chávez took money from the Obras budget to support the immigrants from Anahuac while they cleared their land.[13]

There was also an effort in 1937 to repatriate Mexicans from Texas to the Matamoros region, organized by the government and the Banco de México. In May of 1937 the Jefe de Población in the Secretaría de Gobernación, José Castrejón Pérez, set up the repatriation of some twenty families of the Unión de Agricultores Mexicanos de Saint Paul, Texas, to the lands of the Sauteña. The owner of the land, the Banco de México, sold them the land on the promise that they would pay in ten years. The colony, called the Colonia "La Esperanza," received no aid from the government, had very poor unirrigated land, and by late 1938 had failed.

Repatriation

The long-delayed plan to settle *repatriados* in the Matamoros area outlined in the *Plan Sexenal* and discussed by Cárdenas again in early 1936 began to take concrete form at the end of 1938. José Castrejón, who had organized the Colonia "La Esperanza," submitted a report to Cárdenas suggesting options for settling *repatriados*. The *hacienda* "Río Bravo" (part of the Sauteña) had enough land for a thousand colonists, and since it was owned by the BNCA, Castrejón noted that the government would avoid the issue of expropriation. The "Azúcar" dam project (the Valle Bajo Río San Juan irrigation system), already under construction by the CNI on the Río San Juan, would make another 15,000 hectares of this "Río Bravo" land available upon completion. The land was already divided into lots for colonization, according to the irrigation and development plans made by the *hacienda* in the Porfiriato, and Castrejón suggested the government follow those plans to settle *ejidatarios* and *repatriados*.[14]

Two factors were important to the implementation of the repatriation project after so long, and in the timing of its implementation. First, the Mexican government and the Banco de México were organizing the financing of the 1939 cotton crop in collaboration with William Clayton. Cárdenas and his financial advisors were hoping that the Matamoros region would soon be opened up to cultivation, and that the plan to export a million bales a year would move toward its realization. Repatriation was seen as the way to secure skilled cotton producers for this national *política algodonera* as it took form in the Valle Bajo Río Bravo. On November 20 of 1939 (the anniversary of the Mexican Revolution), Cárdenas made a speech reaffirming his commitment to promoting repatriation, and immediately thereafter plans were announced to provide land to *repatriados* in three irrigation zones: Mexicali, the Río

Fuerte Valley in Sinaloa, and Matamoros.[15] All three were cotton-producing regions. The second reason why repatriation was implemented in early 1939 was that by the end of 1938 the flood control works in Matamoros were almost complete and the SCOP was ready to shift attention to irrigation. This irrigation would allow colonization of the dry rangeland beyond the railroad tracks that defined the southern limit of the old riverside agricultural zone. In December of 1938 Chávez told Cárdenas that he had already settled colonists from Don Martín on lands that had no water, that they had cleared a good deal of land, and that it was time to open up a canal to this new area of colonization. Cárdenas had assured the *colonos* of Anáhuac that construction of this canal would begin in January.[16]

Cárdenas wanted the Anderson Clayton Company to finance the colonization of the Matamoros region. However, in their February 1939 meeting Cárdenas and Clayton reached a verbal agreement that the Anderson Clayton Company would not invest in public works or colonization in Matamoros, providing instead all the cotton financing the Matamoros region should need, once the Mexican government provided the infrastructure. A week after the meeting with William Clayton in the capital, the president ordered the Secretary of Hacienda to authorize the money to build the canal to open up the new lands south of the old agricultural zone for colonization with *repatriados*.[17]

To ensure the success of repatriation and colonization to the Valle Bajo Río Bravo, Cárdenas enlisted the services of Manuel Gamio. On January 19 of 1939, Gamio headed to Matamoros to conduct a regional survey in preparation for the colonization of *repatriados* on the lands of the Sauteña. He was joined in the survey tour by Marte R. Gómez, Eduardo Chávez, Ernesto Reza from the BNCA, and others from the Demographics Department (Departamento Demográfico). Gómez was in the area to distribute some 11,500 hectares to new *ejidos* as part of the regional reaccomodation, and after conferring with the federal commission he instructed the local authorities to lend their support to the colonization project.[18]

Gamio's report evaluated four tracts of lands available for colonization. The best option was a 40,000-hectare parcel of land south and west of Matamoros called the "Valle Bajo Río Bravo," which was once part of the Sauteña and by that time belonged to the BNCA. This was the uncleared land that lay south of the riverbank agricultural zone and fell within the flood control and irrigation district planned by Chávez. Another 6000 hectares to the west of the town of Río Bravo known as "Colombres #1" was discarded as an option until the Presa Azúcar could be put into operation and irrigation could be made available by the CNI. This land was also formerly part of the Sauteña, and at that time was owned by the Banco de México. The third area was the vast expanse of land south of the planned irrigation zone, which still bore the name of "La Sauteña." This land, Gamio said, was more suited for livestock, except for a thin band of lands near the coast where the *rancheros* had been able to grow crops with the moisture from the coastal fog. The success of colonization with *repatriados* in the "Valle Bajo Río Bravo" tract would be ensured by the infrastructural elements of development such as irrigation, flood control, and roads, and by the cultural progressiveness of the native population, which, he believed, would benefit from, rather than retard, the development of the *repatriados*.[19]

Cárdenas sought to make the repatriation of cotton farmers to Matamoros part of a much larger movement of Mexicans southward to their previous homes or to new ones in agricultural regions across Mexico. While work continued in the Valle Bajo Río Bravo, Subsecretary of Foreign Relations Ramón Beteta traveled in the United States, providing information about the government's repatriation plans and identifying candidates for the Matamoros colonization program. In March of 1939 Beteta and Gamio were in Texas, speaking before large crowds, urging them to consider repatriation and assuring them that the government was fully supportive of the project. The consulates were asked to process applications from Mexicans wishing to be colonized on lands provided by the government. This tour led to the movement of *repatriados* into the Matamoros area throughout the month of March. On March 24 a group of 101 *repatriados* from Corpus Christi reached Brownsville in U.S. Immigration Service trucks, and were escorted across the bridge to Matamoros by Mexican consuls Xavier Osorno and Carlos Calderón. Other groups followed, and still others could not make the trip due only to a lack of transportation.

"We all met in the school, in Houston," said Doña Elisa, a repatriate from Houston. "We didn't know what to expect, and we didn't know more than two or three other families." Twenty-five families gathered that morning to begin the long drive down to Mexico. Everybody brought what gear they had: tents, beds, wood and gas stoves, lamps and wicks, tools. They all got on board the buses provided by the U.S. Immigration and Naturalization Service and headed south. Her parents had worked as migrant laborers in central Texas picking strawberries and cotton, but they were not really farmers. Her father was an industrial worker in the petroleum sector in Houston, and he learned about agriculture when he arrived to Matamoros. He did bring his carpentry tools, and his axes, which came in handy for the clearing of the land and the fabrication of a makeshift dwelling. "We were told it was going to be beautiful when we got there," Elisa recalled, "but it wasn't."[20]

Beteta was sent by Cárdenas to convince Mexicans in the United States that the government was sincere in its offer, and would keep its promises. The government, he told the Brownsville press in April of 1939, hoped to repatriate some 500,000 Mexicans and Mexican Americans to Mexico, many of them to the El Azúcar irrigation zone under construction on the Río San Juan and the Valle Bajo Río Bravo zone around Matamoros. "We are not trying to create an artificial demand," said Beteta, "but we have a need for those Mexican nationals who wish to return to their native land, and we are trying to take them back and settle them on land in such a way that they can help themselves and be an asset to the nation."[21] The government's "need" was for skilled agricultural labor, especially for cotton production, more than an ideological or emotional need to fulfill the patriotic promise of returning exiled nationals. Beteta told crowds that the government was prepared to spend 40 million pesos in the effort, a truly enormous amount. The government would evaluate the applications of hopeful colonists and provide transportation to their new colonies in Mexico, where each colonist and his family would be given 20 hectares of land. These lands would be held individually, rather than communally as in *ejidos,* but could not be sold and would revert to the nation if the farmers stopped working them. In return, the repatriated colonists would increase and improve the country's agricultural production.

After twenty years of similar promises and dreadful failures, Beteta encountered far fewer people willing to make the move than he had expected, although in his correspondence with Cárdenas he remarked constantly that there was an immense amount of trust in the president and his administration. But the failure to attract *repatriados* was a result of the government's desire to repatriate a certain kind of Mexican or Mexican American: the one that had "something to lose." Cárdenas, Beteta, and Gamio all agreed that the government needed skilled farmers for repatriation as *colonos* to the cotton zones of the Bajo Río Bravo, Mexicali, and Río Fuerte, and were not interested in placing the nation's export cotton production in the hands of those indigent or unskilled workers who most needed support and who were the most eager to be repatriated. Those who were in such a difficult economic situation were to be given *ejido* lands, but not in these cotton zones. Of course, those who were doing well in the United States and had "something to lose" were the least likely to risk what they had in order to start over in Mexico.[22]

Archival documents show that the pronounced goal of repatriating 500,000 people was less than realistic. On April 20, 1939, a group of officials including Cárdenas's personal secretary Gustavo Leñero, Minister of the Interior (Gobernación) Ignacio García Tellez, Minister of Foreign Relations Eduardo Hay, and Gamio's boss in Gobernación, Fernando Foglio, met to discuss the concrete possibilities for the repatriation plan outlined by Cárdenas and promoted by Beteta. The BNCE was prepared to finance the settlement of up to one thousand skilled farmers in *ejidos* across the country. The SCOP representative announced that it could employ six hundred *repatriados* in its Valle del Bajo Río Bravo project, and Gobernación mentioned that it would continue to repatriate some two or three hundred people a month to their homes. The idea of placing large numbers of *repatriados* in Matamoros ran into a problem of available lands: the Sauteña had still not been expropriated, and irrigation works were still not completed in the region. Fernando Foglio told the group that at that moment in Matamoros there was "not even one hectare available," and that even with increased spending on the Obras de Defensa lands could be opened for only two thousand *repatriados.* In fact, the participants at the meeting proposed that until irrigated lands could be made available, Beteta should be told not to send any *repatriados* southward.[23]

Francisco E. Balderrama and Raymond Rodríguez reach the conclusion that Beteta's 1939 trip to the United States was a resounding failure that resulted in very few repatriations. However, if we look beyond the fantastic proclamations of the state about repatriating hundreds of thousands of Mexicanos, and take the objective of Beteta's trip to have been the selection of a few hundreds *or* thousands of *repatriados* for the colonization of the Matamoros region, the project was successful. The Matamoros zone was central to Cárdenas's *política algodonera,* and it was really the only place where irrigation works under construction made the opening of new lands possible at that time. Both Beteta and BNCA director Manuel Mesa Andraca were eager to split up the holdings of the privileged colonists of the CNI-built irrigation systems, and offer them to *repatriados.* But the time for such radical social intervention had passed by 1939, and at that point the government "needed" *repatriados* to expand cotton production by opening up *new* lands. They also wanted repatriates with "something to lose" to settle as individual smallholders in *colonias,* while the expropriation of *colonia* lands in government irrigation districts had led to the creation of *ejidos* instead.[24]

Cárdenas began to cement the Valle Bajo Río Bravo development project as the cornerstone of the government's repatriation and colonization program. He ordered the BNCE and BNCA to take care of the Colonia La Esperanza, and to renew funding for the Colonia Anáhuac. Then he obtained Eduardo Chavez's assurance that the irrigation works for which he was requesting funding would make 10,000 hectares available to up to five hundred families, and ordered the Secretaría de Hacienda to forward money to Beteta in San Antonio to pay for the transportation of *repatriados* to the border. Accompanied by Gamio, Beteta was at that time conducting a "selection and census of repatriates" for the Valle Bajo Río Bravo project. With this groundwork completed, Cárdenas traveled to Matamoros to personally oversee the colonization of the new agricultural zone with *repatriados.*[25]

After discussing the details of the development project with Chávez, on April 24 Cárdenas issued a presidential accord (*acuerdo*) that established the repatriation and colonization program as part of an integrated, multisecretarial Valle Bajo Río Bravo development project, and named Chávez as the director of that project. A combined system of flood control and irrigation works opened up lands for colonization with *repatriados* and others, but the infrastructure made necessary a total redrawing of the property lines in the region in order to resolve the conflicts between property owners, on the one hand, and *ejidatarios* and recently arrived landless immigrants, on the other. A "*reacomodo*" (reaccommodation) of the population on a reconfigured rural landscape was deemed essential to the further development and colonization of the region.[26] To empower the federal government to do the *reacomodo,* Cárdenas decreed the expropriation of the entire rural area of the *municipio* of Matamoros—98,000 hectares. This presidential decree (*decreto*) also created the intersecretarial Commission for the Development of the Valle Bajo Río Bravo with Chávez as its head, and charged the commission with organizing the expropriation of lands and the redistribution of population in the region. The *decreto* called for the establishment of three main zones in the irrigation zone: the northern zone along the riverbank would be home to the region's *pequeños propietarios,* the central zone would be for collective *ejidos,* and the southern zone was reserved for *colonias* of cotton farmers relocated from the Don Martín system as well as the new *repatriados* from Texas. To ensure that these farmers would have irrigation water, Cárdenas provided the Comisión a three-year budget of 13,819,268 pesos to complete the project. The *ejidos* and *pequeñas propiedades* would receive two-thirds of the water from the Vaso de Culebrón (enough for 30,000 hectares), and the two groups of *colonos* would split the final third. Each *campesino,* regardless of the land he or she owned, was assured water to irrigate 10 hectares, which the government considered to be the amount that one family could cultivate without hired labor. Five hundred repatriated families would be settled, and all were obliged by the *decreto* to plant cotton.[27]

The documents signed by Cárdenas in April of 1939 articulated a vision of agrarian society and development that inherited elements of previous development plans and added new ones. The radical redrawing of regional productive geography and social reconstruction were essential parts of the plans suggested by Múgica and Chávez in 1937, and Chávez's heavy influence in the formulation of these 1939 documents is evident. The "*acuerdo*" and "*decreto*" of 1939 also maintained the earlier focus on collective production, arguing that collective *ejidos* could be created through an "organic" plan of economic, agricultural, and legal transformation. Nevertheless, by 1939 independent small-property-holding colonists were figuring prominently in the development plan, responding to the conjunctural need for skilled cotton farmers, and resurrecting, to some degree, porfirian and *callista* visions of regional development in the Matamoros region. By this time Múgica, a primary proponent of collectivization, had been replaced by the far more centrist Melquiades Angulo as the minister of the SCOP.

Despite the intensive clearing of lands by new settlers, the development plans for the Matamoros region incorporated conservationist elements. Chávez was especially worried that the offshore breeze from the Gulf of Mexico that was a permanent feature of the region's environment would cause the kind of wind erosion that was devastating the U.S. plains states at that time. To preserve windbreaks, he ordered that for every four parcels (800 meters) of land cleared by colonists, one parcel (200 meters) should be left in its original state. These windbreaks would also provide firewood and habitat for game. Another important conservationist element of Chávez's plan was designed into the irrigation infrastructure, which directed the silt-laden floodwaters of the Río Bravo onto the lands that were being opened to cultivation. This system mimicked the seasonal flooding pattern of rivers such as the Bravo and the Nile, whose delta regions owed their productivity and sustainability to the annual deposits of nutrients carried by the waters.[28]

With the irrigation works funded and the development and colonization project placed under the charge of Chávez, the repatriation of cotton farmers could begin. Ramón Beteta met with Cárdenas during his Matamoros visit so as to coordinate the efforts of his team with the Bajo Río Bravo project, and on April 23 the president authorized him to begin the process of repatriating 450 families, choosing the name

"18 de Marzo" (after the date of the oil expropriation) for the new colony. On April 27 Beteta informed Cárdenas that the number of people wishing to be settled in the "18 de Marzo" colony was growing, and that he was "examining the applicants with greater care, so as to choose only true farmers, anxious to go and open lands, and, if possible, knowledgeable of the cultivation of cotton."[29] The first group of *colonos,* not passing one hundred families, would arrive in mid-May. Beteta also visited the area near Austin and New Braunfels, Texas, where he spoke highly "of the qualities of our compatriots as farmers, principally of cotton," and decided to return in September to select a "group chosen for the Colonia '18 de Marzo.'" Meanwhile, Chávez submitted a *memorandum* discussing the establishment of the Colonia "18 de Marzo," and requesting money to fund land clearing, agricultural equipment, roads, temporary and permanent housing, and wells for the *repatriados.*[30]

The "*acuerdo*" and "*decreto*" of Cárdenas, as well as the May 8 "*memorandum*" by Chávez, together represent a reconsolidation of the government's development blueprints for the Valle Bajo Río Bravo. These documents reflect a good deal of continuity with previous development visions for the region, but also show the influence of the conjunctural events confronting the *cardenista* administration. The *política algodonera* developed by Cárdenas in conjunction with the Anderson Clayton Company over the previous three years generated a "need" for settling skilled cotton farmers in Matamoros, and the opening of the irrigation zone in Matamoros made lands available for Cárdenas's repatriation effort. The creation of *ejidos* in the old riverbank agricultural zone was important to the project insofar as it provided a way to defuse social tensions between the various rural social classes, and collectivization was a priority for these *ejidos* because it was considered the most efficient manner of organizing production, and the best way for the government to recover its investment in infrastructure. The newly opened areas of rural Matamoros, however, were reserved for colonies of property-owning *repatriados.*

The Colonia "18 de Marzo"

On May Day of 1939, Eduardo Chávez inaugurated the Retamal floodgates and canal. The water flowed through the canal and began to fill the Vaso de Culebrón, although very little of the system of secondary distribution canals had been completed. Cárdenas was to have been in the region for the May 1 inauguration, but arrived in the region early and left prematurely. Despite the shortcomings, the event was meant to signal the readiness of the zone for colonization and production, and a few days later Chávez held a meeting with *ejido* representatives in the region to explain to them the creation of the Comisión de las Obras del Valle Bajo del Río Bravo (Lower Río Bravo Valley Works Commission), the infrastructure Chávez was to oversee as its director, and the nature of the *reacomodo* of the region's population and land boundaries.[31]

According to Chávez, five hundred families were each to be given 12.5 hectares, of which 2.5 hectares were for windbreaks, roads, canals, and other public works, and 10 hectares for cultivation. To make the movement and installation of the *repatriados* manageable, Chávez suggested that the Commission headed by Beteta bring only one hundred families down from Texas each month. Until they could be settled on their own parcels, the repatriates were to be housed temporarily in large wooden structures that would later be used as storage buildings for the colony. The measurement and delineation of these parcels required the mapping and clearing of 500 kilometers of narrow paths (*brechas*), and the clearing of the parcels was to be contracted to the *colonos* themselves. Once on their land the *colonos* would be given materials to build a modest house, following the style of architecture and using the materials common in the region. Chávez calculated that 65 pesos a week would be enough to support the *colonos* while they cleared their land and built their houses, and Cárdenas approved funding for the project between May 1939 and January 1940. To secure the land for the *colonia*, Marte R. Gómez organized the legal paperwork for an expropriation by the state of Tamaulipas. The money for the colonization and settlement of the *repatriados* arrived at Chávez's office in Matamoros in the second week of May.[32]

Ramón Beteta and Manuel Gamio were touring Texas, choosing colonists. By May 10 they had put together a list of one hundred families (five hundred people) from Houston, Beaumont, Corpus Christi, San Antonio, Karnes, Kennedy, and Raymondville. Chávez had the construction of the provisional housing and roads for the *colonia* under way by mid-May, and Beteta had arranged transportation for the *repatriados* on U.S. Immigration Service buses. On May 16 Mexican consular officials accompanied the first group of sixty-five *repatriados* from San Antonio to the bridge in Brownsville. Another group of fifty-one from the Kennedy area crossed the border on the 23rd, and then fifty more from Corpus Christi on the 24th. By the beginning of June Chávez reported that the *colonia* had five hundred inhabitants, and that ninety-six parcels had been given out. Chávez had been expecting a slower pace for the arrival of *repatriados,* and the large number of arrivals caused difficulties in quickly establishing people on parcels of land, problems that were further exacerbated by torrential rains. By mid-June, San Antonio Consul Omar Josefe reported that 849 people had been settled in the Colonia "18 de Marzo," and that in one more month the *colonia* would reach its limit of five hundred property holders.[33]

Despite the detailed planning of its director, the substantial funding, and the professed support of the various agencies of the federal government, the colonization effort soon ran into problems of two kinds. First, living conditions in the Matamoros area were abysmal, and some of the colonists were not able to clear their lands and build their houses as quickly as Chávez wanted them to. Furthermore, Chávez exercised almost total power over these *colonos,* who were paid in food and required to clear and cultivate their land before they received titles for it. This required an immense effort, as the colonists worked alone or with their older children chopping down brush and trees with hand tools, and had only the help of farm animals to haul away the trees and rip out the stumps. To make some cash to live by, the colonists had to begin to plant cotton and corn as soon as possible, and their agricultural labors took time away from the clearing of their lands.[34] The hardships suffered by the colonists and the extraordinary power exercised by Chávez in the region gave rise to an ongoing conflict between the director and some colonists.

Beteta was worried that the complaints about the Colonia "18 de Marzo" would circulate in the United States and the government's repatriation program would grind to a halt. Upon visiting the area in August he noted that only thirty-four of the six hundred *jefes de familia* given plots were behind in the schedule for clearing their land and were running up debts with the Comisión. However, the living conditions still provided an awful lot to complain about. Many of the *colonos* had not been assigned plots of land. The extreme heat and humidity of the Matamoros summer made the physical work of clearing land miserable, and because the wells had produced salt water, drinking water had to be trucked in from distant *ranchos*. This water was unsanitary, and there was a lack of medical attention for the many children that fell ill from amoebic dysentery and typhoid.[35]

The fact that bad news from the *colonia* did not stop people from applying for repatriation actually created a more serious problem, for the government was faced with an overwhelming number of applications and a scarcity of land. By July the colony had reached its limit of five hundred families and 2500 inhabitants, but when Beteta announced to the press that the repatriation program would be suspended, ten thousand people were waiting for their applications to be processed. Despite Beteta's suspension of the repatriation process, Cárdenas authorized the colonization of some 145 more families from communities in the Texas side of the lower Rio Bravo/Río Grande Valley, which further kindled the hopes of potential colonists. Beteta warned Cárdenas that the government would be forced to break its promise of repatriation: "a grave and urgent situation that we ourselves have provoked."[36]

The *colonia* soon had more *colonos* than Chávez could handle. As part of the regional *reacomodo*, *colonia* land had been assigned to regional smallholders such as those from the *rancho* "Vallitas," who had to be relocated because a levee turned their lands into a flood channel. Others who worked for the SCOP clearing *brechas* and digging the canals were assigned lots as well. Thus by the time of Beteta's visit to the Colonia "18 de Marzo" in early August, there were already six hundred plots given out—one hundred more than Chávez could confidently promise irrigation water for. In his Presidential Address of September 1, Cárdenas told the nation that the *colonia* had 627 families, and that nine hundred men over sixteen years of age had received a parcel. With so many people arriving in such a short space of time, the *repatriados* were slow in receiving their land.[37]

The regional *reacomodo* and the project to settle repatriates in the Colonia "18 de Marzo" superseded the government priority of re-settling workers from the Don Martín region in Matamoros, and these workers mounted a sustained attack on Eduardo Chávez. These workers were unionized since their days in Don Martín, and many of them were repatriates themselves. Some of them had worked to build the infrastructure of that CNI irrigation system, and had moved to the Bajo

Río Bravo both because of the jobs that were offered by the Obras and the promise made by Cárdenas in 1934, and again in 1936 and 1937, of redistributing hundreds of thousands of hectares of Sauteña land.

In June of 1939 a group of these workers was brought to the Bajo Río Bravo by a Presidential Accord, and settled in the Colonia "Magueyes" (better known in its earlier years as the Colonia "Nicolás Lenin") on land right next to the Colonia "18 de Marzo." Chávez immediately began to make plans to integrate these industrial-style, syndicalized workers into the regional development plan, telling Cárdenas that because of the costs implied in outfitting all the colonists with agricultural implements, the government should encourage the Spanish Republicans entering Mexico at the time to invest in an agricultural implements factory in Reynosa, where natural gas had been discovered, and where, he implied, these *obreros* could be put to work. Chávez was very reluctant to settle them on irrigated *parcelas,* and while the accord had provided for four hundred colonists, the workers maintained, only 250 were given plots of land. In October Chávez had already passed his limit for the Colonia "18 de Marzo" by some 276 *colonos,* and he refused to settle more in "Magueyes." The director asked Cárdenas to end the movement from Ciudad Anáhuac to Matamoros, warning that the development disaster of Don Martín could be repeated.[38]

To secure the remaining 150 plots, in December of 1939 the workers rallied the support of unions across the country, who sent telegrams to Cárdenas denouncing Chávez as an "enemy of the proletariat," and charging him with disobeying Cárdenas's accord. Families continued to arrive to the Commission's headquarters in Control, and a caravan of more than one hundred families left Don Martín for the Matamoros region to raise publicity about the situation. Once in Matamoros, they launched a hunger strike in an effort to obtain land, water, and financial support for colonization. Chávez pleaded with Cárdenas to end the immigration, saying that "authorized budgets have been exceeded by the congestion produced in this zone; irrigation resources have turned out to be dangerously insufficient; available lands have been exhausted forcing bad-quality areas to be put into use."[39] The hunger strike apparently worked, for in June of 1940 Cárdenas signed another accord that increased the payments for *desmontes,* and secured 110 more parcels for the workers from Don Martín.[40]

As an alternative to what they considered an excessive concentration of power in the hands of Chávez, the immigrants from Don Martín proposed the democratization of the decision-making process in the Commission and the colonies. In June of 1939 the General Secretary of the "Josefa Ortiz de Domínguez" Revolutionary Municipal Women's League wrote to Cárdenas suggesting that "their husbands, and not Engineer Chávez, be those who administer the colonization" of refugees from the Don Martín System.[41] This movement for self-determination made some headway in mid-1940, when Chávez agreed to form a council including members from the colonies and the Commission. Apparently unhappy with the shape the council took, Chávez later refused to acknowledge its existence.[42]

The breakdown in communication led to open conflicts between the *colonos* and Chávez. In February 1940 Chávez gave notice to some two hundred *colonos* that the stipends they had been receiving would be reduced, due to their lack of progress in clearing their lands. The *colonos* responded by marching on the work camp of the SCOP in Valle Hermoso, and demanding that the stipends be continued. According to Chávez, the "circumstance [was] taken advantage of by agitators to rally the colonists to burn down the offices and sack the colony stores," but the five federal soldiers stationed at the camp intervened to maintain order.[43] When the June 30 "*acuerdo*" signed by Cárdenas failed to produce the results hoped for by the *colonos*, another demonstration was held at the Valle Hermoso camp, where, according to the *colonos*, Chávez once again brought out the federal troops in an attempt to "apprehend the speakers."[44]

Throughout the latter part of 1940 the *colonos* continued to complain to Cárdenas of Chávez's failure to enact the measures stipulated in the *Acuerdo* of June 30, and with the presidential succession looming on the horizon, they began to question Chávez's allegiance to the ruling party, the PNR. The Don Martín colonists got Graciano Sánchez, general secretary of the CNC, to convey a message to Cárdenas that Chávez was bypassing the official *campesino* organizations in an effort to create new "societies of socialist farmers" under the leadership of the president of the Partido Democratico Nacional, Cipriano Villanueva Garza. CTM leader Vicente Lombardo Toledano sent a similar message. These accusations resonated among the politicians in Mexico City concerned about the political pretensions of *norteño* Juan Andreu Almazán, who declared his renegade PRUN candidacy in early September with a call to revolution that was heard strongly in the borderlands. The *Brownsville Herald* reported that two hundred *almazanistas* were headed for Mexico to stir up trouble, and shortly thereafter the houses of *almazanistas* in Matamoros were searched for weapons. *Campesinos* in Jamauve, in central Tamaulipas, rose up in arms to support Almazán's candidacy, and Cárdenas publicly warned Almazán to stop agitating support in South Texas. Seizing the moment, the workers charged Chávez with being an *almazanista*—"an utmost enemy of the worker and peasant organizations."[45] None of these accusations seriously placed Cárdenas's support for Chávez in question, however.

The Discourse of Regional Development in the Valle Bajo Río Bravo

The Mexican government had, since at least the 1920s, framed its relationship to the northern borderlands as one of regional development, and an idiom of territorial community and historical progress shaped the conflicts and negotiations between the government and the new colonists. During a trip to the border with his entourage in 1936, Cárdenas told the *Brownsville Herald* "this northern part of México is one of the richest sections of the entire nation, and it will undoubtedly develop into a prosperous country."[46] Speaking in Matamoros's Teatro de la Reforma, the head of the federal government's Departamento Agrario spoke to a crowd of *campesinos* about the progress assured to the region. The flood control and immigration works were, he said, "transforming the danger of destruction and death into a positive hope of fertile lands . . . that assure the rural workers a rosy future."[47] The governor of Tamaulipas shared this vision and language of regional development. "The northern part of the state is unquestionably going to develop into a big producing area," he told a reporter in Brownsville.[48]

On May Day (May 1) of 1939 the director of the Valle Bajo Río Bravo, Eduardo Chávez, spoke before an assembly of some three thousand *campesinos* to commemorate the inauguration of the irrigation system. "This enormous extension of the Valle Bajo Río Bravo," he proclaimed, "was a green ocean of dense forests, watered by the fecund floodwaters of the river, that made it one of the most fertile regions in the world. . . . The works of the Federal Government . . . brought forth the great development that we are witnessing, and will make this the most important agricultural, industrial and commercial zone of the Republic."[49] Chávez's speech reflects the understanding of historical change at the basis of the government's developmentalist thinking about the region. Chávez felt that this developmentalist language would have a deep impact on the *campesinos* gathered before him, who were "familiarized with social concepts and economic problems, and for whom these words have a repercussion of understanding in their intellects and feelings in their hearts." It was in public ceremonies where speeches like this were given that the region's *campesinos* heard the powerful language of regional development.

The *campesinos* and workers of the region internalized the language of regional development articulated in public pronouncements, and used it when making formal statements directed at, or concerning, state actors. For example, in response to the April 1939 accord that formalized institutional relationships within the Valle Bajo Río Bravo project, the agricultural credit cooperatives set up by the government banks in the region congratulated the president for his "generous help in converting these rich lands into an emporium of work."[50] The SCOP workers who were building the irrigation project also lauded the patriotism that they said would surely bring enormous benefits to the region, and the nation.[51] These statements display a use of developmental language within formalized exchanges commemorating the harmonious relation between rulers and the ruled.

Documentation of how people spoke or wrote to each other without the mediation of the state is extremely scarce, because it usually doesn't end up in the state's archives. However, a letter from a member of the Colonia "18 de Marzo" to his brother in Texas provides a sense of how many *repatriados* imagined themselves on the path to development. He contrasted the difficulties presented to the recently arrived *colonos* with the "rosy future" that the region was destined for. "I'm not saying that here in Mexico things don't work," the *repatriado* wrote, "No, not that, because here in Matamoros in any hamlet you visit they are building. And as for lands, everything they say is true, and I've seen that they are very good and fertile.

In a very short time it will be as pretty as if it were the Valley of Texas."[52] Despite the optimism shown by this colonist, it was not an easy life by any means, and the *colonos* had absolutely none of the conveniences of their previous homes in Texas. They were paid with food ("just potatoes and beans" said the *colono*), nothing was available for purchase, and Matamoros was 50 miles away by bad dirt roads. Nevertheless, this *colono* considered the repatriation an opportunity—an opportunity to progress, to develop, to improve, to build. "Here it is very good," he told his brother, "for he who is very strong."

Developmental language is historical and programmatic: it articulates a sense of movement from past to future, and postulates a certain future condition. It does not lend itself to the quotidian business of building or maintaining flood control levees, organizing credit, digging canals, establishing *ejidos,* and all the other things that make up development, although this daily language of the bureaucracy and work may help to realize long-term development goals. For example, in April of 1939 the regional committee of the CNC wrote to Cárdenas about the state of agriculture within the emergent irrigation zone. A drought, the influx of workers and *campesinos* into the region, and the hostility of the region's cotton companies to the farmers on the *ejidos* had caused an economic crisis, and forced many *ejidatarios* to abandon their newly cleared lands in search of work in Texas. Clearly this was not the "development" that Eduardo Chávez spoke of at the May Day demonstration a month later; in fact, the *campesinos* were describing the failure to develop. Couching their suggestions in quite straightforward technical terms, they proposed a series of concrete measures concerning financing from the Banco Ejidal to get the plan back on track. Only when this business was finished did the *campesinos* conclude the letter with a developmentalist flourish: "that all this will serve to improve the conditions of living for the workers and popular classes."[53]

The language of development was not used by all people, in all contexts, and neither did terms like *desarrollo* (development) and *progreso* (progress) have only one meaning. Official declarations and newspaper reports about the development plans for Matamoros are full of descriptions of the irrigation project as a progressive march of economy, society, and culture into the future. The difficulties experienced in colonizing and building the development project, however, moved one *repatriada* to imagine a quite different historical process at work. "We feel that if we continue this way in a short time instead of preparing ourselves to be good citizens for our beloved country, we will form a good cemetery," she wrote.[54] In asking for more attention from the state—more development—she presented a dystopic vision of the future of the repatriation project, the antithesis of the one propagated by the government and the regional press.

The hardships suffered by the *repatriados* may have limited the believers in the golden future of the region to "those that were very strong." As time passed, however, the initial period of suffering served as an important point of reference for understanding the growth and progress of regional society. As the irrigation works proceeded and farmers cleared their lands, built houses, and produced cotton, the emerging prosperity of the region was measured against the deprivations of the colonization period. The developmentalist prophecies spoken during the lean years of 1939 to 1941 seemed to be coming true just three years later, and as the *colonos* experienced the change, a direct understanding of historical process formed. Already in 1944 the Colonia "18 de Marzo" was celebrating the anniversary of its founding, and the Matamoros press took the opportunity to laud the "undeniable development of the colony."[55] The development seen by the newspaper reporter was defined in relation to the "penalties that these colonists had to suffer during the first season."[56] At the 1944 anniversary celebration in Valle Hermoso the director of the BNCA in Matamoros told the *colonos repatriados* assembled for the event that they were "converting unproductive lands into agricultural centers . . . full of hope and faith and with thousands of sufferings and sacrifices, registering the second liberation of Mexico, economic liberation."[57] This developmental tale mapped onto the future laid out in the plans for the Valle Bajo Río Bravo project in the mid-1930s, incorporating as well the suffering of the repatriated colonists and their political struggles against the state development apparatus into a trajectory of regional progress. Over the next twenty years, ideas of historical trajectory (development) and political community (region) central to the narration of regional development in the Valle Bajo Río Bravo were reshaped in the context of political struggles to control the benefits of cotton production.

Conclusion

The effort to realize the vision of rural society contained in the government declarations of April 1939 immediately confronted a number of limitations. The agents of the national state—who had already reformulated their development goals in order to deal with both the changing conditions present in the regional social field of the Valle Bajo Río Bravo and the national and global political economy of cotton—found themselves unable to keep abreast of the social effervescence generated by their own development interventions. Migrants brought to the region by promises and hopes of settling down and farming constructed their own idea of development and their own political projects. Overwhelmed by these popular movements, Chávez was forced to retrench within the more narrow limits afforded by the state's social engineering project.

Despite the shortcomings of the government's colonization project and the conflicts that arose in the region between *colonos* and Chávez, the success for the colony on the whole was quite notable. By May 1940 only 5 percent of the colonists had abandoned their parcels, which Chávez said compared favorably to a "normal" failure rate for colonization of 20 percent. And on a cold, windy day in late November of 1940, a group of government officials came to Valle Hermoso to hand out titles to the *colonos* for the parcels they had cleared and settled. These titles transformed the land from the patrimony of the nation to the inalienable patrimony of the individual colonists and their descendants. Apart from the support of the government, much of this success had to do with the fact that many *repatriado* families were able to harness the financial resources of the relatives they left behind in Texas, or were able to send family members to work in Matamoros or Brownsville. The dissonance between the totalizing optimism of the statements of social engineering made by Cárdenas and Chávez and the harsh experience of hacking a living out of the mesquite forests of northern Tamaulipas with very limited resources and serious shortcomings in the regional infrastructure gave rise to a heroic and mythic history of the origins of the Colonia "18 de Marzo." This historical memory was solidified between 1940 and 1960, in the course of struggles to control the benefits of the enormous cotton boom that defined postwar Matamoros.[58]

CHAPTER 8
DEFINING DEVELOPMENT IN THE RÍO BRAVO DELTA, 1940–1963

In this chapter I discuss the intertwined socioeconomic process and language of regional development as it continued to shape regional dynamics in the Bajo Río Bravo through the cotton boom years of the 1940s and 1950s. In tracking the material discourses of regional development, I take Judith Irvine's suggestion that we look not at an economy of signs with complex linkages to a material economy, "but, instead, just at an economy, from which the verbal must not be included."[1] In Mexico, where ritualized, material, discursive interactions with a central state have, since at least the colonial period, played a large role in the acquisition of economic resources and the establishment of rule, this understanding of language and political economy is particularly useful.[2] By speaking the common language of regional development, the various social actors in the Bajo Río Bravo sought to obtain resources and legitimize political and economic projects. At the same time that they reproduced the dominant mode of framing politics in terms of region and development, they also gave new inflections to those idioms, with varied, often unintended, and sometimes counterhegemonic political effects.

Two events in the history of the Valle Bajo Río Bravo were especially important in the construction of this political culture of regional development. The first was a fight between the federal government and the region's cotton industrialists to manage the sale and export of the 1944 harvest. Although the expansionist course set by Cárdenas for cotton production and exports was maintained throughout World War II, the severance of trade routes reduced exports to a trickle, which resulted in an accumulation of surplus cotton stocks within the country. The Mexican government sought to ameliorate the situation by wresting control over the Matamoros cotton economy from the regional elite. Both sides fought to enlist the region's industrial workers, private farmers, *colonos,* and *ejidatarios* by deploying notions of region and development in an effort to universalize their interests and establish a unified political bloc.

The second event was the creation, in 1953, of the independent municipality of Valle Hermoso. During the late 1940s and early 1950s increased demand and decreased production elsewhere in the world made cotton a hugely profitable business in Mexico, and particularly in Matamoros, the epicenter of the government's long-term expansionist *política algodonera*. Faced with the presence of cantinas, gunfights, large numbers of migrant workers, as well as a lack of electricity, telephones, water, education, and other services during the height of the cotton boom, the farmers and businessmen of Valle Hermoso mounted their own effort to bring "development" to that part of the irrigation zone that was founded by the *cardenista* colonization of 1938–1940. They were opposed vehemently by the political and economic elite of Matamoros and their allies in the government of Tamaulipas, who sought to retain Valle Hermoso within the political community and geography of Matamoros. This movement reinforced an alternate definition of regional community and historical development, and led to the establishment of an independent *municipio*.

Cotton and World War II

By 1939 Cárdenas's *política algodonera* was unfolding in the Matamoros region, and the plan to turn the region into a "limitless expanse of cotton"[3] seemed destined for success. But while Cárdenas and his government were able to provide capital, land, labor, planning, and other key elements for this project, they did not anticipate two crucial factors that would have a serious impact on cotton production in Mexico and Matamoros. The first was the establishment of import quotas and export subsidies by the U.S. government in late 1939 in response to the accumulation of large cotton surpluses by the Commodity Credit Corporation. The second turn of events was World War II, which closed shipping lanes to Japan and Europe, and caused a glut of cotton in producing countries such as the United States and Mexico. These two events generated a struggle between regional capital and the national state to control the Matamoros cotton harvest of 1944.

While the cotton policies of the New Deal brought a measure of protection to landowning American farmers, they led to a steep rise in cotton production outside the United States: from 13 million bales in 1935 to 19.5 million bales in 1937. Cotton businessman William Clayton contributed to this tendency by relocating production to countries such as Mexico. The record-breaking world harvest of the 1937–1938 crop year spurred the U.S. government to take measures to eliminate the enormous amount of surplus cotton it held as collateral for loans extended under the provisions of the Agricultural Adjustment Act, and to reclaim some of the market share it had lost to other countries. Roosevelt's government called an international conference to announce that it would subsidize the export of 7 million bales of U.S. cotton, and limit imports from other countries to 50 percent of the average levels during the previous ten years: 17,519 bales for Mexico. While the import quota may not have seriously threatened those conference participants that exported little cotton to the United States, or, like Peru, did not compete with particular fiber lengths produced in the U.S., it was a serious blow to Mexico, whose borderlands irrigation zones were dedicated to the export of upland varieties of cotton. The quota was set based on statistics covering the period of economic crisis during the 1930s when borderlands cotton production for export fell dramatically, and when the nationalization of the cotton economy in the Laguna and Mexicali led to even further declines in production. Most important, the quotas did not consider the immanent huge expansion of cotton exports from the Matamoros region that was the cornerstone of the government's *política algodonera*.[4]

Mexico's state cotton experts were aware of the threat to the nation's cotton development strategy posed by the wartime trade limitations, but did not change their course. In a study made in preparation for the International Cotton Conference of September 1939, the SAF reported that because "since 1926, official credit, colonization and the improvement of the Irrigation Systems have given a constant impulse to cotton cultivation, the government has decided to continue with the same intensity until it satisfies its economic and social necessities."[5] Arguments by the Mexican ambassador Rafael Fuentes failed to increase or eliminate the quotas established by the U.S. government on cotton imports from Mexico, and in 1940 wartime hostilities shut down Mexico's cotton trade with Europe, and cut exports to Japan by 90 percent. Although the SAF reiterated its position supporting cotton agriculture, national industry was consuming only 50 percent of the country's production, and the Mexican government was confronted with large surpluses of cotton fiber.[6]

Nationalist and state-centered economic stances gained strength in the difficult economic conditions of the war period. The Mexican government defended the *política algodonera* and insisted that changes to it could not be made. "It is not possible to even think about limiting the areas of cotton cultivation in our country," Julián Rodríguez Adame wrote; "cotton is in an initial phase, whose limits are still far off."[7] Complaints about the continuing centrality of foreign and private cotton houses in the Mexican cotton business laid the basis for a proposal by Pascual Ortiz Rubio to President Ávila Camacho for a national cotton bank. Secretary of National Economy (Secretaría de Economía Nacional or SEN) Javier Gaxiola argued that in order to curtail the power of foreign cotton capitalists such as the Anderson Clayton Company, Paul King, William Woodward, and De la Mora and Figueroa, Mexican cotton should be financed and marketed by the government. Gaxiola told President Ávila Camacho that the problem was a lack of coordination among the different actors involved in the cotton economy, rather than overproduction.[8]

Despite the nationalist tenor of these proposals, the role of the Anderson Clayton Company in the cotton economy was protected by President Ávila Camacho. Anderson Clayton representative Lamar Fleming Jr. sent a letter to Ávila Camacho detailing the company's role, established by Cárdenas and Clayton, in Mexico's cotton development strategy, and explaining that in 1941 the Anderson Clayton Company invested 21 million pesos, 11 million of which went to the BNCE. Fleming received Ávila Camacho's assurance that the central position held by the Anderson Clayton Company would not be threatened by any nationalization of Mexico's cotton economy.[9]

The continued support for the *política algodonera* notwithstanding, between 1942 and 1945 various branches of the Mexican government did make plans to limit cotton production. A consortium of government banks was empowered to buy unlimited amounts of cotton at guaranteed base prices through the state's Mexican Import and Export Company (Compañía Exportadora e Importadora Mexicana, S.A., or CEIMSA), and the SEN was awarded control over the exports of the fiber. These price floors actually promoted the increase in fiber production in 1943 and 1944 and counteracted Secretary of Agriculture Marte R. Gómez's desire to reallocate cotton land to wheat and corn. In June 1944 the CEIMSA lowered the guaranteed base prices for cotton, and instituted severe price penalties for low-quality fibers, in the hope that farmers would take lands poorly suited for cotton out of production, and that Mexican fiber would become competitive on the international market. Despite these measures, the 70 percent increase in cotton production between 1941 and 1944 combined with U.S. import quotas and the closing of shipping lanes to produce a rapid accumulation of surplus, from an average of about 100,000 bales in the late 1930s to 552,000 bales at the end of the 1944–1945 season. A Mexican tax on domestic consumption was passed in order to fund a subsidy for fiber exports, but, faced with the continued inability to sell its product, the Mexican government used tax money instead to pay for the storage of this surplus cotton in the United States, and for the construction of new storage facilities in Mexico.[10]

During World War II the Mexican government was both unwilling and unable to abandon the expansionist borderlands cotton development strategy implemented by the Cárdenas government. Even after 1942, when the government did make efforts to confront the conditions generated by the war, these were unsuccessful in reducing production or surplus cotton stocks. Finally, in 1945, the government scaled back its efforts at controlling prices, production, exports, and other aspects of the cotton economy. The withdrawal of direct government intervention in the cotton economy was, to a large degree, the result of the government's loss of a protracted political and economic struggle with private cotton capital over the control of the harvest. This struggle emerged clearly in the Matamoros region as a fight between private regional cottonmen and the federal government.

The 1944 Cotton Freeze in Matamoros: Class and Region

The Matamoros cotton zone expanded from 37,000 hectares in 1937 to nearly 100,000 hectares in 1944. Between 1940 and 1943, thirty-eight *ejidos* were formally created or expanded, and many more awaited the government's legal recognition. In 1944 irrigation had still only reached 17,500 hectares, and regional yields depended on rainfall and other climatic factors. Production hovered around 40,000 bales before rocketing to more than 100,000 bales in 1944. In that year, the nearly two thousand

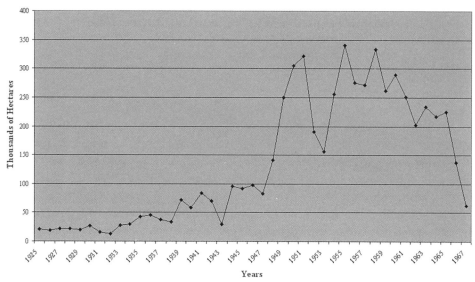

Area dedicated to cotton: northern Tamaulipas.

repatriados of the "Anáhuac," "18 de Marzo," and "Magueyes" colonies planted about 20,000 hectares; the remaining 80,000 hectares in the greater Matamoros region were cultivated by *ejidatarios* or *pequeños propietarios.*[11]

The social field constituted by cotton development was a complex, changing web of cooperative and conflictive social relations. U.S. capital—namely the Anderson Clayton Company—joined the existing regional cotton merchant-industrialists in financing and commercializing the anticipated enormous expansion of the Matamoros cotton crop. The old landholding elite of Matamoros, dispossessed of its large cattle and cotton ranches, maintained its leading role in regional society by moving its capital into the emerging cotton industries: gins, compresses, and cottonseed oil extraction. However, the entrance of the BNCE and BNCA into the region during the late 1930s, and the attempts by the government to regulate cotton surplus during the 1940s, fueled a struggle between the state and the private merchant-industrialists to control the production and sale of the fiber. This distinction between state and private capital had repercussions among the rural social classes: the private cotton-men worked with the private property owners, and the government banks worked with the *ejidatarios* and *colonos*. Furthermore, there was a clear divide between the smaller Mexican cotton capitalists in the region and the large foreign firms.

The regional social formation was unstable, as the wealth generated by cotton was distributed unequally among the region's inhabitants. Because of family and social ties, the region's large landowners (often now also industrialists) were able to organize the capital to clear land and grow cotton, and because they had from two to seven times more land than the *ejidatarios* and *colonos,* they prospered accordingly. Among the *colonos* and *ejidatarios,* there were many who, because they lacked agri-

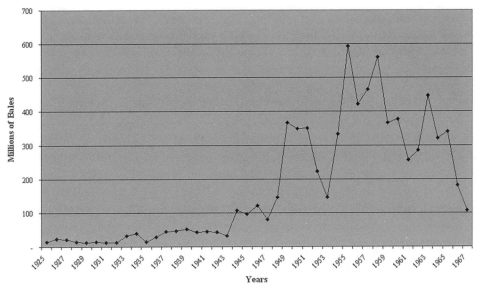

Cotton production: northern Tamaulipas.

cultural experience or resources, simply did not succeed as cotton farmers, and they gave up the land to those who did succeed. As would be expected, the industrialists prospered enormously from the cotton trade, while the workers in the cotton industries, although well paid, did not have the earning power of the successful cotton farmers. The cotton houses (*casas algodoneras*) found their clients in that privileged agricultural class of small and medium-sized private cotton ranchers, but they also bought contraband cotton produced by *ejidatarios,* who were legally obliged to do business only with the government's BNCE.

The structural tensions in Matamoros society were articulated and accentuated by the political activity of the region's more radical worker and *campesino* groups. *Agrarismo* was a key element of the *cardenista* land reform in the region, and remained present. Communists and socialists participated in regional *campesino* organizations, and independent labor organizers unsettled the relations between labor and cotton capital. These organizers built upon the language of class and social justice generalized during the Cárdenas period to raise consciousness about the unequal nature of social relations in the region.[12]

The language and identity of class, however, were not as strong as the language and identity of region. In *The German Ideology,* Marx and Engels argued that political rule depends on the ability of the dominant class to "represent its interest as the common interest of all the members of society, that is, expressed in ideal form: it has to give its ideas the form of universality."[13] Much like the process of ideological production described by Marx and Engels, the bourgeoisie formed by cotton production in the Valle Bajo Río Bravo sought to make its interest universal, and it did this by fomenting the idea of a united region, for which it spoke. But this political-cultural effort by the bourgeoisie to naturalize its role as the leading element in the region did not occur just on the level of ideas. The discourse and identity of region was produced in the course of a material struggle between the industrialists of Matamoros and the federal government to control the organization, financing, processing, and marketing of the region's cotton crop.

At first the political claims and arguments of the merchant-industrialists of Matamoros were couched in nationalist terms. In June of 1941, a group of cottonmen representing the "totally Mexican cotton houses" of Matamoros sent complaints to President Ávila Camacho that four or five foreign firms in Matamoros were receiving tax breaks injurious to both them and the region's cotton farmers. The industrialists from Matamoros presented themselves as the guardians and spokesmen of the region, arguing that if they, rather than the foreign firms, were awarded those tax breaks they would pass them along to the farmers. By 1942 the *casas algodoneras* in Matamoros organized themselves into a professional association called the Asociación Algodonera Mexicana (Mexican Cotton Association, or AAM), which sought to guide regional development by coordinating and promoting cotton production in the region, to improve the quality of regional cotton, and to increase consumption of its cotton in other countries. The group also adopted a "social mission" that consisted of raising funds for the paving of roads, the provisioning of clean water, and other civic initiatives in the city of Matamoros. The AAM was formed to defend the interests of the region's cottonmen, who never failed to "represent their interests as the interests of all members of society," to use Marx's words. Thus a major part of the AAM's labors consisted of representing the region of Matamoros in negotiations with the federal government over taxes, labor policies, prices, export quotas, and the like.[14]

As the government increased its efforts to establish control over the cotton economy during the war years of the early 1940s, the regionalist dimension of the Matamoros cottonmen's political stance began to outweigh its nationalism, as their primary competitors switched from foreign merchant industrialists to the agencies of the Mexican state. A key period in this process was late 1943 and 1944. The crop harvested in Matamoros during the summer of 1944 was enormous, and outstripped the ability of the region's industrial sector to process and store it. This was especially true for the BNCE and BNCA, which lacked gins, oilseed factories, compresses, and warehouses to accommodate the rapidly expanding production of the *ejidos* and *colonias* they provided with credit. The *ejidatarios* and *colonos* thus turned to the private cotton houses for the ginning of their bulk cotton (*algodón en hueso*), and then presented the baled fiber to the official banks as payment for their loans. This trade in *algodón de hueso* was common throughout the cotton regions of northern Mexico.[15]

Contraband cotton markets flourished in these conditions. *Ejidatarios,* who did not hold title to their land, could not use their land as collateral to obtain credit in private markets, and were therefore restricted legally to the credit provided by the BNCE. But because the BNCE had no control over the industrialization of the cotton during these years, its clients often delivered only a fraction of their product in payment of the loans, or sold the rest of the *algodón en hueso* to *coyotes,* or middlemen, who in turn sold the cotton to the cotton houses. These transactions were often performed at night, which gave rise to the description of contraband cotton as "moonlight cotton" (*algodón de luna*). Although the prices paid by *coyotes* were far lower, illegal sales of cotton provided these undercapitalized small producers with immediate cash. Some *ejidatarios* turned to their property-owning neighbors for credit and seed.[16]

In Matamoros, *ejidatarios* often contracted directly with the cotton houses, despite the fact that they did not hold title to their land. This was certainly due, in part, to the fact that many of the *ejidatarios* in the region were smallholders who, lacking titles, entered *ejidos* out of fear of losing their land, but who continued to farm their parcels as if they were private. By the time the BNCE began to provide credit in the late 1930s, these *ejidatarios* enjoyed established credit relations with regional cotton factors, who apparently saw little risk in continuing their investments given the positive conditions set by the federal government's *política algodonera.* Another large group of *ejidatarios* (perhaps 2500) had not yet, by 1944, received the official award (*dotación*) of land that brought with it access to BNCE credit, and were thus forced to use the resources provided by the cotton houses. For the cotton houses, the provision of seed to *ejidatarios* and the acceptance of unginned cotton in payment was not much different from the relationship they had long held with sharecroppers in the region.[17]

Faced with huge surpluses, in August of 1943 the Secretary of the Interior (Secretaría de Gobernación) sought to increase state control of cotton and credit by prohibiting the free trade of *algodón en hueso* in all the major cotton regions except Matamoros, where the processing capacity of the official banks fell far short of production, and where the government expected production to expand greatly. Control over exports was conferred to the SEN by decree in September, and what remained of the cotton harvested earlier that year in Matamoros and Mexicali was "frozen" in those border zones until the sale or storage of the fiber could be organized by the federal government. The National Railways were ordered not to move any cotton from the border, despite the fact that private cottenmen and the BNCE had outstanding contracts to fill with industrialists in the center of the country.[18]

The AAM protested the interference of the federal government in what it considered to be its rightful control over production in the region. And, given its embeddedness in regional society and its predominance in the financing, provisioning, industrialization, and commercialization of the region's crop, the regional cotton bourgeoisie had a good deal of leverage. At the beginning of the 1943–1944 crop year, the industrialists refused to invest their money until they were provided with an official price and assured the free trade of the cotton they received in payment. While the *algodoneros* constricted their operations, the official state banks stepped up their distribution of seed and credit to the *ejidatarios* and *colonos,* and the CEIMSA declared that at harvest time the government would buy all cotton ginned by the *algodoneros* at the guaranteed prices, as well as the raw cotton delivered by *colonos* and *ejidatarios* to the gins of the official banks. Then, as the cotton ripened in the fields, the *algodoneros* declared that they would not buy and gin any cotton because, they maintained, their only buyer—the CEIMSA—offered them a price below that which the industrialists were forced to pay to the farmers.[19]

Most of the region's inhabitants believed and sided with the *algodoneros,* and the struggle between the *algodoneros* and the state resulted in massive protests by farmers and workers. The Association of Medium and Small Property Owners and Colonists (Asociación de Pequeños y Medianos Propietarios y Colonos, or APMPC) sent a telegram to Ávila Camacho calling for the government to release its control over the regional cotton crop, which, they argued, would permit the cotton companies to resume their normal operations and allow their farmer clients to harvest and sell their cotton. On August 3, more than five thousand of these small farmers assembled before the municipal palace to protest the disruption to the cotton harvest caused by the cotton freeze. A representative of the BNCE was shouted off the podium, as the crowd voiced its demand that the CEIMSA leave the region. Joined by the workers who labored in the gins of the regional cottonmen, these farmers organized a general strike that shut down the city.[20]

The cottonmen and their spokesmen represented the conflict as one between a united region and distant center, rather than between the private and state sectors of the region's cotton economy. Rather than argue that the cotton freeze hurt their profits, they took the position that the government's actions were hurting the "development" of the workers and *campesinos* of the region. One industrialist wrote in a newspaper editorial that while the regional representatives proudly defended the region, federal government officials "seem to go out of their way to protect the interests of the CEIMSA to the detriment of thousands of modest *campesino* households, squashing their aspirations of progress and their efforts to improve themselves."[21] The cottonmen couched their argument in the same language of regional development propagated by the federal government, attacking the government for endangering the "progress" and developmental aspirations of the region.

Faced with this regional political mobilization behind the *algodoneros,* Secretary of Agriculture Marte R. Gómez met with Anderson Clayton Company officials in Mexico City to reconsider the price the government could offer for the region's cotton. He then reiterated the government's pledge to purchase all the cotton produced in the region, and threatened the local industrialists with the confiscation of their gins unless they agreed to process the harvest at the same prices offered by the BNCE and BNCA. The cottonmen ceded before Gómez's threats, and agreed to pay official prices 10 to 15 percent higher than those they had offered. In a long telegram read by Municipal President Ladislao Cárdenas to a large assembly of farmers in the main plaza, Marte R. Gómez explained the government's position in relation to regional cotton production, outlined why the measures were taken, and described how they were to be enacted. This time, rather than shouting the government official's words down, most of the audience listened patiently.[22]

Once it became known that the cottonmen were consistently underpaying the farmers, the universalizing claim lodged in the idea of a unified region was untenable, and the regional bloc assembled behind the cottonmen began to fragment. The industrialists accepted the price for cotton established by the government, but when the farmers delivered their product to the gins, the industrialists imposed price cuts of between 3 and 20 percent, claiming that the cotton was of inferior quality. These cuts effectively reinstated the prices offered by the cottonmen before they were forced to accept the government's guaranteed prices. The actions of the region's cottonmen infuriated many of their former supporters among the agricultural classes, and the press reported that the leaders of the earlier general strike were now "profoundly displeased" with the cotton companies. A group of cotton farmers invaded the municipal palace to demand that the Secretary of Agriculture confiscate the gins of those industrialists who imposed price cuts. Although the municipal president stepped in to prevent another mass mobilization, the conflict between the farmers and the regional cottonmen continued to simmer throughout the rest of the harvest season.[23]

In the 1943–1944 conflict between the state and regional capital, a language and ideology of regional development served to paper over the structural social tensions between the private farmers, *ejidatarios* and *colonos,* on the one hand, and the cotton industrialists on the other. It was a language imbued with a sense of unity and historical destiny that helped congeal a regional bloc that supported the bourgeoisie of Matamoros. After the government's purposes and cotton prices were made clear, however, and the regional cottonmen were seen actively disregarding federal price guarantees, many of the farmers changed their minds. In fact, the APMAC, which had earlier rallied its members in support of the region's cotton capitalists, went so far as to form a credit union in order to gain independence from the cotton companies. Despite the blow dealt to the authority of regional cottonmen, by 1945 "free trade" was once again regnant in Matamoros and Mexico, as the government refocused its controlling efforts on managing just *ejidal* cotton production, and on taxation and other fiscal measures applied to the private sector. By the admission of a cotton expert who worked in the CEIMSA and the BNCE, the government had, in fact, lost the struggle to make the cottonmen of Matamoros (and their regional political bloc) respect its price controls.[24]

The move away from direct control was also strongly influenced by events in the international political economy of cotton, especially in the United States. Faced with surplus stocks of many agricultural products, in the late 1930s the U.S. government made efforts to establish international regulation of the production of commodities such as cotton and wheat, and as soon as the war started it began to plan postwar agreements to manage surpluses and minimize national protectionism. As the war drew to a close, the promise of supplying a rebuilding Europe and Japan generated optimism in the United States and Mexico that both the accumulated stocks and the product of expanded cotton production would find a ready market, making the intensive government efforts of the Depression and war years unnecessary.[25]

During the war William Clayton worked to monopolize U.S. control over the world's strategic materials from his positions as vice president of the U.S. Export-Import Bank and Assistant Secretary of Commerce. In 1944 he was sworn in as Assistant Secretary of State for Economic Affairs, and his first important assignment was to head the economics section of the U.S. delegation to the Interamerican Conference held in Mexico City in mid-February, 1945. At the conference Clayton made it clear that although the United States was interested in supporting Latin American economies after the war, the Export-Import Bank would make no loans for enterprises that depended on subsidies or tariffs. Recognizing U.S. domination over the postwar global economy, and its own inability to control national cotton production, the CEIMSA concluded that it could no longer directly subsidize cotton production, except through its agricultural banks.[26]

With the help of Clayton, the U.S. government placed cotton at the heart of its efforts to rebuild and manage the postwar economy of the noncommunist world. As was the case after World War I, in 1945 the United States controlled a large part of the world's cotton supply, as well as most of the credit needed to purchase that cotton. For overseas industries to buy fiber they needed dollars, and in 1945 a special cotton loan program was initiated by the Export-Import Bank that distributed $100 million over the next few years to countries such as China, Italy, and Czechoslovakia. At the same time, a cotton-for-textiles program was implemented by which German and Japanese industries were provided with $215 million worth of CCC cotton, in exchange for three-fifths of the textiles produced. The remaining textiles stayed in Germany and Japan. With the implementation of the Marshall Plan between 1948 and 1950, over a billion dollars was advanced to foreign countries through the Economic Cooperation Administration to pay for 6 million bales of U.S. cotton. More than 60 percent of the cotton exported by the United States during this time was bought with credit extended by the government.[27]

El Oro Blanco: 1948–1952

In the late 1940s and early 1950s a number of factors contributed to make cotton agriculture in Mexico immensely profitable. With the United States providing credit to the world's industrialized nations, world cotton consumption far exceeded production, and the all-time high of 28 million bales of accumulated surplus cotton was cut in half between 1945 and 1948. Although U.S. cotton was still expensive compared to that of other countries, the Assistant to the U.S. Secretary of Agriculture asserted that "the outlook for cotton is brighter than it has been in many years."[28] When, in late 1949, the supply of excess cotton once again threatened to increase due to credit shortages among consumers, the U.S. government implemented acreage reduction measures. The U.S. harvest in 1950 was a little more than half that of the previous year, and when the U.S. government limited exports to assure supplies for its Korean War preparation effort, prices for cotton from other countries rose dramatically.[29]

Mexico never abandoned the strategy of increasing cotton production for export that was born in the irrigation development projects of the 1920s and strengthened during the Cárdenas period. Although the government had to take extraordinary measures to deal with surpluses during World War II, irrigation spending was higher during the Ávila Camacho presidency (1940–1946) than ever before, reaching 15 percent of the federal government's budget in 1946. Equally important was the completion during the 1940s of the five big-dam irrigation projects begun by the Cárdenas government. Four of these were located in the river valleys of the north, and much of the land they watered was dedicated to cotton. The "Azúcar," or "Marte R. Gómez" dam on the Río San Juan, was completed in 1946, irrigating 66,000 hectares of the Valle Bajo Río San Juan irrigation district adjacent to the Valle Bajo Río Bravo. And between 1947 and 1952, 47,000 additional hectares of cotton land were irrigated in the Valle Bajo Río Bravo district. The extraordinarily high prices of the late 1940s and early 1950s also allowed profits to be made from growing cotton on land without irrigation, and large areas were opened to this marginal dryland cultivation. The Matamoros region reached the apex of its cotton boom at this moment: 147,000 bales were grown on 142,000 hectares in 1948; by 1951 350,000 bales were grown on 322,200 hectares. Nationally, there was an 82 percent increase between the harvest of 1949 and that of 1951: from 540,000 to 1 million bales (see graphs, pp. 97, 158, and 159).[30]

The social formation in the cotton region of the lower Río Bravo changed dramatically as the agricultural zone boomed. After the initial period of settlement by *ejido* and *colonia* (1934–1943), most of what was left of the government's Sauteña land was sold by the BNCA as private properties to investors eager to participate in the storied prosperity of the region. Many cotton ranches were taken by government officials for themselves or their friends. The Mexican comedic film star Cantínflas, for example, owned a large cotton ranch in the Río Bravo delta. Because of these political connections the new landowners were able to purchase the land for ridiculously low prices, and by registering different 100-hectare parcels under names of family members, were able to establish cotton ranches well beyond the limits established by federal law—often over 500 hectares. The *ejidatarios* and *colonos* settled in the late 1930s and early 1940s held their new neighbors in disdain, calling them "*agricultores nylon*"—artificial, synthetic, "nylon" farmers. Nevertheless, by 1948 *colonos* and *ejidatarios* each only controlled 20 percent of the land, while the private property owners had the other 60 percent. The shift in the overall pattern of land tenure toward private property resulted in an expansion of the private cotton houses and industries, and the influence of these over the region's economy. In 1945 there were twelve gins in the region; by 1950 there were seventy-four, of which only a few were managed by the government banks. After 1945 private banks began operating in force in the region.[31]

The expansion of private capital and the inability of the government banks to provide sufficient credit for the rapidly expanding cotton production meant that even *ejidatarios* were commonly contracting loans with private houses or selling their cotton to *coyotes*. The sale of contraband "*algodón de luna*" contributed to the very unhealthy state of the government's agricultural banks in Matamoros. Between 1948 and 1952, the peak years of cotton prices and production, the BNCE never recuperated as much as it lent. And in 1952, at a time when farmers and private cotton capitalists were earning fabulous amounts of money, 70.9 percent of the BNCE's loans were unpaid. The government made efforts to stop "*coyotage*," posting soldiers in the fields and repossessing the agricultural implements of those *ejidatarios* caught selling their cotton illegally. Nevertheless, by 1949 the massive flow of cotton from the social sector to the private cotton houses combined with a devaluation of the peso to drain the regional BNCA of capital, and the government bank was forced to borrow 12 million pesos from the five leading cotton companies in the region in order to stay solvent.[32]

Despite the cotton freeze of 1944, and the ongoing latent and open conflicts among various social classes and state actors in the region, the AAM continued to promote an ideology of unity, social harmony, and developmental progress. In 1948 the AAM published a glossy promotional pamphlet that served to describe the region's progressive nature to the world's cotton buyers, and to assure them that "Matamoros is one of the cotton producing regions with the most promising future." "The businessmen of Matamoros," the AAM claimed, "work with absolute faith in the future of their region, and will continue striving to make it greater." In publications and through the local press, the cotton capitalists proclaimed themselves the defenders and guides of this future, relentlessly universalizing their interests.[33]

These claims about the leading role of the AAM may have been exaggerated, but with the conflict of the 1943–1944 period behind them, the government and the regional elite forged a clearly cooperative relationship in promoting cotton production to its fullest: the businessmen for profits and the federal government for taxes. Indeed, the very separation between state and regional elite collapsed as the sale of lands to government officials after 1946 turned politicians into farmers. Examples abound. In early 1948, when the inadequacy of the rail facilities in Matamoros threatened to hinder the cotton business, the AAM provided 150,000 pesos for the improvement of the station, and the National Railways made sure the cottonmen would have enough rail cars to move their product. As was mentioned before, in 1949 the BNCA was rescued from bankruptcy by a 12-million-peso loan from the five largest members of the AAM. At the popular level, the AAM provided money for the improvement of local water services, and for the establishment of an agricultural school.[34]

Another important way that the government supported the large landowners and cotton capitalists in the region was to secure property rights against further requests for *ejidos* or outright land seizures by migrant workers. With the region producing more than 100,000 bales of cotton by 1944, a sizable mass of migrant laborers was needed, especially during the harvest (*pizca*), which took place during the end of summer and early fall. By 1950 some 120,000 people arrived each season, and many of them stayed. In 1930 the *municipios* of Matamoros and Reynosa had 37,000 inhabitants; by 1940 this number had risen to 77,000; and by 1950 there were 198,000 people in the Bajo Río Bravo cotton zone. Throughout the late 1940s groups of agricultural laborers established themselves on uncleared or unused parcels in the hinterlands of Matamoros, and sought recognition as *ejidos* or *colonias*. These attempts were rebuffed with military force by the federal government, which had the full support of the AAM and the region's newspaper editors, who denounced the squatters as "communists."[35]

Despite the AAM's claims of regional unity and harmony, independent unions and wildcat strikes provide evidence that labor was by no means convinced of the harmony of social relations under the leadership of the cottonmen. Furthermore, the improvements wrought by AAM spending in the city of Matamoros did not benefit those living in the city's hinterlands. As we shall see, the AAM's claims of leadership, unity, and harmony would be contested by the *colonos, ejidatarios, agricultores,* intellectuals, and businessmen of Valle Hermoso when, in their struggle to establish an independent *municipio* in order to control the material benefits of the cotton boom, they appropriated and redefined the language of regional development.[36]

Redefining Regional Development: The Independence of Valle Hermoso, 1949–1953

Many of the people old enough to remember the 1940s and 1950s describe a time of opulence when money grew like cotton in the fields. A friend raised in Valle Hermoso during that period told me that he and his schoolmates would find change lying in the dust of the road, thrown away by *campesinos* flush with money. During the harvest time farmers would walk around town with brown paper bags full of money. Little boys and girls who came to the region with their families would pick cotton as well, and children from the town would earn money selling food and drinks to the migrant workers. "In those times, there was money for everyone," he told me wistfully.[37]

This view of the Valle Bajo Río Bravo as a rotund development success was also taken by Manuel Gamio, who helped organized the repatriation of colonists to the zone in 1939. In an article published in 1952, Gamio attributed the fact that Matamoros was "the leading cotton zone in Mexico" to the racially, economically, socially, and culturally advanced status of its colonists, and the "integrated" development blueprints of the federal government. He contrasted Matamoros with the Valle de Mezquital, where, he argued, the government's economic and technological development efforts failed to account for the cultural, racial, and social particularities of the region's largely indigenous population, resulting in a resounding failure to develop.[38]

Gamio's comparison between Matamoros and the Mezquital mapped the positive aspects of development onto Matamoros, and the negative dimensions on the Mezquital. Had he actually visited the border region and spoke with the colonists he wrote about, he might have seen things differently. Along with the memories of the positive aspects of development held by people in Valle Hermoso today, there are a lot of memories of the negative aspects. The same person who spoke of the late 1940s and 1950s as a time "when there was money for everyone," later described the avenue leaving town packed with cantinas serving alcohol to rowdy masses of migrant workers from "the south." Without a doubt, many of these migrant workers made the trip to the Matamoros cotton fields from their homes in the Valle de Mezquital on the Mexico–Laredo highway. Gunfights were so common that his mother put the children to bed on the floor. "It was the wild west," he said—definitely not the modern, progressive town of independent smallholding farmers described in the popular narrative of progress.[39]

Archival sources corroborate these oral histories. After ten years of steady increases in production, earnings, and taxes, the *colonos* of Valle Hermoso complained that they were not seeing the economic benefits of their labors. Basic services such as water, telephones, schools, police, and mail were deficient and the *colonos* lacked the political power to make their demands heard. The astounding economic growth of the region had not led to the kind of positive development they desired and had been promised. Despite the division and colonization of the land in parcels small enough for one family to work, the use of migrant labor was ubiquitous. The immense amount of money generated at harvest time gave rise to all kinds of improvised and shady businesses, and everywhere the residents of Valle Hermoso looked, they found homeless migrant workers, cantinas, and gunfighting. Respect for the laws prohibiting the sale of hard liquor was, like the respect for laws prohibiting contraband cotton, notable for its absence in the *colonias*. Police efforts to close the cantinas resulted in armed battles, and the death of a police chief in a shoot-out brought alarmed warnings in the press of a return to prohibition-era gangsterism.[40]

Around 1950 a political movement emerged in Valle Hermoso that sought to limit the negative aspects of rapid growth. In the process, the movement gave new content to the concepts of region and development. A group of leaders mounted their own development initiative, forming the "Junta de Mejores Materiales de Valle Hermoso." This effort led to the installation of electricity, the establishment of schools, and other material gains, but the leaders were dissatisfied with the lack of security in the town, and the fact that they did not control the use of the taxes they paid. The next step, therefore, was to secure the independence of the zone as a municipality separate from Matamoros, and residents implemented a strike against paying cotton taxes to achieve this end. The various social groups that comprised the regional political bloc led by the cotton bourgeoisie of Matamoros opposed independence fiercely. The press published a statement signed by the AAM, the Chamber of Commerce, as well as union and *campesino* groups, arguing that it was precisely because Valle Hermoso was not yet developed that the town needed to remain within the territorial and political jurisdiction of Matamoros. Despite this opposition, which was backed by the governor of Tamaulipas, a group was formed in Valle Hermoso to take over the tasks of government, and the *municipio* was legally constituted in March of 1953.[41]

At the heart of the political struggle over the creation of the *municipio* of Valle Hermoso was a conflict over the concept of region. The *colonos* and *ejidatarios* of Valle Hermoso did not feel the unity implicit in the definition of the Matamoros region espoused by the industrialists of Matamoros. They viewed the *agricultores nylon* with resentment, and accused them of betraying the *cardenista* social vision of a rural Mexico populated by small, independent, hardworking farmers. Many criticized the corruption that forged the alliance between *agricultores nylon,* Matamoros cottonmen, and the federal government. With the creation of huge cotton ranches around the towns of Río Bravo and Reynosa, the Water Ministry (Secretaría de Recursos Hidraúlicos) focused its attention on new irrigation works, neglecting the system built a decade earlier by Eduardo Chávez and the colonists.[42]

Rather than submit to regional "unity," the *colonos, ejidatarios, rancheros,* and businessmen of Valle Hermoso labored to construct a new geopolitical identity based to a large degree on historical memories of repatriation, colonization, *cardenismo,* the struggle to clear the lands, and other elements of a shared history and historical consciousness. The struggle to establish the *municipio* of Valle Hermoso was conceived as a struggle to unite the *colonias, ejidos,* and small private farms around Valle Hermoso as a distinct region, with its own historical destiny of progress and prosperity.[43] This region was defined both by space and by the people who inhabited that space. The *agricultores nylon* were not included in this imagined community, and neither were the industrialists and politicians of Matamoros. The legitimacy of the new polity was claimed by placing it on an historical trajectory that began with the developmentalist social engineering project of the *cardenista* government, passed through the hardship years of colonization, and culminated in the extraordinary boom years of the late 1940s and early 1950s. Political independence was the next logical step in the evolution of Valle Hermoso.

U.S. "Dumping" and the End of the "Milagro Mexicano" in the Valle Bajo Río Bravo

The independence of Valle Hermoso in 1953 led to an increased amount of spending in the new *municipio,* but it was not long before the foundations of the region's prosperity began to crumble. Mexico had harnessed its agricultural sector to a global political economy of cotton that was held steady and lucrative by U.S. domestic and foreign policy, as well as demand for the fiber generated by the rebuilding industries in Japan and Europe. Cotton exports provided foreign currency for import substitution industrialization in Mexico, and the increase and modernization of textile production fueled the demand for cotton fiber within the country as well. The same year of the independence of Valle Hermoso, however, the United States began to scale back its lending programs, and U.S. cotton exports fell some 55 percent. Rising cotton surpluses in the United States forced the government to accept foreign currency for its cotton, and even to authorize the donation of free cotton. In 1953 and 1954, the Valle Bajo Río Bravo suffered through a drought that eliminated all but irrigated cotton in the region, and lowered national production levels. A peso devaluation that year made production costs higher for farmers in the borderlands, where many of the inputs for the cotton crop were imported and bought in dollars. Despite government relief in the form of a cut in the export tax, profits fell as farmers found it necessary to apply pesticides ten or fifteen times a season, and as the soil, exhausted by monocrop cotton and wind erosion, yielded less. By 1955, the role of Matamoros as the largest cotton-producing region in the country was being challenged by the Mexicali zone and the rapidly expanding irrigation zones of Sinaloa and Sonora.[44]

In late 1955 the U.S. government announced what every other cotton-producing country feared: the subsidized export of its surplus cotton. At first the United States supported the export of only the less desirable shorter lengths of cotton, but in February 1956 the Secretary of Agriculture announced that the CCC would offer all lengths and sizes of cotton at subsidized prices, beginning on August 1. Mexico was, by that time, the second leading exporter of cotton in the nonsocialist world, and her government officials, businessmen, and farmers led an alarmed protest against the U.S. "dumping" of 12 million bales of cotton. The Secretary of Agriculture and Livestock (Secretaría de Agricultura y Ganadería), Julián Rodríguez Adame, declared that "the fundamentals of commerce based in healthy competition will disappear," turning the U.S. government's own discourse on free trade against it.[45] The loss of cotton exports would have meant losing almost 30 percent of its total income of dollars, and to avoid this the government supported domestic cotton production with a tax cut. Nevertheless, government earnings from cotton fell 25 percent in 1956. The U.S. government continued to provide export subsidies for cotton throughout the late 1950s, defending its actions by saying that it simply wanted to reduce its surpluses and recover its "just participation" in the world's cotton market.[46]

In the international debate that ensued, the world's cotton-producing countries strove to assert their notion of economic justice, a notion based in the premises and language of development. Julián Rodríguez Adame, president of the Interamerican Cotton Federation (Federación Interamericana del Algodón, or FIDA), an organization representing cotton-producing countries in the Americas other than the United States, articulated the main objections to the U.S. cotton politics. The United States had reached its original goal of selling 6.5 million bales of surplus cotton, and the continuance of the subsidy raised serious questions about what "just participation" in the cotton market really meant. The cotton-producing countries that suffered from the U.S. policy argued that their development was being compromised by the actions of the United States, which, they maintained, was trying to avoid a painful resolution of its own domestic problem of overproduction by passing the damages on to them. For Mexico and the rest of the FIDA, "just participation" in the cotton market meant U.S. domestic price guarantees that supported cotton agriculture development strategies around the world, and the end of export subsidies that compromised that development.[47]

The Mexican government received support for its attack on U.S. dumping from its traditional ally in the international political economy of cotton: U.S. cotton capital. The president of the Anderson Clayton Company, Lamar Fleming Jr., wrote an open letter of protest in early 1959. The other producing countries of the world were already reducing their harvests by 1959, Fleming argued, and the United States could have saved its taxpayers a great deal of money and saved the cotton producers overseas a great deal of anguish by reducing the cotton subsidy. "The succession of dumpings by the United States of America," he concluded, has "bitter consequences for the farmers and the national economies of all the cotton exporting countries."[48] Arguments in defense of Mexican cotton production were also provided by Bank of America Vice President Henry W. Drath. At this time 80 percent of Mexican cotton was financed by American banks and cotton merchants, and any damage to that business would have repercussions in the U.S. credit market. "When we help Mexican cotton producers," Drath stated, "we are helping ourselves."[49] None of these arguments was strong enough to convince the U.S. government to reduce its production, restore the price floors through purchase of surplus, or refrain from dumping that surplus on the world market. The world's cotton producers were left to contend with conditions radically different from those that they had enjoyed since the 1930s.

In a few years the fields of cotton disappeared from the Valle Bajo Río Bravo. Despite the falling profits, the farmers of Matamoros continued to plant cotton until 1963, each year with less success, and with more acreage dedicated to corn and sorghum. In 1962 Matamoros's cotton production fell 33 percent from the previous year, and by 1964 the manager of the BNCA in the region described "a real agrarian transformation, consisting of having abandoned cotton for the harvesting of grains such as corn and sorghum."[50] Attempts to rescue cotton production through tax breaks met with no success. Cotton production in Matamoros went south, figuratively and literally. Transnational companies and U.S. banks foreclosed on many farmers who could not pay their debts. The gins and compresses were dismantled and shipped to southern Tamaulipas, Michoacan, and Sonora, where cotton was gaining strength. New areas were opened to cotton in Chiapas and Central America during the late 1950s and 1960s as well. After 1963, the Bajo Río Bravo agricultural zone remained productive, but the crops shifted to sorghum and maize.[51]

The production of basic grains over the next twenty years coincided with efforts by the Mexican government to achieve food security. Subsidies of various kinds were provided to farmers so that the countryside would produce as much corn and wheat as the country consumed. The *ejidatarios* and *colonos* settled in the 1930s and 1940s on 12.5- and 20-hectare plots of land continued to eke out an existence with the help of family members working in other occupations, but the only farmers prospering were those who had hundreds of hectares. The economic crisis of the early 1980s hit at a moment when many of these small farmers were old enough to quit the business, and pass the farm along to their children. But few of the next generation were willing to enter into agriculture in these conditions. Even many of these large producers were forced out of business. The crisis finally ushered out the social fields established during the age of cotton. Small producers were increasingly rare after 1982, and big operators farming hundreds or thousands of acres of sorghum were the norm.[52]

Conclusion

The world of cotton in the Valle Bajo Río Bravo ended not with a bang, but a whimper. Most farmers I spoke with simply said that by 1963 it was no longer profitable to produce cotton, so they stopped. When questioned further, they mentioned a variety of problems. "The pests were uncontrollable: *gusano* (worms), *picudo* (weevils)," a well-to-do farmer from the town of Río Bravo told me. "Every year we had to use more pesticide: at the end we were doing 15 applications, and each time they got stronger. We created a super-race of bugs."[53] "No," another wealthy *agricultor* from Río Bravo opined, "what really did us in was the *pudrición texana* ("Texas rot," a soil fungus); we couldn't fight it."[54] An engineer who had worked on the irrigation system before becoming an *agricultor nylon* in the late 1940s told me that "we just couldn't keep making profits. Because of the U.S. selling cheap cotton, the price of cotton fell, and because of pests, the costs rose. And by then the soil just didn't have the strength anymore."[55] He was the only person I spoke with who identified the dumping of cotton by the United States as a factor in the demise of that crop in the Bajo Río Bravo.

Others placed the blame on moral faults found in both the farmers and the government. "What the state sold us as pesticide was brick dust," Jaime told me. "I remember there was a fellow in the *ejido* who got us all together to tell us that the company that was selling us pesticide was ripping us off. 'I'll prove it,' he said, taking a handful of the powder and eating it. He survived so I guess he was right. They kept growing cotton on the other side of the river, because they had legitimate pesticides. Cotton failed in Mexico because of corruption."[56] Another voiced a common opinion when he told me that "the *ejidatarios* didn't know how to respond to fall of cotton. The government maintained them so long with subsidies—it was a political thing; they voted for the PRI—they didn't know how to make a profit on their own."[57]

By the late 1990s, when I spoke with them, the farmers that survived in the Bajo Río Bravo since the cotton years had experienced thirty-five years of lackluster earnings from corn and sorghum and, at times, crushing environmental and economic disasters. The farmers remembered the cotton years as a time of exceptional prosperity, but acknowledged the negative dimensions of that development as well. Perhaps interpreting my interest in the history of cotton to be rooted in a desire to reintroduce the crop in the region, many went to lengths to explain to me that it would not, could not, be brought back. Those who attempted to grow cotton in response to high prices in the early 1990s met with failure when the prices crashed at harvest time. There was no credit, no initiative on part of the farmers, no help from the state, the farmers explained. It was easier just to go along growing sorghum, because everything was set up to do so.

The 1944 and 1953 conflicts hinged on the struggle to control both the historical process and narrative definition of regional development in the Valle Bajo Río Bravo, and the language of regional development continues to frame political discourse in Valle Hermoso. The municipal president of Valle Hermoso from the National Action Party (PAN) made a conscious effort to commemorate the struggles and achievements of the people of her *municipio* during the colonization and cotton boom years. "We won't know where we are going unless we recover this history," she told me.[58] Various events were held in which local historians and notable historical figures from the region spoke before assemblies of townspeople or schoolchildren. The public spaces of the town center were adorned with murals depicting important people and events from the founding of the region: Eduardo Chávez, Lázaro Cárdenas, Marte R. Gómez, the arrival of the *repatriados* to the Colonia 18 de Marzo, cotton. These dominant local histories of Valle Hermoso usually include the negative dimensions of development only insofar as they serve as a basis against which to compare the positive dimensions. There are, of course, many alternate histories that tell the tale of cotton smuggling, economic failure, and vice, and that turn the focus of the narrative away from the colonists and repatriates that arrived in 1938 and 1939. These narratives also have a place in the regional economy, describing and facilitating the long-standing, subterranean practices of smuggling that, by legal definition, fall beyond the reach of state control but that, in practice, incorporate many state actors in a fundamental way. The language spoken between the government and the governed, however, remains that of regional development. As the town historian of Valle Hermoso told an audience assembled in the Municipal Palace in 1998, "we would like to have something more: we are not developing to the level we want."[59]

CHAPTER 9

CONCLUSION: HISTORICIZING THE BORDERLANDS

Don Marcelo, Don Fausto, and Don Roberto had known each other since the 1930s, and as they sat talking on Roberto's porch, they helped each other remember names, dates, events, and places.[1] Don Marcelo was born and raised on the Rancho Santa Adelaide, a rural outpost at that time, now being swallowed by the city of Matamoros as it grows southward along the Sendero Nacional, the highway that runs to the Colonia Anáhuac and Valle Hermoso. Although he had no land himself, the young Marcelo picked cotton on local ranches even before the construction of the irrigation district in the mid-1930s. With the construction and colonization of the irrigation district he found an easier job driving a school bus. Don Roberto and Don Fausto arrived with the rest of the *colonos* from the Don Martín irrigation system to settle the Colonia Anáhuac, and still cultivated their 20-hectare parcels. In their eighties when I interviewed them in 1997, these men spoke about their lives as farmers in the Valle Bajo Río Bravo. "I've cultivated these twenty hectares all my life," said Don Roberto. "At this point growing sorghum only pays the costs. No profit. I don't need much; and I have children that help me out. It's just nice to see the plants grow up; that's why I keep doing it."

As we sat on his porch looking out over the stubble on that hot September afternoon, Roberto confessed that it might be the last time he harvested those fields. Water deliveries to the irrigated district were down recently, he said, and it was unclear what water the farmers would get during the next growing season. Without water, Fausto agreed, it was not worth investing in seed and diesel to plant the crop. It was not like the old days, all three concurred, when there was plenty of water, credit, and land to go around and the crops grew with hardly an effort. Don Fausto and Don Roberto were migrants and had just what they carried with them to their new home: land reform allowed them to acquire parcels of land, and cotton turned them into comfortable middle-class farmers.

The astounding boom of irrigated cotton agriculture remembered so fondly by these men was based on the wholesale reorganization of environment, production, and society in the lower Río Bravo Valley by Mexico's postrevolutionary state, transnational cotton capital, and a highly mobile borderlands population of farmers and agricultural workers. The dense, subhumid Tamaulipan scrub forest was ripped out of the ground by tractors, draft animals, and human hands, and replaced by level, uniform agricultural fields that offered little habitat to the wild animals that lived in the region. Irrigation and flood control works built by government engineers channeled water to dry lands and protected crops and people from disastrous inundations. Land reform remapped the landscape, establishing new forms of property and placing production in the hands of new classes of small producers— *ejidatarios, colonos,* and *pequeños propietarios*—many of whom were repatriated from the United States during the 1930s. Cotton, the world's quintessential industrial cash crop, occupied 95 percent of the agricultural zone, which grew to almost 300,000 hectares by the early 1950s. Those who experienced this boom felt it to be their development destiny.

The creation of a transnational borderlands cotton economy with high rates of capital accumulation and generalized prosperity was based in a series of physical infrastructures such as dams, canals, level fields, houses, cotton gins, and roads, and social infrastructures such as education, agrarian reform (*ejidos* and *colonias*), and health care. A developmentalist "structure of feeling" made sense of the experience.[2] As I have argued throughout the book, development is as much a response to social and economic crisis as it is a blueprint for proactive social engineering. The social and physical infrastructures of irrigated cotton erected in the borderlands between 1880 and 1960 should be seen in a similar way: as a response to crisis conditions such as decreasing productivity in the cotton fields of the old South, unemployment and migration. David Harvey explains how the recurrent crises in capitalist economy and society are crises of overaccumulation of capital, and argues that they are ameliorated through spatial and temporal displacement.[3] The cotton economy moved into the borderlands to take advantage of relatively cheap land, new soils, and innovations in the productive process, such as mechanization and irrigation. At the same time, the physical and social infrastructures of irrigated cotton built in the borderlands constituted a temporal fix: they were investments that soaked up stagnant capital and put it back into circulation. These infrastructures were built in response to the crisis of overaccumulation that came to a head around 1930, and stretched the returns on those investments out over the following forty years. As we have seen, the infrastructures of irrigated cotton laid the foundations for the now legendary era of "white gold" in northern Mexico.

The irrigated agriculture that created affluence and optimism in the Valle Bajo del Río Bravo is now in crisis. Cotton gave way to corn and sorghum in the early 1960s, as the federal government promoted basic grains as part of a national food system designed to support the rural sector and provide security in an increasingly volatile and politicized world market. Since the early 1980s, peso devaluations and the erosion of market price and government subsidies for these grains have translated into lowered earnings for most farmers. To make matters worse, seventy-five years after the massive floods that periodically swept the delta region were first

harnessed for irrigation, the hydraulic society that grew up there is facing a scarcity of water. Agricultural and urban growth has met and surpassed the availability of water from the rivers and regional aquifers. This became especially appar-
ent between 1993 and 2004, when a sustained drought besieged the borderlands.
Because urban uses have priority over agricultural uses, water deliveries to farmers
in the irrigation districts of the lower Río Bravo/Rio Grande Valley were severely
cut, and denied altogether.

Without secure supplies of irrigation water, only drought-resistant sorghum is
a relatively safe gamble when it comes time to plant, and more profitable crops are
unthinkable. Even sorghum yields much less grain without adequate water. As a
result of these changes in water availability, grain markets, and government support
for agriculture, while in 1950 a family lived quite well farming 10 hectares, now only
those few families with access to 200 hectares or more can maintain such a standard
of living solely from agriculture. Most of the smallholders established sixty years ago
who have not sold their land now rent it to big producers, and the few that still farm
10- or 20-hectare parcels make a living by incorporating into the domestic economy
maquiladora work, commerce, contraband, agricultural day labor, and remittances
from relatives in the United States. "Only the big survive" in these conditions, an
ejidatario explained to me.[4]

The effects of water scarcity in the agricultural borderlands include conflict and
restructuring. The failure to deliver water to the users of the irrigation districts in
the delta of the Río Bravo/Rio Grande led to struggles between groups and governments across northern Mexico and Texas. A similar fight is taking shape between
urban and agricultural users of the Colorado River in southern California and Mexico, as the U.S. government stepped in to ensure a water transfer from the Imperial
Valley to the city of San Diego. This water transfer agreement involves the lining of
the All-American Canal, which will most likely prevent water from filtering into
Mexico and have a negative impact on agriculture in Mexicali. The realization that
both the Río Bravo/Rio Grande and the Colorado River are overconcessioned—that
there are more rights to water in these rivers than there is water—has state and federal governments reviewing their water treaties, preparing for legal battles, regulat-
ing water use, and investing in infrastructure.[5]

This book shows us that borderlands economy, society, and culture were built
upon the use of water for irrigated cotton agriculture, and this history can help in
understanding current conflicts over water and in anticipating possible outcomes.
Scarcity and conflict are indicators of the environmental limits of irrigated agriculture in the borderlands, and symptoms of its crisis and restructuring. In Matamoros,
there is no significant freshwater aquifer, and irrigation water must be sent by canal
from distant upriver dams. Even in the best of conditions, the lower Río Bravo
Valley receives only a few large waterings a year, a situation that is ideal for cotton
or grain production but makes growing thirsty, high-profit crops such as vegetables
impossible. With delicate, high-priced crops ruled out, so is the possibility of pay-

ing for the kind of infrastructural renovation that would enable a more efficient and precise administration of the water resources in the region. This is a vicious circle that destines the region to producing sorghum, which is the most drought-resistant of the basic grains. And because the lower Río Bravo Valley receives an average of about 500 millimeters of rain a year, an amount that permits sorghum production, there is even less incentive to renovate the irrigation system and plant more profitable crops. In the case of Matamoros, economic, environmental, and infrastructural conditions have combined to create a situation in which a few farmers cultivate large extensions of sorghum on rented land.

The crisis of irrigated agriculture will take different forms and have different outcomes depending on the particular social field present in each zone where irrigated agriculture is practiced. These regional social fields, each defined by a particular combination of land tenure, infrastructure, commodity production, environment, and social formation, need to be studied historically and anthropologically. In Mexicali's irrigation district, for example, the Treaty of 1944 assures a steady amount of water delivered more or less continuously from the Colorado River to the distribution system of canals. The proximity and security of this water source, as well as the presence of groundwater apt for irrigation, makes the production of vegetables in this region possible, and since the 1950s farmers have grown and exported scallions, asparagus, grapes, and other crops to the markets of southern California. But even Mexicali, with its relatively low population, is beginning to see pressure on its agriculture as Colorado River water is transferred to the rapidly growing urban sprawl along the Mexican coastline between Tijuana and Ensenada. In the Laguna region of Coahuila and Durango, the switch from cotton to milk production in the 1950s accelerated a process of aquifer depletion that is having grave consequences on the water supply and environmental health of the region. Agriculture in the Laguna is now largely dedicated to producing alfalfa for cattle feed, a crop that uses a great deal of water. Water levels in the Principal Aquifer are so low that the pumps are now extracting water saturated with heavy metals such as arsenic. The Nazas and Aguanaval rivers, once the sources of a great lake after which the region was named, are dry vestiges that rarely carry water. With the North American Free Trade Agreement (NAFTA) treaty, *maquiladoras* have moved into the Laguna region, spurring urban growth that also increases demand on the water supply.

As water use grows and its availability for agriculture decreases, the borderlands irrigation systems will need to adjust and restructure. Today many of the physical and social infrastructures upon which the regions were built at the beginning of the twentieth century are fond memories. There are no farmers supporting families on 10-hectare cotton plots. The canal systems are in disrepair after decades of neglect, and the federal government has recently "decentralized" them, placing financial and managerial responsibility for them in the hands of their users. In the place of smallholder irrigated cotton a variety of regionally specific productive arrangements are emerging. In all cases, however, the rents accrued during the twentieth century by the agricultural sector from an ample supply of water and state infrastructures are now in question.

The changing social use of water and the crisis of irrigated agriculture in the borderlands signal a larger transition from an economy and society driven by irrigated agriculture to one driven by urban industries and services, a transition that has been under way since World War II in the Southwest United States, and since the 1960s in Mexico. This urban and industrial society has given rise to social actors, formations, and identities, which are growing out of and slowly displacing those generated in the context of irrigated agricultural development that dominated the region during most of the twentieth century. Perhaps the agricultural sector in northern Mexico will respond to the crisis by building more efficient social and hydraulic infrastructures and choosing a more capital- and labor-intensive production of luxury commodities such as berries and salad greens, a path taken in Californian and Chilean agriculture. Regardless of the particular form they take, these new productive arrangements will engender new kinds of border crossings and new social and cultural precipitates of state and capital. The people who live and work building and rebuilding the borderlands—their experiences and stories—can only be understood as part of this history.

NOTES

ABBREVIATIONS

AET: Archivo Histórico del Estado de Tamaulipas, Ciudad Victoria, Tamaulipas.

AGN: Archivo General de la Nación, Mexico City, Mexico.

CONDUMEX: Fondo Luis Montes de Oca, Centro de Estudios de Historia de Mexico de Condumex, Mexico City, Mexico.

FJM: Fondo Francisco J. Múgica, Centro de Estudios de la Revolución Mexicana "Lázaro Cárdenas," Jiquilpan, Michoacán, Mexico.

JFB: Fondo Juan F. Brittingham, Archivo Histórico "Juan Agustín de Espinoza, S.J.," Universidad Iberoamericana, Torreón, Coahuila, Mexico.

PEC: Fondo Plutarco Elias Calles, Archivo Histórico Calles/Torreblanca, Mexico City, Mexico.

RAC: Rockefeller Archive Center, Tarrytown, NY.

SEP: Archivo Histórico de la Secretaría de Educación Pública, Mexico City, Mexico.

USNA: United States National Archives, Department of State, College Park, MD.

CHAPTER 1

1. Elisa, interview with author, Valle Hermoso, Tamaulipas, 1997. I follow standard anthropological practice in changing all names of informants to pseudonyms.

2. Benito, interview with author, Valle Hermoso, Tamaulipas, 1998.

3. Benito interview.

4. Fernando and Elisa, Interview with author, Valle Hermoso, Tamaulipas, 1997.

5. Rogelio, conversation with author, Valle Hermoso, Tamaulipas, 1998.

6. Luis Aboites, *La Irrigación Revolucionaria: Historia del Sistema Nacional de Riego del Río Conchos, Chihuahua, 1927–1938.*

7. Neil Foley, *The White Scourge: Mexicans, Blacks and Poor Whites in Texas Cotton Culture*; David Montejano, *Anglos and Mexicans in the Making of Texas, 1836–1986*; Devra Weber, *Dark Sweat, White Gold: California Farm Workers, Cotton, and the New Deal.*

8. Fernando Coronil, *The Magical State: Nature, Money and Modernity in Venezuela*; Sidney Mintz, *Sweetness and Power: The Place of Sugar in Modern History*; Ángel Palerm, *Antropología y Marxismo*; William Roseberry, *Coffee and Capitalism in the Venezuelan Andes*; Steve Striffler, *In the Shadows of State and Capital: The United Fruit Company, Popular Struggle, and Agrarian Restructuring in Ecuador, 1900–1995*; Steven Topik and Allen Wells, "Introduction: Latin America's Response to International Markets during the Export Boom," in *The Second Conquest of Latin America: Coffee, Henequen and Oil During the Export Boom, 1850–1930*, Steven Topik and Allen Wells, eds., 1–36; Casey Walsh and Elizabeth Ferry, "Introduction: Production, Power and Place" in *The Social Relations of Mexican Commodities: Production, Power, and Place*, Casey Walsh et al., eds., 19–54; Arturo Warman, *La Historia de un Bastardo: Maíz y Capitalismo*; Eric Wolf, *Europe and the People without History.*

9. Aboites, *Irrigación Revolucionaria;* Maria Eugenia Anguiano, *Agricultura y Migración en el Valle de Mexicali;* Foley, *White Scourge;* Milo Kearney and Anthony Knopp, *Boom and Bust: The Historical Cycles of Matamoros and Brownsville;* Dorothy Pierson Kerig, "Yankee Enclave: The Colorado River Land Company and Mexican Agrarian Reform in Baja California, 1902–1944"; William K. Meyers, *Forge of Progress, Crucible of Revolt: The Origins of the Mexican Revolution in La Comarca Lagunera, 1880–1911;* Montejano, *Anglos and Mexicans;* Manuel Plana, *El Reino del Algodón en México. La Estructura Agraria de la Laguna;* Weber, *Dark Sweat.*

10. For a review of how the term was used by Max Gluckman, see William Roseberry, "Political Economy and Social Fields," in *Building a New Biocultural Synthesis: Political-Economic Perspectives on Human Biology,* Alan H. Goodman and Thomas L. Leatherman, eds., 75–92; William Roseberry, "Social Fields and Close Encounters," in *Close Encounters of Empire: Writing the Cultural History of U.S.–Latin American Relations,* Gilbert Joseph, Catherine Legrand, and Ricardo Salvatore, eds., 518–523.

11. Susana Narotzky, *Antropología Económica: Nuevas Tendencias.*

12. Wolf, *Europe,* 76.

13. Pierre Bourdieu, *Distinction: A Social Critique of the Judgement of Taste,* chapter 4; Pierre Bourdieu, *The Logic of Practice.*

14. Michael Kearney, "The Local and the Global: The Anthropology of Globalization and Transnationalism," *Annual Review of Anthropology* 24 (1995): 547–65; George Marcus, "Ethnography in/of the World System: The Emergence of Multi-Sited Ethnography," *Annual Review of Anthropology* 24 (1995): 95–117.

15. For an initial presentation of the area studies concept, see Julian Steward et al., *The People of Puerto Rico: A Study in Social Anthropology.* For a discussion of the history and current rethinking of area studies, see David Nugent, "Introduction," in *Locating Capitalism in Time and Space: Global Restructurings, Politics, and Identity,* David Nugent, ed. Authors that have parted with the area concept include: Roberto Álvarez, "The Mexican-U.S. Border: the Making of an Anthropology of the Borderlands," *Annual Review of Anthropology* 24 (1995): 447–70; Roberto Álvarez, *Mangos, Chiles and Truckers: The Business of Transnationalism;* Arjun Appadurai, *Modernity at Large: Cultural Dimensions of Globalization;* Linda Basch, Nina Glick Schiller, and Cristina Szanton Blanc, *Nations Unbound: Transnational Projects, Postcolonial Predicaments, and Deterritorialized Nation-States;* Carmen Bueno Castellanos, *Globalización: Una Cuestión Antropológica;* James Clifford, "Diasporas," *Cultural Anthropology* 9.3 (1994): 302–38; Ulf Hannerz, *Transnational Connections: Culture, People, Places;* Kearney, "The Local"; Marcus, "Ethnography"; Ana Tsing, *Friction: An Ethnography of Global Connections.* For an earlier statement of global connectivity, see Wolf, *Europe,* 13–19.

16. Akhil Gupta and James Ferguson, "Beyond 'Culture': Space, Identity, and the Politics of Difference," *Cultural Anthropology* 7 (1992): 6–23; Claudio Lomnitz, "Concepts for the Study of Regional Culture," in *Mexico's Regions: Comparative History and Development,* Eric Van Young, ed., 59–89.

17. Paul Baran, *The Political Economy of Growth;* Arturo Escobar, *Encountering Development: The Making and Unmaking of the Third World,* chapter 3; David Harvey *The Condition of Postmodernity,* part II; Albert Hirschman, "The Political Economy of Latin American Development: Seven Exercises in Retrospection," *Latin American Research*

Review 22.3 (1987): 7–36; Victor Urquidi, *Otro Siglo Perdido. Las Políticas de Desarrollo en América Latina (1930–2005)*.

18. Escobar, *Encountering Development*; James Ferguson, *The Anti-Politics Machine: "Development," Depoliticization, and Bureaucratic Power in Lesotho*; Akhil Gupta, *Postcolonial Developments: Agriculture in the Making of India*; Wolfgang Sachs, *The Development Dictionary: A Guide to Knowledge as Power*.

19. Héctor Alimonda, ed., *Ecología Política: Naturaleza, Sociedad y Utopía*; Coronil, *Magical State*; James Greenberg and Thomas Park, "Political Ecology," *Journal of Political Ecology* 1.1 (1994): 1–12; Susan Paulson and Lisa L. Gezon, eds., *Political Ecology across Spaces, Scales and Social Groups*; Richard Peet and Michael Watts, *Liberation Ecologies: Environment, Development, Social Movements*; Thomas Sheridan, *Where the Dove Calls: The Political Ecology of a Peasant Corporate Community in Northwest Mexico*; Susan Stonich, *"I Am Destroying the Land": The Political Ecology of Poverty and Environmental Destruction in Honduras*.

20. David Harvey, "The Nature of Environment: The Dialectics of Social and Environmental Change," *Socialist Register* 29 (1993): 1–51; Mark Fiege, *Irrigated Eden: The Making of an Agricultural Landscape in the American West*.

21. Karl Wittfogel, *Oriental Despotism: A Comparative Study of Total Power*.

22. Ángel Palerm and Eric Wolf, "Irrigation in the Old Alcohua Domain, Mexico," *Southwestern Journal of Anthropology* 11 (1954): 265–81; Ángel Palerm, *Agricultura y Sociedad en Mesoamérica*; Julian Steward et al. *Irrigation Civilizations: A Comparative Study*; Ángel Palerm and Eric Wolf, *Agricultura y Civilización en Mesoamérica*.

23. Robert McCormick Adams, *The Evolution of Urban Society: Early Mesopotamia and Pre-Hispanic Mexico*.

24. Clifford Geertz, *Negara: The Theater State in Nineteenth-Century Bali*; Stephen Lansing, *Priests and Programmers: Technologies of Power in the Engineered Landscape of Bali*; 1991. For a review and critique of the literature, see Brigitte Hauser-Schaublin, "The Precolonial Balinese State Reconsidered: A Critical Evaluation of Theory Construction on the Relationship between Irrigation, the State, and Ritual," *Current Anthropology* 44.2 (2003): 153–70.

25. Aboites, *Irrigacion Revolucionaria*; Lisa J. Lucero, "The Collapse of the Classic Maya: A Case for the Role of Water Control," *American Anthropologist* 104.3 (2002): 814–26; Donald J. Pisani, *Water and American Government: the Reclamation Bureau, National Water Policy and the West, 1902–1935*; Marc Reisner, *Cadillac Desert: The American West and Its Disappearing Water*; Donald Worster, *Rivers of Empire: Water, Aridity, and the Growth of the American West*.

26. Luis Aboites, *El Agua de la Nación: Una Historia Política de México (1888–1946)*; Robert Glennon, *Water Follies: Groundwater Pumping and the Fate of America's Fresh Waters*; Emlen G. Hall, *High and Dry: The Texas–New Mexico Struggle for the Pecos River*; Michael C. Meyer, *Water in the Hispanic Southwest: A Social and Legal History, 1550–1850*; Donald Pisani, *Water, Land, and Law in the West: The Limits of Public Policy, 1850–1920*; Pisani, *Water and American Government*.

27. Victoria Bernal, "Colonial Moral Economy and the Discipline of Development: The Gezira Scheme and 'Modern' Sudan," *Cultural Anthropology* 12.4 (1997): 447–79; Kjell Enge and Scott Whiteford, *The Keepers of Water and Earth: Mexican Rural Social*

Organization and Irrigation; Wendy Espeland, *The Struggle for Water: Politics, Rationality and Identity in the American Southwest;* Eva Hunt and Robert Hunt, "Canal Irrigation and Local Social Organization," *Current Anthropology* 17 (1976): 389–411; Daniel McCool, *Command of the Waters: Iron Triangles, Federal Water Development, and Indian Water;* Paul Trawick, *The Struggle for Water in Peru: Comedy and Tragedy in the Andean Commons.*

28. Aboites, *Irrigación Revolucionaria;* Rocio Castañeda González, *Irrigación y Reforma Agraria: Las Comunidades de Riego del Valle de Santa Rosalía, Chihuahua 1920-1945;* Fiege, *Irrigated Eden;* Tomás Martínez Saldaña, *El Costo Social de un Exito Político;* Evan Ward, *Border Oasis: Water and the Political Ecology of the Colorado River Delta, 1940–1975.*

29. Harvey, "Nature of Environment."

30. Adolfo Orive Alba, *La Irrigación En México;* Philip L. Fradkin, *A River No More: The Colorado River and the West;* Reisner, *Cadillac Desert.*

31. Patrick McCully, *Silenced Rivers: The Ecology and Politics of Large Dams. Enlarged and Updated Edition.*

32. David Barkin, ed., *Innovaciones Mexicanas en el Manejo del Agua;* Paul Gelles, *Water and Power in Highland Peru: The Cultural Politics of Irrigation and Development;* Tomás Martínez and Jacinta Palerm, eds., *Antología Sobre Pequeño Riego [vol. I],* Paul Trawick, "The Moral Economy of Water: Equity and Antiquity in the Andean Commons," *American Anthropologist* 103.2 (2001): 361–79.

33. Vivienne Bennet, *The Politics of Water: Urban Protest, Gender and Power in Monterrey, Mexico* ; Vandana Shiva, *Water Wars: Privatization, Pollution and Profit;* Casey Walsh, "Aguas Broncas: the Regional Political Ecology of Water Conflict in the Mexico–U.S. Borderlands," *Journal of Political Ecology* 11 (2004): 45–60.

34. Susan Michel, ed., *The U.S.-Mexican Border Environment: Binational Water Management Planning;* Scott Whiteford and Roberto Melville, eds., *Protecting a Sacred Gift: Water and Social Change in Mexico.*

35. Ángel Palerm, "The Agricultural Bases of Urban Civilization in Mesoamerica," in *Irrigation Civilizations: A Comparative Study,* Julian Steward et al., eds.; Palerm, *Agricultura y Sociedad en Mesoamérica;* Palerm and Wolf, *Agricultura y Civilización.*

36. Ana Maria Alonso, *Thread of Blood: Colonialism, Revolution and Gender on Mexico's Northern Frontier;* Marjorie Becker, *Setting the Virgin on Fire: Lázaro Cárdenas, Michoacán Peasants, and the Redemption of the Mexican Revolution;* Gilbert Joseph and Daniel Nugent, eds., *Everyday Forms of State Formation: Revolution and the Negotiation of Rule in Modern Mexico;* Florencia Mallon, *Peasant and Nation: The Making of Postcolonial Mexico and Peru;* Daniel Nugent, *Spent Cartridges of Revolution: An Anthropological History of Namiquipa, Chihuahua;* Jeffrey Rubin, *Decentering the Regime: Ethnicity, Radicalism, and Democracy in Juchitán, Mexico;* Mary K. Vaughan, *Cultural Politics in Revolution: Teachers, Peasants, and Schools in Mexico, 1930–1940.*

37. Claudio Lomnitz, "Barbarians at the Gate? A Few Remarks on the Politics of the 'New Cultural History of Mexico,'" *Hispanic American Historical Review* 79.2 (1999): 367–83; Eric Van Young, "The New Cultural History Comes to Old Mexico." *Hispanic American Historical Review* 79.2 (1999): 211–47.

38. Mallon, *Peasant and Nation;* Vaughn, *Cultural Politics.*

39. Alan Knight, *The Mexican Revolution*; Friedrich Katz, *The Secret War in Mexico*; Jane-Dale Lloyd, *El Proceso de Modernización Capitalista en el Noroeste de Chihuahua (1880–1910)*; William K. Meyers, *Forge of Progress*; William K. Meyers, "Seasons of Rebellion: Nature, Organisation of Cotton Production and the Dynamics of Revolution in La Laguna, Mexico, 1910–1916," *Journal of Latin American Studies* 30 (1998): 63–94.

40. William Roseberry, *Anthropologies and Histories: Essays in Culture, History and Political Economy*; Scott Cook, *Understanding Commodity Cultures: Explorations in Economic Anthropology with Case Studies from Mexico.*

41. Alonso, *Thread of Blood*; Nancy Appelbaum, "Whitening the Region: Caucano Mediation and 'Antioqueño Colonization' in Nineteenth-Century Colombia," *Hispanic American Historical Review* 79.4 (1999): 631–67; Marisol De la Cadena, *Indigenous Mestizos: The Politics of Race and Culture in Cuzco, Peru, 1919–1991*; Greg Grandin, *The Blood of Guatemala: A History of Race and Nation*; Jeffrey Gould , *To Die in This Way: Nicaraguan Indians and the Myth of Mestizaje, 1880–1965*; Alan Knight, "Racism, Revolution and Indigenismo: Mexico, 1910–1940," in Richard Graham, ed., *The Idea of Race in Latin America, 1870–1940*; Deborah Poole, *Vision, Race and Modernity: A Visual Economy of the Andean Image World*; Deborah Poole, "An Image of 'Our Indian': Type Photographs and Racial Sentiments in Oaxaca, 1920–1940," *Hispanic American Historical Review*, 84.1 (2004): 37–82.

42. Stephen J. Gould, *The Mismeasure of Man*; Adam Kuper, *The Invention of Primitive Society: Transformation of an Illusion*; George Stocking, *Race, Culture and Evolution: Essays in the History of Anthropology.*

CHAPTER 2

1. Ana María Alonso, *Thread of Blood: Colonialism, Revolution and Gender on Mexico's Northern Frontier* ; Martínez Saldaña, *La Diáspora Tlaxcalteca, la Expansión Agrícola Mesoamericana*; Nugent, *Spent Cartridges of Revolution.*

2. Friedrich Katz, *La Servidumbre Agraria En México En La Época Porfiriana*; William K. Meyers, "Seasons of Rebellion."

3. Barry Carr, "Las Peculiaridades del Norte Mexicano: Ensayo de Interpretación," *Historia Mexicana*, 22.3 (1973): 321–46.

4. Josiah McC. Heyman, "The Mexico-United States Border in Anthropology: A Critique and Reformulation," *Journal of Political Ecology* 1.1 (1994): 43–65.

5. María Eugenia Anguiano, *Agricultura y Migración en el Valle de Mexicali*, 37; Richard Ciolek-Torrello, *Early Farmers of the Sonoran Desert: Archaeological Investigation at the Houghton Road Site, Tucson, Arizona*; Emil Haury, *The Hohokam: Desert Farmers and Craftsmen. Excavations At Snaketown, 1964–1965*; Carlos Vélez-Ibañez, *Border Visions: Mexican Cultures of the Southwest United States*, chapter 1; Martínez Saldaña, *Diáspora Tlaxcalteca.*

6. Rivera Saldaña, *Frontera Heroica*, 23.

7. Philip W Porter, "Note on Cotton and Climate: A Colonial Conundrum," in *Cotton, Colonialism and Social History in Sub-Saharan Africa*, Allen Isaacman and Richard Roberts, eds., 43–49.

8. Donna Guy, "'El Rey Algodón': Los Estados Unidos, la Argentina y el Desarrollo de la Industria Algodonera Argentina, *Mundo Agrario: Revista de Estudios Rurales* 1 (2000);

Allen Isaacman and Richard Roberts, eds., *Cotton, Colonialism and Social History in Sub-Saharan Africa;* Meyers, *Forge of Progress;* Vincent C. Peloso, *Peasants on Plantations: Subaltern Strategies of Labor and Resistance in the Pisco Valley, Peru;* Richard L. Roberts, *Two Worlds of Cotton: Colonialism and the Regional Economy in the French Soudan, 1800–1946.*

9. Robert Potash, *El Banco de Avio de México. El Fomento de la Industria, 1821–1846.*

10. Dawn Keremitsis, *La Industrial Textil Mexicana En El Siglo XIX,* 24–26.

11. Keremitsis, *Industria Textil,* 14; Aboites, *Irrigación Revolucionaria,* 120; Charles Hale, *Mexican Liberalism in the Age of Mora;* Jesus Reyes Heroles, *El Liberalismo Mexicano;* Luis Aboites, *Norte Precario: Poblamiento y Colonización En México (1760–1940).*

12. Isaacman and Roberts, *Cotton, Colonialism,* 5; Roberts, *Two Worlds,* 48–50.

13. Amos Taylor, "Cotton and the Postwar World Trade," *Proceedings of the Eighth Cotton Research Congress* (1946), 20.

14. Keremitsis, *Industria Textil,* 67; Isaacman and Roberts, *Cotton, Colonialism,* 7; Roberts, *Two Worlds,* 50–51; James Daddysman, *The Matamoros Trade: Confederate Commerce, Diplomacy, and Intrigue,* 180.

15. Mario Cerutti, *Burguesía y Capitalismo En Monterrey (1850–1910);* Manuel Plana, *El Reino.*

16. Keremetsis, *Industria Textil,* 36–37, 44, 67–69.

17. Daddysman, *Matamoros Trade,* 154–155.

18. Cerutti, *Burguesía;* Plana, *El Reino.*

19. Plana, *El Reino.*

20. John Coatsworth, *Growth against Development: The Economic Impact of Railroads in Porfirian Mexico;* Stephen Haber, *Industry and Underdevelopment: The Industrialization of Mexico, 1890–1940.*

21. Meyers, *Forge of Progress,* 28, 33, 34.

22. Meyers, *Forge of Progress,* 43–66; Plana, *El Reino,* 193–202; María Vargas Lobsinger, *La Hacienda de "La Concha": Una Empresa Algodonera de la Laguna, 1883–1917.*

23. Meyers, *Forge of Progress.*

24. Meyers, *Forge of Progress,* 116, 186. William K. Meyers, "Seasons of Rebellion: Nature, Organisation of Cotton Production and the Dynamics of Revolution in La Laguna, Mexico, 1910–1916," *Journal of Latin American Studies* 30 (1998): 70.

25. W. D. Hunter, "The Present Status of the Mexican Cotton-Boll Weevil in the United States," *Yearbook of the Department of Agriculture,* (1901): 369–80.

26. Isaacman and Roberts, *Cotton, Colonialism,* 9.

27. In Mexico the river is called the Río Bravo; in the United States it is called the Rio Grande. When referring to both sides of the river, I use both names: Río Bravo/Rio Grande. When I am referring to only one side of the river, I use the name used in that country.

28. United States Department of the Interior, Bureau of Reclamation, Rio Grande Federal Reclamation Project: New Mexico–Texas; *International Cotton Bulletin* 3 (1924–1925): 261, 269; Neil Foley, *White Scourge.*

29. John Turner, *White Gold Comes to California,* 29–31.

30. Kerig, "Yankee Enclave," 480.

31. Kerig, "Yankee Enclave," 481; Carey McWilliams, *Ill Fares the Land: Migrants and Migratory Labor in the United States,* 72–75.

32. Anguiano, *Agricultura y Migración,* 56; Kerig, "Yankee Enclave," 42–127.

33. Anguiano, *Agricultura y Migración,* 75, 77, 118–119; Kerig, "Yankee Enclave," 160; Gerardo Renique, "Sonora's Anti-Chinese Racism and Mexico's Postrevolutionary Nationalism, 1920s-1930s," in Nancy Applebaum, Anne MacPherson, and Karin Rosemblatt, eds., *Race and Nation in Modern Latin America,* 211–236.

34. William Clayton, "What Price Cotton?" *International Cotton Bulletin* 8 (1929–1930): 476.

35. William Clayton, "The Struggle for the World's Cotton Markets," *International Cotton Bulletin* 9 (1930–1931): 349; Mark Reisler, *By the Sweat of Their Brow: Mexican Immigrant Labor in the United States,* chapters 2 and 3; Snyder, *Cotton Crisis,* xvi; United States Department of Agriculture, *1921 Yearbook of Agriculture.*

36. "Recent Expansion of Cotton Cultivation in Southern California," *International Cotton Bulletin* 4 (1925–1926): 365–369; Arno Pearse, "New Cotton Districts in the U.S.A.," *International Cotton Bulletin* 3 (1924–1925): 260–71; Henry Wallace, "The World Cotton Drama," *Foreign Affairs* 13.4 (1935): 546.

37. A. B. Cox, "New Cotton Areas for Old," *International Cotton Bulletin* 5 (1927): 556; Wallace, "World Cotton," 547.

38. Brian R. Mitchell, *International Historical Statistics: The Americas, 1750–1993,* 214; Arno Pearse, "Ceará Cotton: The Irrigation Works of Ceará," *International Cotton Bulletin* 1 (1922–1923): 360–65; Ernest L. Tutt, "Marketing Cotton in South America," *International Cotton Bulletin* 5 (1926–1927): 117–127.

39. Henry Richards, *Cotton and the A.A.A;* "World's Cotton Production 1927–1928," *International Cotton Bulletin* 6 (1927–1928): 650; "The United States Cotton Problem," *International Cotton Bulletin* 17 (1938–1939): 37–39.

40. Aboites, *Irrigación Revolucionaria,* 41; Ignacio López Bancalari, *Work Done by the Mexican Government in the Execution of Water Works,* 17–53; Adolfo Orive Alba, *La Irrigación En México,* 73.

41. Kerig, "Yankee Enclave," 46, 58–60; Worster, *Rivers of Empire,* 208.

42. Norris Hundley Jr., *Dividing the Waters: A Century of Controversy between the United States and Mexico,* 21–30; Jorge L. Tamayo, "Las Aguas Internacionales del Norte de México y el Tratado de 1944," *El Trimestre Económico* 12.47 (1945): 469.

43. Javier Sánchez Mejorada, *Obra Social de la Comisión Nacional de Irrigación,* 6.

44. Fortunato Dozal, "La Irrigación En México," *Estudios Publicados en los Números 9 y 10 del Volumen 1 de la Revista Mexicana de Ingeniería y Arquitectura,* 2, 5.

45. Hundley Jr., *Dividing the Waters,* 38–40.

CHAPTER 3

1. Alan Knight, "Popular Culture and the Revolutionary State in Mexico, 1910–1940," *Hispanic American Historical Review* 74.3 (1994): 398.

2. Arturo Escobar, *Encountering Development: The Making and Unmaking of the Third World;* James Ferguson, *The Anti-Politics Machine: "Development," Depoliticization, and Bureaucratic Power in Lesotho.*

3. Escobar, *Encountering Development,* 23–24.

4. Stacey Leigh Pigg, "Constructing Social Categories through Place: Social Representations and Development in Nepal," *Comparative Studies in Society and History* 34.3 (1992): 491–513.

5. M. P. Cowen and R. W. Shenton, *Doctrines of Development,* 116.

6. Kerig, "Yankee Enclave," 132.

7. Lowell Blaisdell, *The Desert Revolution: Baja California, 1911;* Dirk W. Raat, *Revoltosos: Mexico's Rebels in the United States, 1903–1934;* Douglas Lawrence Taylor, *La Campaña Magonista de 1911 en Baja California: El Apogeo del Partido Liberal Mexicano.*

8. Kerig, "Yankee Enclave," 144.

9. Kerig, "Yankee Enclave," 140–147.

10. Álvaro Obregón, cited in Arnaldo Córdova, *La Política de Masas del Cardenismo,* 277.

11. Córdova, *Política de Masas,* 278.

12. Andrés Molina Enríquez, *Los Grandes Problemas Nacionales,* 239–77.

13. Roberto Gayol, *Dos Problemas de Vital Importancia para México. La Colonización y la Irrigación.*

14. Abdiel Oñate, *Banqueros y hacendados.*

15. Orive Alba, *Irrigación,* 61–63.

16. "Mexico," *International Cotton Bulletin* 1 (1922–1923): 399; Kerig, "Yankee Enclave," 202–237; "Mexican Cotton," *International Cotton Bulletin* 2 (1923–1924): 399.

17. Lawrence Cardoso, "La Repatriación de Braceros en la Epoca de Obregón: 1920–1923," *Historia Mexicana* 26.4 (1977): 576–95; "Sociedad to Obregón" (11-6-22), Archivo General de la Nación, Mexico (hereafter AGN), Ramo Presidentes, Obregón/Calles, 803-A-31; "Memorandum," AGN, Obregón/Calles, 823-O-4; "Obregón to Ferrocarriles Nacionales," AGN, Obregón/Calles, 823-O-4; "Obregón to Madero," AGN, Obregón/Calles, 823-O-4.

18. "Obregón to Santa Ana Almada Jr," AGN, Obregón/Calles, 823-O-4; Benvenutti, "Informe," AGN, Obregón/Calles, 823-O-4.

19. "Sifuentes to Obregón," AGN, Obregón/Calles, 823-O-4; "Obregón to Aduana, Ciudad Juarez," AGN, Obregón/Calles, 823-O-4.

20. "Obregón to the Departamento de Salubridad Pública" (11-22-23), AGN, Obregón/Calles, 823-O-4; "Gómez to Obregón" (12-4-23), AGN, Obregón/Calles, 823-O-4; "León to Obregón" (4-11-25), AGN, Obregón/Calles, 823-O-4; Manuel Gamio, "Sugestiones Sobre la Colonización de los Territorios," Archivo Historico de la Secretaría de Educación Pública (hereafter SEP), Instituto de Orientación Socialista, 5382/13.

21. "Estudio Presentado por el Presidente de la Junta, Gustavo P. Serrano" (7-8-24), Archivo Plutarco Elias Calles (hereafter PEC), Caja 74, Expediente 5361, 1/13.

22. Ignacio López Bancalari, *Work Done by the Mexican Government in the Execution of Water Works,* 10–11; Aboites, *Irrigación Revolucionaria,* 34.

23. Aboites, *Irrigación Revolucionaria,* 28; López Bancalari, *Work Done,* 14.

24. CNI, "La Labor del Colono en los Sistemas de Riego," *Irrigación en México* 1.4 (1930): 8.

25. Aboites, *Irrigación Revolucionaria,* 11, 23.

26. CNI, "La Labor," 11.

27. CNI, "La Política Agrícola de la Comisión," *Irrigación en México* 2.4 (1931): 293; CNI, "La Labor," 10–11; Arturo Warman, *El Campo Mexicano en el Siglo XX,* 61.

28. CNI, "La Labor," 11; CNI, "Ley Federal De Colonización," *Irrigación en México* 1.5/6 (1930): 90.

29. CNI, "La Labor," 10.

30. CNI, "Política Agrícola," 294; CNI, "La Labor," 12.

31. Nugent, *Spent Cartridges.*

32. CNI, *Estudio Agrícola y Económico, Sistema de Riego "Río Salado,"* 151–153.

33. CNI, *Estudio Agrícola,* 12.

34. Aboites, *Irrigación Revolucionaria,* 35.

35. CNI, *Estudio Agrícola,* 14–15.

36. Alejandro Brambila, "Estudio Agrícola del Proyecto de Riego de Santa Gertrudis, Tamaulipas," 22–23.

37. Roberto Quiros Martínez, "Tamaulipas: Sus Elementos De Riqueza," *Irrigación en México* 5.3 (1932): 248.

38. Alonso, *Thread of Blood;* Casey Walsh, "Eugenic Acculturation: Manuel Gamio, Migration Studies, and the Anthropology of Development in Mexico," *Latin American Perspectives* 31.5 (2004): 118–145.

39. López Bancalari, *Works Done,* 37.

40. Moisés Rangel, "La Colonización de los Sistemas Nacionales de Riego," *Irrigación en México* 2.6 (1931): 526.

41. CNI, *Estudio Agrícola,* 201.

42. CNI, "Nuestro Concepto de la Colonización" *Irrigación en México* 2.5 (1931): 390.

43. Jose D. Pazuengo, "La Cooperativa Agrícola dentro de Los Sistemas Nacionales de Riego," *Irrigación en México* 2.6 (1931): 536–38; CNI, *Estudio Agrícola,* 141–149.

44. CNI, "Nuestro Concepto," 390–91.

45. Adolfo Orive Alba, *Ciudades Agrícolas,* 6–7.

46. Orive Alba, *Ciudades Agrícolas,* 11.

47. Brambila, "Casas," 34–35.

48. Manuel Gamio, *Mexican Immigration to the United States: A Study of Human Migration and Adjustment;* Manuel Gamio, *The Mexican Immigrant: His Life Story;* Walsh, "Eugenic Acculturation"; CNI, *Estudio Agrícola,* 181; Manuel Gamio, *Hacía un México Nuevo: Problemas Sociales,* 127.

49. Gamio, *Hacia,* 72, 76.

50. Orive Alba, *Ciudades Agrícolas,* 7, 13.

51. James Scott, *Seeing Like a State: How Certain Schemes to Improve the Human Condition Have Failed.*

52. Fausto, interview with author, Colónia Anáhuac, Tamaulipas, 1998.

53. Rangel, "La Colonización."

54. Francisco Vázquez del Mercado, "Irrigation in Mexico" *Bulletin of the Pan American Union* 71.3 (1937): 264.

55. Lorena, interview with author, Valle Hermoso, Tamaulipas, 1997.

56. Mexico. Secretaría de Agricultura y Fomento, *Estadisticas Sobre Algodón, Decenio 1925–1934,* 35; Laura, interview with author, Valle Hermoso, Tamaulipas, 1998; Fausto, interview with author, Poblado Anáhuac, Tamaulipas, 1998.

57. Rangel, "La Colonización," 526; "Sousa to Consejo," Archivo Histórico de la Secretaría de Relaciones Exteriores, México (hereafter SRE), "Gobernación," IV-577-5.

58. Orive Alba, *Ciudades Agrícolas,* 29; Orive Alba, *Irrigación,* 70–73.

59. Michael Omi and Howard Winant, *Racial Formation in the United States: From the 1960s to the 1980s.*

CHAPTER 4

1. Octavio Herrera Pérez, "Del Señorío a la Posrevolución. Evolución Histórica de una Hacienda en el Noreste de México: El Caso de la Sauteña," *Historia Mexicana* 63.1 (1993): 5–7; 43; Carlos Martínez Cerda, *El Algodón en la Región de Matamoros, Tamaulipas,* 2–25; Oscar Rivera Saldaña, *Frontera Heróica I Colonización del Noreste de México (1748–1821);* Milo Kearney and Anthony Knopp, *Boom and Bust: The Historical Cycles of Matamoros and Brownsville,* 7–25.

2. Compañía Agrícola del Río Bravo, S. A., *Constitución de la Cía Agrícola del Río Bravo,* 186–191.

3. Compañía, *Constitución,* 137, 228–230; John M. Hart, *Revolutionary Mexico: The Coming and Process of the Mexican Revolution,* 105–128.

4. J. L. Allhands, *Gringo Builders,* 114; Hart, *Revolutionary Mexico,* 115–117; Kearney and Knopp, *Boom to Bust,* 175, 192; David Montejano, *Anglos and Mexicans in the Making of Texas, 1836–1986,* 96–110.

5. Allhands, *Gringo Builders,* 163–164.

6. Armondo Alonzo,*Tejano Legacy: Rancheros and Settlers in South Texas, 1734–1900,* 17–22. Elisa, interview with author, Valle Hermoso, Tamaulipas, 1997.

7. Herrera, "Del Señorío," 16, 20; Compañía, *Constitución,* 5, 36, 138.

8. Compañía, *Constitución,* 83, 183.

9. Compañía, *Constitución,* 230; CNI, *Estudio Agrícola y Económico, Sistema de Riego "Río Salado,"* 54; Herrera Pérez, "Del Señorío," 22.

10. Herrera Pérez, "Del Señorío," 22–23; Hart, *Revolutionary Mexico,* chapter 5; Aboites, *El Agua,* 105–107; Compañía, *Constitución,* 73–74, 85, 170, 232.

11. Herrera Pérez, "Del Señorío," 19.

12. *Periodico Oficial del Estado de Tamaulipas,* Feb. 25, 1939.

13. Herrera Pérez, "Del Señorío," 31–33; *Periodico Oficial del Estado de Tamaulipas,* March 20, 1937; *Periodico Oficial del Estado de Tamaulipas,* March 24, 1937; "Mexican Cotton" *International Cotton Bulletin* 2 (1923–1924): 399.

14. "Anglo" is the word used by the inhabitants of the region to refer to white, non-Mexicans. "Anglo" and "Anglo-Saxon" do not refer to those Northern European groups, and people of German, Irish, and many other extractions are called "Anglo" for their whiteness.

15. *Brownville Herald,* October 23, 1935; *Brownville Herald,* September 13, 1943; "The Rapid Development of Texas: Its Irrigation Possibilities," *International Cotton Bulletin* 4 (1925–1926): 549; *Brownsville Herald,* September 28, 1936.

16. *International Cotton Bulletin* 3 (1924): 269; USDI, *Rio Grande Federal Reclamation Project: New Mexico-Texas;* Reisner, *Cadillac Desert;* Elwood Mead, "Making the American Desert Bloom," *Current History* 31 (1929): 123–32.

17. George Coalson, *The Development of the Migratory Farm Labor System in Texas: 1900–1954;* Foley, *White Scourge;* McWilliams, *Ill Fares the Land;* Selden Menefee, *Mexican*

Migratory Workers of South Texas; Montejano, *Anglos and Mexicans;* Harry Schwartz, *Seasonal Farm Labor in the United States: With Special Reference to Hired Workers in Fruit and Vegetable and Sugar-Beet Production,* chapter 1.

18. United States National Archives, Department of State (hereafter USNA), "Diversion of Waters of Rio Grande in Lower Valley," 711.1216A/528; USNA, "Report on Preliminary Investigations for Flood Control Lower Rio Grande Valley, Texas, 1931," 711.1216A/352.

19. McWilliams, *Ill Fares the Land; Brownsville Herald,* December 21, 1937; *Brownsville Herald,* January 23, 1938; *Brownsville Herald,* May 18, 1936.

20. Montejano, *Anglos and Mexicans,* 109; Kearney and Knopp, *Boom and Bust,* 194.

21. Alonzo, *Tejano Legacy.*

22. The town of Reynosa had only 2107 people, with 4281 inhabiting the countryside (Mexico, Department de Estadistica Nacional, "Censo General de Habitantes, Estado de Tamaulipas," *Quarto Censo de Población*). By 1930 the city of Matamoros had 9733 inhabitants, and the rural area had 15,222. In 1930 the city of Reynosa had only 4840 inhabitants, but the rural population density was the same as Matamoros, with a few settlements numbering above 250 inhabitants (Mexico, Secretaría de Economía Nacional. Dirección General de Estadísticas, "Tamaulipas," *Quinto Censo de Poblacion*).

23. Mexico, Departamento de Estadística Nacional, "Censo General de Habitantes, Estado de Tamaulipas," *Cuarto Censo de Población.*

24. Manuel Teran, *Agua, Tierra, Hombre: Semblanza de Eduardo Chávez,* 54; *Periódico Oficial del Estado de Tamaulipas,* February 23, 1944; *Periódico Oficial del Estado de Tamaulipas,* June 14, 1944.

25. Arturo Alvarado Mendoza, *El Portesgilismo en Tamaulipas: Estudio Sobre la Constitución De La Autoridád En El México Posrevolucionario,* "Anexo Estadístico, Cuadro III"; *Periódico Oficial del Estado de Tamaulipas,* July 12, 1944; *Periódico Oficial del Estado de Tamaulipas,* July 16, 1941.

26. *Periódico Oficial del Estado de Tamaulipas,* July 27, 1938. For a discusión of land tenure in the region, see: CNI., *Estudio Agrícola y Económico, Sistema de Riego "Río Salado,"* 149–155.

27. *Periódico Oficial del Estado de Tamaulipas,* January 4, 1939; "Gómez to Cárdenas" (3-5-37), AGN, Cárdenas, 404.1/206.

28. "Gómez to Cárdenas" (3-5-37).

29. Archivo Histórico de la Secretaría de Educación Pública, México (hereafter SEP), IV/161(IV-14)/20176.

30. *Periódico Oficial del Estado de Tamaulipas,* July 28, 1938.

31. *Periódico Oficial del Estado de Tamaulipas,* October 12, 1940.

32. *Periódico Oficial del Estado de Tamaulipas,* October 10, 1936.

33. Mexico, Secretaría de Agricultura y Fomento (SAF), *Estadísticas sobre Algodón, Decenio 1925–1934,* 14–18. Statistics on cotton production in Matamoros must, like all statistics from this period in Mexico, be treated with suspicion. The methods of collecting data were often haphazard, and always selective. Reliable production statistics are especially difficult to attain because producers were eager to avoid paying taxes on their product and income. Furthermore, given the porous nature of the border, and the different price regimes on each side, contraband has always been quite common in the region. For

scattered reports on Mexican cotton production, see *The International Cotton Bulletin* 1923–1939.

34. These calculations were made with the statistics provided for the *municipios* of Reynosa and Matamoros, Tamaulipas, in the Mexican censuses of 1920 and 1930: Mexico, Departamento de Estadística Nacional, "Censo General de Habitantes, Estado de Tamaulipas," *Cuarto Censo de Población;* Mexico, Secretaría de Economía Nacional, Dirección General de Estadísticas, "Tamaulipas," *Quinto Censo de Población.*

35. Terán, *Agua, Tierra, Hombre,* 19. Even the absentee landlord of La Sauteña insisted on sharecropping relations with those on its land (Herrera, "Del Señorio," 28).

36. Jane-Dale Lloyd, *Cinco Ensayos Sobre Cultura Material de Rancheros y Medieros del Noroeste de Chihuahua, 1886–1910,* 4.

37. Terán, *Agua, Tierra, Hombre,* 19.

38. *Brownsville Herald,* January 13, 1936.

39. *Periódico Oficial del Estado de Tamaulipas,* January 7, 1939; *Periódico Oficial del Estado de Tamaulipas,* October 12, 1940.

40. Alvarado, *El Portesgilismo,* 148.

41. Martínez Cerda, *El Algodón.*

42. CNI, *Estudio Agrícola,* 55.

43. *Periódico Oficial del Estado de Tamaulipas,* January 7, 1939.

44. "El Goliat," SEP, IV/161(IV-14)/20175.

45. CNI, *Estudio Agrícola,* 152.

46. Oscar Rivera Saldaña, *Los Longoria; Trabajo, Dedicación y Triunfo; Periódico Oficial del Estado de Tamaulipas,* March 29, 1939; Alvarado, *El Portesgilismo,* 148.

47. Oscar Rivera Saldaña, *Historia del PRI en Matamoros: Semblanza de Sus Políticos de 1924 a 1947,* 17–18; "Measures Taken for Combatting the Pink Bollworm, and Data Relating to Cotton Growing and Harvesting, in the Matamoros, Mexico, Consular District," USNA, 800.612/102: 591; "Report on the 1927 Journey through the USA Cotton Belt," *International Cotton Bulletin* 6 (1927): 27; *Brownsville Herald,* January 13, 1936.

48. Rivera, *Los Longoria.*

49. Herrera, "Del Señorio," 28.

50. Alvarado, *El Portesgilismo,* Tabla I, Cuadro III.

51. Alvarado, *El Portesgilismo,* 149.

52. Alvarado, *El Portesgilismo,* 149; Rivera, *Historia del PRI,* 41–45.

53. Alvarado, *El Portesgilismo,* 150; "Report on the 1927 Journey," 27.

CHAPTER 5

1. Fernando Henrique Cardoso and Enzo Faletto, Dependency and Development in Latin America, CEPAL, Economic Survey of Latin America, 1949; Rosemary Thorpe, ed., *Latin America in the 1930s: The Role of the Periphery in World Crises.* On Mexico: Enrique Cárdenas, *La Industrialización Mexicana Durante la Gran Depresión;* Enrique Cárdenas, "La Política Económica en la Época de Cárdenas," *El Trimestre Económico* 60.239 (1993): 675–97; E. V. K. Fitzgerald, "Restructuring through the Depression: The State and Capital Accumulation in Mexico, 1925–1940," in *Latin America in the 1930s: The Role of the Periphery in World Crises,* Rosemary Thorpe, ed.; Stephen Haber, *Industry and Underdevelopment: The Industrialization of Mexico, 1890–1940,* chapter 9; Friedrich

Schuler, *Mexico between Hitler and Roosevelt: Mexican Foreign Relations in the Age of Lázaro Cárdenas, 1934–1940.*

2. Cynthia Hewitt de Alcantara, *Modernizing Mexican Agriculture: Socioeconomic Implications of Technological Change, 1940–1970;* Warman, *El Campo Mexicano.*

3. Antonio Gramsci, *Selections from the Prison Notebooks,* Quintin Hoare and Geoffrey Nowell Smith, eds. and trans., 177–178.

4. Snyder, *Cotton Crisis,* chapter 3; Richards, *Cotton and the A.A.A,* 12.

5. The "new countries" were those that had responded to the favorable conditions after World War I to begin, or dramatically increase, production of cotton: Argentina, Australia, and Turkey, for example.

6. Henry Wallace, "The World Cotton Drama," *Foreign Affairs* 13.4 (1935): 543–56; William Clayton, "Our National Cotton Policy," *International Cotton Bulletin* 12 (1933–1934): 452; Richards, *Cotton and the A.A.A.,* 16–17; Alston Garside, "Domination of American Cotton Threatened," *International Cotton Bulletin* 9 (1930–1931): 355.

7. Mexico, Secretaría de Agricultura y Fomento, *Estadísticas Sobre Algodón, Decenio 1925–1934,* 8–9.

8. "Brownsville, Consulado," SRE, 30-29-278; "Informe Comercial Feb 1932," SRE, 30-29-278; Mexico, Secretaría de Agricultura y Fomento, *Estadísticas Sobre Algodón,* 8; Rivera, *Historia del PRI.*

9. "J. F. Brittingham to Clark," Archivo Histórico "Juan Agustín de Espinoza, S.J.," Universidad Iberoamericana, Torreón, Coahuila, México, Fondo Juan F. Brittingham (hereafter, JFB), #0061605; "J. F. Brittingham to Chandler," JFB, #0067489; "J. F. Brittingham to Clark," JFB, #0068029; "J. F. Brittingham to Chandler," JFB, #0068654; "Testimonio," JFB, #19-0024; "Chandler to J. F. Brittingham," JFB, #38-0306; "J. F. Brittingham to Chandler," JFB, #38-0231; "J. F. Brittingham to Chandler," JFB, #38-0295; "J. F. Brittingham to N. Chandler," JFB, #38-0291; "J. F. Brittingham to Plutarco Elias Calles," (PEC), expediente 173, inventario 726, legajo 1/3.

10. Mexico, Secretaría de Agricultura y Fomento, *Estadísticas Sobre Algodón,* 8.

11. "Olachea to Rodríguez," AGN; Ramo Presidentes—Abelardo Rodríguez, 550/50; *International Cotton Bulletin* 10 (1931–1932): 493; *International Cotton Bulletin* 11 (1932–1933): 329–330.

12. "Memorandum," JFB, #38-0108.

13. *International Cotton Bulletin* 10 (1931): 178.

14. Richards, *Cotton and the A.A.A.,* 1–9, 27, 194–230.

15. Wallace, "World Cotton Drama," 555.

16. United States Department of Agriculture, *The World Cotton Situation: Foreign Cotton Production (Preliminary),* 2–3; Curtis Vinson, "Can America Retain Cotton Leadership?" *International Cotton Bulletin* 12 (1933–1934): 278–80; "Latins Hike Cotton Crop" *Brownsville Herald,* March 10, 1937.

17. Every year five or ten thousand bales of cotton were imported into Mexico—except for 1933, when 35,825 bales were introduced into the country. Exports in 1928 were 120,242 bales, which dropped to 22,280 bales in 1930, and then to a low of 11,417 bales in 1933. Exports increased to 33,642 bales in 1934, and to 115,598 bales in 1935 (Mexico, Secretaría de Agricultura y Fomento, *Estadísticas Sobre Algodón,* 99, 143–144).

18. Brian Mitchell, *International Historical Statistics: The Americas, 1750–1993,* 213.

19. Cox, "New Cotton Areas for Old," 554–61; Mexico, Secretaría de Agricultura y Fomento, *Estadísticas Sobre Algodón,* 55–57.

20. Assuming it takes 70 person-hours to pick a bale of cotton, the Valley's 100,000-bale crop required about seven million hours of labor. The harvest would require 14,000 workers to labor fifty 10-hour days (excluding Sundays) over the two-month harvest period. The number of workers at the peak of the harvest period was probably much higher, and often entire families would work and live in the fields.

21. R. Reynolds McKay, "The Federal Deportation Campaign in Texas: Mexican Deportation from the Lower Río Grande Valley during the Great Depression," *Borderlands* 5.1 (1981): 95–99; R. Reynolds McKay, "Texas Mexican Repatriation during the Great Depression," chapter 4.

22. "López Montero to Consul General in San Antonio," SRE IV-86-32; "López Montero to Consul General in San Antonio" SRE IV-104-24; "López Montero to SRE," SRE IV-88-129); "López Montero to Mexican Consul in Hidalgo County," SRE, IV-88-129; "William A. Whalen to López Montero," SRE, IV-88-129.

23. *Brownsville Herald,* September 13, 1929.

24. Mexico's cotton production dropped 58 percent between 1926 and 1927, and that of United States, 28 percent ("World's Cotton Acreage and Production," *International Cotton Bulletin* 7 [1928–1929]: 265, 268–69).

25. CNI, *El Desarrollo de la Irrigación en México. Publicaciones de la Comisión Nacional de Irrigación, Número 10.*

26. "López Montero to Subsecretario de Relaciones Exteriores," SRE, IV-108–61.

27. SRE, Brownsville, Consulado; IV-108–61; "López Montero to Subsecretario de Relaciones Exteriores" (6-20-29).

28. Herrera, "Del Señorío," 34; "Informe, E.A. González, Consulate Inspector, 1930," SRE, IV-28-13; "López Montero to Subsecretario de Relaciones Exteriores," SRE, IV-108-61.

29. In defending their holdings against the *ejidal* reforms that began in earnest in 1934, some landowners in Mexico argued that the *campesinos* soliciting lands were not Mexicans (*Periódico Oficial del Estado de Tamaulipas,* October 28, 1936; *Periódico Oficial del Estado de Tamaulipas,* November 11, 1936).

30. "Report on Preliminary Investigations for Flood Control, Lower Rio Grande Valley, Texas, 1931," USNA, 711.1216a/352.

31. "Saldaña to SEP," SEP, Escuelas Federales Rurales, IV/16 (IV-14)/20217.

32. "Informe Comercial," SRE, IV-635-1.

33. PNR, *La Gira del General Lázaro Cárdenas,* 253.

34. Ibid., 70–75, 219–25, 250–54.

35. Ibid., 74.

36. Terán, *Agua, Tierra,* 27; Lucrecia Chávez y Barragán de Martín, "El Retamal," in *XVII Jornadas de Historia de Occidente: Lázaro Cárdenas en las Regiones,* Luis Prieto Reyes and Carolina Figueroa, eds., 164–208.

37. Martínez, *El Algodón,* 74–83; Herrera, "Del Señorío"; Rivera, *Historia del PRI.*

38. AGN, Cárdenas, 404.1/179; "Informe de Comisión," AGN, Cárdenas, 404.1/206; "Castañeda to Cárdenas," AGN, Cárdenas, 404.1/206; "Contreras to Cárdenas," AGN, Cárdenas, 404.1/206; "Benavides to Cárdenas," AGN, Cárdenas, 404.1/206.

39. "Informe de Comisión," AGN, Cárdenas, 404.1/206; "Villareal to Cárdenas," AGN, Cárdenas, 404.1/206; "Agrarians May Be Given Land," *Brownsville Herald*, January 28, 1935; "Agrarians Get American's Land," *Brownsville Herald*, January 31, 1935; "Repartirán la Hacienda de 'Las Rusias,'" *Heraldo de Brownsville*, January 31, 1935.

40. "Esparza to Cárdenas," AGN, Cárdenas, 508.1/178; "Villarreal to Cárdenas," AGN, Cárdenas, 508.1/178.

41. "Manifestación de Campesinos," *Heraldo de Brownsville*, July 22, 1935; "Gangs Beseige Matamoros," *Brownsville Herald*, July 23, 1935.

42. "Manifestación de Campesinos," *Heraldo de Brownsville*, July 22, 1935.

43. "Tamaulipas Approaches Crisis," *Brownsville Herald*, July 26, 1935.

44. "Will Not Resign" *Brownsville Herald*, July 24, 1939; "Troops to Resist Agrarians," *Brownsville Herald*, July 25, 1935; "Agrarians Still Insist on Action," *Brownsville Herald*, July 25, 1935; "Tamaulipas Approaches Crisis," *Brownsville Herald*, July 26, 1935; "Train Leaves for Border," *Brownsville Herald*, July 28, 1935; "Agrarians See Victory," *Brownsville Herald*, July 28, 1935; "Matamoros Mayor Ousted," *Brownsville Herald*, November 3, 1935; "Protestan los Campesinos," *Heraldo de Brownsville*, July 23, 1935; "Marcharán a Matamoros" *Heraldo de Brownsville*, July 24, 1935; "No Renunciaré" *Heraldo de Brownsville*, July 24, 1935; "Se Resolverá la Situación Hoy en Matamoros, Tamaulipas?" *Heraldo de Brownsville*, July 25, 1935; "Lo Que Dicen los Informes de la Ciudad de México," *Heraldo de Brownsville*, July 25, 1935; "Se Aproxima Hoy la Crisis Política," *Heraldo de Brownsville*, July 26, 1935; "Se Cree Inminente la Renuncia," *Heraldo de Brownsville* July 28, 1935.

45. PNR, *La Gira del General Lázaro Cárdenas*, 74; "Conferenciarán con el Presidente," *Heraldo de Brownsville*, February 22, 1935.

46. Chávez, "El Retamal," 167. "Memorandum para el Señor Presidente de la República: El Programa de Desarrollo Rural de la Compañía Explotadora y Fraccionadora del Valle del Bajo Río Bravo, S.C.P.," AGN, Cárdenas, 521.7/151.

47. "Garza to Cárdenas," AGN, Cárdenas, 508.1/178; "Munguia to Cárdenas," AGN, Cárdenas, 508.1/178; "Villarreal to Cárdenas," AGN, Cárdenas, 508.1/178; "Calles to Cárdenas," AGN, Cárdenas, 508.1/178; "Construirán una Presa," *Heraldo de Brownsville*, October 10, 1935; "Aumenta el Volúmen del Río," *Heraldo de Brownsville*, May 21, 1935; "Aumentará el Volúmen del Río Bravo," *Heraldo de Brownsville*, May 22, 1935; "Hay Alarma en la H. Matamoros," *Heraldo de Brownsville*, May 26, 1935; "Controlaron la Creciente," *Heraldo de Brownsville*, May 27, 1935; "Importantes Obras en Matamoros," *Heraldo de Brownsville*, June 11, 1935; "El Ingeniero G. Serrano en Mats.," *Heraldo de Brownsville*, June 13, 1935; "Another Rise in Río Grande on Way Down," *Brownsville Herald*, May 22, 1935; "Calles' Son to Visit Valley Sunday," *Brownsville Herald*, June 7, 1935; "Mexico Plans Big Jobs in This Section," *Brownsville Herald*, June 11, 1935; "Giant Irrigation Project," *Brownsville Herald*, October 10, 1935.

48. "Flood Control Official Visits," *Brownsville Herald*, August 20, 1935; "Llegó el Subsecretario," *Heraldo de Brownsville*, August 20, 1935; "Las Obras de Control," *Heraldo de Brownsville*, August 23, 1935.

49. "Se Envian los Contratos a Agricultores," *Heraldo de Brownsville*, September 5, 1935.

50. "Embarcarán Algodón por Brownsville," *Heraldo de Brownsville*, July 5, 1935; "Shipments from Mexico," *Brownsville Herald*, July 5, 1935; "Free Zone Is Proposed," *Brownsville Herald*, July 7, 1935.

51. "Informe Comercial," SRE, IV-635-1; "Hoy Inauguran las Obras de Defensa," *Heraldo de Brownsville,* October 15, 1935.

52. "Mexico Plans Water System," *Brownsville Herald,* December 15, 1935.

53. Leticia, interview with author, Mexico City, 1998.

54. "Report on Preliminary Investigations for Flood Control, Lower Rio Grande Valley, Texas, 1931," USNA, 711.1216a/352, p. 11.

55. *Brownsville Herald,* October 10, 1935.

56. "Construirán mas Presas en México," *Heraldo de Brownsville,* September 8, 1935; "Work at Last Gets Under Way," *Brownsville Herald,* December 29, 1935; *Brownsville Herald,* August 23, 1935; Chávez, "El Retamal."

57. "Cardenas May Delay Visit," *Brownsville Herald,* February 12, 1936; "Pizcadores en Huelga," *Heraldo de Brownsville,* July 21, 1935; Lázaro Cárdenas, *La Irrigación del Nordeste: Plan Económico;* México, Secretaría de Relaciones Exteriores, *El Gobierno de México ante los Problemas Sociales y Económicos;* "Peralta to Cárdenas," AGN, Cárdenas, 565.4/346.

58. "Leader Due Later in Day," *Brownsville Herald,* February 17, 1936.

59. Chávez, "El Retamal," 170–175.

60. "Mexico Cotton Acreage Hiked," *Brownsville Herald,* January 13, 1936.

CHAPTER 6

1. Eyler Simpson, *The Ejido: Mexico's Way Out;* Clarence Senior, "The Laguna Region: Mexico's Agrarian Laboratory" *Quarterly Journal of Inter-American Relations* 1.2 (1939): 67–78; Clarence Senior, "Mexico in Transition," *League for Industrial Democracy Pamphlet Series, Volume 6.*

2. Nora Hamilton, *The Limits of State Autonomy: Post-Revolutionary Mexico;* Alan Knight, "Cardenismo: Juggernaut or Jalopy?" *Journal of Latin American Studies* 26 (1994): 73–107; Gilbert Joseph and Daniel Nugent, "Popular Culture and State Formation in Revolutionary Mexico" in *Everyday Forms of State Formation: Revolution and the Negotiation of Rule in Modern Mexico,* Gilbert Joseph and Daniel Nugent, eds.

3. Marjorie Becker, "Torching La Purisima and Dancing at the Altar: The Construction of Revolutionary Hegemony in Michoacán, Mexico, 1934–1940," in *Everyday Forms of State Formation: The Negotiation of Rule in Modern Mexico,* Gilbert Joseph and Daniel Nugent, eds., 264.

4. Adolfo Gilly, *El Cardenismo: Una Utopía Mexicana.*

5. For a similar treatment of the regional dynamics of *cardenismo,* see: Ben Fallaw, *Cárdenas Compromised: The Failure of Reform in Postrevolutionary Yucatán.*

6. Barry Carr, *Marxism and Communism in Twentieth Century Mexico.*

7. James Scott, *Seeing Like a State: How Certain Schemes to Improve the Human Condition Have Failed.*

8. Bernal, "Colonial Moral Economy," 449.

9. Gramsci, *Selections from the Prison Notebooks.* The idea of "trusteeship" is proposed in M. P. Cowen and R. W. Shenton, *Doctrines of Development.*

10. Scott, *Seeing Like a State,* 196; Paul Lucas, "Como Trata La 'U.R.S.S.' de Producir Algodón en su Territorio," *Agricultura* 1.5 (1938): 45–47.

11. "Pizcadores en Huelga," *Heraldo de Brownsville,* July 21, 1935; Lázaro Cárdenas, *La Irrigación del Nordeste: Plan Económico,* 16; México, Secretaría de Relaciones Exteriores, *El Gobierno de México,* 17–18; R. Reynolds McKay, "Texas Mexican Repatriation," 496–509.

12. Cárdenas, *Irrigación del Nordeste,* 13–14.

13. Ibid., 23.

14. Ibid., 24.

15. "Memorandum para el Señor General de División Don Lázaro Cárdenas, Presidente de la Repúblic," Centro de Estudios de la Revolución Mexicana Lázaro Cárdenas, Jiquilpan, Michoacán; Fondo Francisco J. Múgica (hereafter FJM), Caja 3, Expediente 151, Documento 39.

16. Ibid.

17. "Cárdenas to Clayton," Archivo Histórico de CONDUMEX, Fondo Montes de Oca (hereafter CONDUMEX), 326/493, #30332.

18. "Palabras," AGN, Cárdenas, 508.1/490.

19. Mexico, Secretaría de Agricultura y Fomento, *Estadísticas Sobre Algodón,* 1; Lázaro Cárdenas, *Resolución del Problema Agrário de la Comarca Lagunera.*

20. Lázaro Cárdenas, *Ideario Político,* 112.

21. "Clayton to Montes de Oca," CONDUMEX, document # 28195.

22. Enrique Cárdenas, "La Política Económica en la Época de Cárdenas," *El Trimestre Económico* 60.239 (1993): 675–97; Lázaro Cárdenas, *Condiciones Económicas de México.*

23. "Latins Hike Cotton Crop," *Brownsville Herald,* March 10, 1937.

24. "Clayton to Montes de Oca," CONDUMEX, document # 28195.

25. "Latins Hike Cotton Crop," *Brownsville Herald.*

26. Maria Eugenia Anguiano, *Agricultura y Migración en el Valle de Mexicali,* 96–97; "J. W. Stone to Gabino Vázquez," CONDUMEX, document #28141; "Anderson Clayton to Cárdenas," CONDUMEX, 306/493, document #28213; "Montes de Oca to Cannafax," CONDUMEX, 306/493, document #28246; "Anderson Clayton to Montes de Oca," CONDUMEX, 321/493; "Montes de Oca to Anderson Clayton," CONDUMEX, 322/493, document #29867; "Sharp to Montes de Oca," CONDUMEX, 323/493, document #29938; "Montes de Oca to Cárdenas," AGN, Cárdenas, 705.2/26.

27. "Gómez to Cárdenas," AGN, Cardenas, 404.1/206; "Montes de Oca to Cárdenas," AGN, Cárdenas, 705.2/26.

28. "BNCA to Guerra," CONDUMEX, 321/493, document #29766.

29. "Development South of Rio Is Foreseen," *Brownsville Herald,* April 2, 1937.

30. "Early Adjustment of Water Treaty Is Seen by Visiting Official," *Brownsville Herald,* April 1, 1937; "Clayton to Montes de Oca," CONDUMEX, 305/493, document #28194; "Montes de Oca to Clayton," CONDUMEX, 306/493, document #28246.

31. "Clayton to Cárdenas," CONDUMEX, 311/493, document #28692; "Cárdenas to Clayton," CONDUMEX, 326/493, document #30332.

32. CONDUMEX; 311/493, document #28692; "Clayton to Cárdenas" (6-1-37), 4.

33. "Clayton to Suárez," CONDUMEX, 311/493, document #28693; "Cárdenas to Clayton," CONDUMEX, 326/493, document #30332.

34. "Sharp to Montes de Oca," CONDUMEX, 319/493, document #29478; "Sharp to Montes de Oca," CONDUMEX, 354/493, document #32889; "Montes de Oca to Suarez," CONDUMEX, 327/493, document #30377; "Sharp to Montes de Oca," CONDUMEX, 327/493, document #30378; "National City Bank to Suárez," CONDUMEX, 327/493, document #30401; "Montes de Oca to Richardson," CONDUMEX, 327/493, document #30429.

35. "De la Mora to Montes de Oca," CONDUMEX, 318/493, document #294337.

36. CONDUMEX, 355/493, document #32973.

37. Clayton, "Our National Cotton Policy," 444–55; Fredrick, Dobney, ed., *Selected Papers of Will Clayton;* CONDUMEX, 355/493, document #32973; "Agriculture Head Attacks Cotton Sales," *Brownsville Herald,* February 14, 1939; "New Cotton Sale by Mexico Is Seen," *New York Times,* February 12, 1939.

38. L. Cárdenas, *Condiciones Económicas,* 10–11.

39. CONDUMEX; 355/493, document #32973.

40. *International Cotton Bulletin* 17 (1938–1939): 147.

41. Carlos Martínez Cerda, *El Algodón en la Región de Matamoros, Tamaulipas,* 74–85.

42. "Cortes Herrera to Cárdenas," AGN, Cárdenas, 508.1/178; Mexico, Departamento de Estadística Nacional, *Quinto Censo de Población.* "Tamaulipas."

43. "Felipe Vázquez to Cárdenas," AGN, Cárdenas, 565.4/346; "Agrarian Plan Changes Seen," *Brownsville Herald,* February 2, 1936.

44. "Mexico Cotton Acreage Hiked," *Brownsville Herald,* January 13, 1936; "Cárdenas May Delay Visit," *Brownsville Herald,* February 12, 1936; "Peralta to Cárdenas," AGN, Cárdenas, 565.4/346; "BNCE to Cárdenas," AGN, Cárdenas, 565.4/346; "Felix Castro to Cárdenas," AGN, Cárdenas, 565.4/346; "Victoria Road Routed along Original Plan," *Brownsville Herald,* February 20, 1936.

45. "Memorandum para el Señor General de División Don Lázaro Cárdenas, Presidente de la República," FJM, Caja 3, Expediente 151, Documento 39.

46. México, Secretaría de Relaciones Exteriores, *El Gobierno de México ante los Problems Sociales y Económicos,* 23.

47. "Castro to Cárdenas," AGN, Cárdenas, 565.4/346; "Cervera to Cárdenas," AGN, Cárdenas, 565.4/346; "BNCE to Cárdenas," AGN, Cárdenas, 565.4/346; "López García to Cárdenas," AGN, Cárdenas, 404.1/206; "González to Cárdenas," AGN, Cárdenas, 404.1/206.

48. "Múgica to Cárdenas," AGN, Cárdenas, 404.1/1982; "A. Cárdenas to L. Cárdenas," AGN, Cárdenas; 508.1/178; "Cámara de Comercio de Matamoros to Cárdenas," AGN, Cárdenas, 508.1/178.

49. *Periódico Oficial del Estado de Tamaulipas,* July 16, 1938; "Pérez to Cárdenas," AGN, Cárdenas, 403/857; "Pequeños Copropietarios to Cárdenas," AGN, Cárdenas, 404.1/3264.

50. AGN, Cárdenas, 508.1/178; "Gómez to Cárdenas," AGN, Cárdenas, 404.1/206.

51. "Gómez to Cárdenas," AGN, Cárdenas, 404.1/206.

52. "Dam Work on Mexican Side Is Resumed," *Brownsville Herald,* October 10, 1936; "Múgica to Cárdenas," AGN, Cárdenas, 404.1/206; "Cárdenas to Rodríguez," AGN, Cárdenas, 404.1/206, November 18, 1936; "Cárdenas to Múgica," AGN, Cárdenas, 404.1/206; "Informe: Bajo Río Bravo—Organización Agrícola," FJM, Caja 3, Expediente 151, Documento 103.

53. "Gómez to Cárdenas," AGN, Cárdenas, 404.1/206.

54. *Periódico Oficial del Estado de Tamaulipas,* March 20, 1937; *Periódico Oficial del Estado de Tamaulipas,* March 24, 1937; *Periódico Oficial del Estado de Tamaulipas,* June 16, 1937.

55. "Cárdenas to Cortes Herrera," FJM, Caja 3, Expediente 151, Documento 226; "Gómez to Cárdenas," AGN, Cárdenas, 508.1/178; *Periódico Oficial del Estado de Tamaulipas,* February 26, 1938; "Alemán to Cárdenas," AGN, Cárdenas, 565.4/346; "SCOP—Departmento de Obras Hidráulicas: Comisión del Bajo Valle del Río Bravo," FJM, Caja 7, Expediente 300, Documento 2; "Gómez to Cárdenas," AGN, Cárdenas, 565.4/950.

56. "Múgica to Cárdenas," AGN, Cárdenas, 508.1/178; *Periódico Oficial del Estado de Tamaulipas,* October 9, 1937; *Periódico Oficial del Estado de Tamaulipas,* October 13, 1937; *Periódico Oficial del Estado de Tamaulipas,* October 16, 1937; "3870 Acres Land Divided," *Brownsville Herald,* October 17, 1937.

57. Gregorio, interview with author, Río Bravo, Tamaulipas, 1997; Alfonso, conversation with author, Matamoros, Tamaulipas, 2001.

58. Amalia, interview with author, Valle Hermoso, Tamaulipas, 1998.

59. Gregorio, interview with author, Río Bravo, Tamaulipas, 1997; Linda Campbell, *Endangered and Threatened Animals of Texas: Their Life History and Management.*

60. *Periódico Oficial del Estado de Tamaulipas* (10-16-37).

61. "Farmer Shot at Meeting," *Brownsville Herald,* October 19, 1937; "Man Hunted as Slayer of Colony Chief," *Brownsville Herald,* October 27, 1937; "Ayala to Cárdenas," AGN, Cárdenas, 521.7/151; "Castro to Cárdenas," AGN, Cárdenas, 404.1/206; "Avalos to Cárdenas," AGN, Cárdenas, 404.1/206; "Garza to Cárdenas," AGN, Cárdenas, 404.1/206; "Gómez to Cárdenas," AGN, Cárdenas, 404.1/206.

62. "Gómez to Cárdenas," AGN, Cárdenas, 508.1/178.

63. "Cervera to Cárdenas," AGN, Cárdenas, 565.4/346; "BNCE to Cárdenas," AGN, Cárdenas, 565.4/346; "Tension Is Abating," *Brownsville Herald,* February 1, 1938; "Delgado to Cárdenas," AGN, Cárdenas, 565.4/346; "Comite Agraria Matamoros to Cárdenas," AGN, Cárdenas, 508.1/178; AGN; "Idar to Cárdenas," Cárdenas, 508.1/178; "Múgica to Cárdenas," AGN, Cárdenas, 508.1/178; "Gómez to Cárdenas," AGN, Cárdenas, 508.1/178; "Múgica to Cárdenas," AGN, Cárdenas, 508.1/178.

64. "Four Killed in Mexican Outbreaks," *Brownsville Herald,* January 29, 1938; "Rebellion Charge Lodged," *Brownsville Herald,* February 10, 1938; "Mexico Sends Regular Troops," *Brownsville Herald,* February 3, 1938.

65. "Tension Is Abating," *Brownsville Herald,* February 3, 1938; "Cámara Nacional de Comercio de Matamoros to Cárdenas," AGN, Cárdenas, 508.1/178; "Gómez to Cárdenas," AGN, Cárdenas, 508.1/178; "Mexico to Aid Borderlands," *Brownsville Herald,* February 14, 1938; "Victoria Road Workers Added," *Brownsville Herald,* February 4, 1938; "Mexico Work to Give Jobs to 2000 Men," *Brownsville Herald,* February 6, 1938; "Cárdenas to Cortes Herrera," FJM, Caja 3, Expediente 151, Documento 226.

66. "Cárdenas to the Secretaría de Defensa Nacional," AGN, Cárdenas, 565.4/346; "Ladislao Cárdenas to President Cárdenas," AGN, Cárdenas, 404.1/206; "Sociedad Pequeños y Medianos Propietarios to Cárdenas," AGN, Cárdenas, 404.1/206; "Hinojosa to Cárdenas," AGN, Cárdenas, 404.1/206.

67. "Gómez to Cárdenas," AGN, Cárdenas, 404.1/206; "Mexican Land Division Made," *Brownsville Herald,* March 20, 1938; "Gómez to Cárdenas," AGN, Cárdenas, 508.1/178;

"Cámara to Cárdenas," AGN, Cárdenas, 508.1/178; "Asociación to Cárdenas," AGN, Cárdenas, 404.1/206; "Gómez to Cárdenas," AGN, Cárdenas, 508.1/178; "Elizondo to Cárdenas," AGN, Cárdenas, 404.1/206; "Castellanos to Cárdenas," AGN, Cárdenas, 404.1/206; "Arriola to Cárdenas," AGN, Cárdenas, 508.1/178; "Solis to Cárdenas," AGN, Cárdenas, 404.1/206.

68. "Agrarians Ask Cardenas' Aid," *Brownsville Herald,* October 30, 1938; "Ladislao Cárdenas to Lázaro Cárdenas," AGN, Cárdenas, 404.1/206; "Garza Sánchez to Cárdenas," AGN, Cárdenas, 404.1/206.

69. "Another Slain across River," *Brownsville Herald,* December 7, 1938.

CHAPTER 7

1. Ruth Allen, *The Labor of Women in the Production of Cotton;* Emory Bogardus, *The Mexican in the United States;* Ernesto Galarza, "Life in the United States for Mexican People: Out of the Experience of a Mexican," *Proceedings of the National Conference of Social Work, 1929;* Max Sylvius Handman, "The Mexican Immigrant in Texas," *The Southwestern Political and Social Science Quarterly* 7.1 (1926): 33–41; Agnes K Hanna, "Social Services on the Mexican Border," *Proceedings of the National Conference of Social Work, 1935;* Anita Edgar Jones, "Mexican Colonies in Chicago," *The Social Service Review* 2 (1928): 579–97; Robert McLean, "Mexican Workers in the United States," *Proceedings of the National Conference of Social Work, 1929.*

2. Ricardo Griswold del Castillo, "The 'Mexican Problem:' A Critical View of the Alliance of Academics and Politicians during the Debate over Mexican Immigration in the 1920s," *Borderlands* 4.2 (1981): 251–74.

3. Walsh, "Eugenic Acculturation," 118–145.

4. Mercedes Carreras de Velasco, *Los Mexicanos que Devolvió la Crisis;* Lawrence Cardoso, "Labor Emigration to the Southwest, 1916 to 1920: Mexican Attitudes and Policy," *Southwestern Historical Quarterly* 79.4 (1976): 400–16; Lawrence Cardoso, "La Repatriación de Braceros en la Epoca de Obregón: 1920–1923," *Historia Mexicana* 26.4 (1977): 576–95; Abraham Hoffman, *Unwanted Mexicans in the Great Depression: Repatriation Pressures, 1929–1939.*

5. Camille Guerin-Gonzales, *Mexican Workers and American Dreams: Immigration, Repatriation and California Farm Labor, 1900–1939;* McKay, "Texas Mexican Repatriation"; Dennis Nodin Valdés, "Mexican Revolutionary Nationalism and Repatriation during the Great Depression," *Mexican Studies/Estudios Mexicanos* 4.1 (1988): 1–23.

6. Francisco E. Balderrama and Raymond Rodríguez, *Decade of Betrayal: Mexican Repatriation in the 1930s.*

7. Scott Cook, *Mexican Brick Culture in the Making of Texas, 1880s–1980s.*

8. "Informe: Chávez to Múgica," FJM, Volumen 160, Documento 429; "Paredes to Múgica," FJM, Caja 3, Expediente 151, Documento 426.

9. McKay, "Texas Mexican Repatriation."

10. Mexico, Secretaría de Relaciones Exteriores, *El Gobierno de México;* "Unión to Cárdenas," AGN, Cárdenas, 503-11/177; "Rangel to Cárdenas," AGN, Cárdenas, 503-11/177; "Almaguer to Cárdenas," AGN, Cárdenas, 503-11/177; "Robles to Cárdenas," AGN, Cárdenas, 503-11/177; "Santoyo to Cárdenas," AGN, Cárdenas, 503-11/177; "Contreras and Bermea to Cárdenas," AGN, Cárdenas, 503-11/177.

11. Fausto, interview with author, Poblado Anáhuac, Tamaulipas, 1998; Renato Vásquez, "Memorias del Municipio No. 41," *El Bravo,* March 27, 1989.

12. Isidro, interview with author, Valle Hermoso, Tamaulipas, 1998.

13. Fausto, interview with author, Poblado Anáhuac, Tamaulipas, 1998; "Pedraza to Cárdenas," AGN, Cárdenas, 508.1/490.

14. "Castrejón to García Téllez," AGN, Cárdenas, 503.11/3.

15. McKay, "Texas Mexican Repatriation," 532–23; Balderrama and Rodríguez, *Decade of Betrayal,* 148.

16. "Chávez to Cárdenas;" AGN, Cárdenas, 508.1/490; "Pedraza to Cárdenas," AGN, Cárdenas, 508.1/508.

17. "Cárdenas to Subsecretario de Hacienda," AGN, Cárdenas, 508.1/490.

18. "Gamio to Cárdenas," AGN, Cárdenas, 404.1/10302; SRE, Algodón, III-403-1; "Gómez to Cárdenas," AGN, Cárdenas, 606.6/27.

19. Manuel Gamio, "Consideraciones Previas," AGN, Cardenas, 565.4/1940.

20. Elena, interview with author, Valle Hermoso, Tamaulipas, 1998.

21. "Cárdenas to Visit Border on Repatriation Project," *Brownsville Herald,* April 17, 1939.

22. "Beteta to Cárdenas," AGN, Cárdenas, 503.11/3; "Informe," AGN, Cárdenas, 503.11/3-1.

23. "Foglio to Secretario de Gobernación," AGN, Cárdenas, 503.11/3; "Puntos Sobresalientes," AGN, Cárdenas, 503.11/3.

24. Balderrama and Rodríguez, *Decade of Betrayal,* 147–150; "Beteta to Cárdenas," AGN, Cárdenas, 503.11/3; Aboites, *Irrigación Revolucionaria,* 46–49.

25. "Cárdenas to Beteta," AGN, Cárdenas, 565.4/1940; "Cárdenas to Suárez," AGN, Cárdenas, 565.4/1940; "García Tellez to Cárdenas," AGN, Cárdenas, 565.4/1940; "Cárdenas to Beteta," AGN, Cárdenas, 503.11/3; "Cárdenas to Beteta," AGN, Cárdenas, 503.11/3-1; "García Tellez to Cárdenas," AGN, Cardenas, 503.11/3.

26. "Acuerdo," AGN, Cárdenas, 508.1/490.

27. "Decreto," AGN, Cárdenas, 508.1/490.

28. Juan B. Fierro, *Informe Relative a la Utilización Que Debe Darse a las Cortinas Llamadas Rompevientos del Distrito de Riego del Bajo Río Bravo, Tamaulipas.*

29. "Beteta to Cárdenas," AGN, Cárdenas, 503.11/3.

30. "Beteta to Leñero," AGN, Cárdenas, 503.11/3-1; "Cárdenas to SRE," AGN, Cárdenas, 503.11/3; "Cárdenas to SAF," AGN, Cárdenas, 503.11/3; Eduardo Chávez, "Memorandum," AGN, Cárdenas, 503.11/3-1.

31. "Chávez to Cárdenas," AGN, Cárdenas, 508.1/490.

32. "Memorandum, Establecimiento," Chávez, AGN, Cárdenas, 503.11/3-1; "Beteta to Cárdenas," AGN, Cárdenas, 503.11/3.

33. "Beteta to Cárdenas," AGN, Cárdenas, 503.11/3.AGN; "Chávez to Cárdenas," Cárdenas, 508.1/490; "65 Repatriates Cross into Mexico," *Brownsville Herald,* May 17, 1939; "51 Repatriates Go to Colony," *Brownsville Herald,* May 23, 1939; "Repatriation Total Swells," *Brownsville Herald,* May 30, 1939; "Vázquez to Cárdenas," AGN, Cárdenas, 508.1/490; "Josefe to Cárdenas," AGN, Cárdenas; 503.11/3.

34. Elisa, interview with author, Valle Hermoso, Tamaulipas, 1997; Fausto, Marcelo, and Roberto, interview with author, Poblado Anáhuac, 1997.

35. "Gallardo to Gómez," AGN, Cárdenas, 503.11/3-1; "Beteta Explains Re-Colonization," *Brownsville Herald,* August 8, 1939; "Informe," Ramón Beteta, AGN, Cárdenas, 503.11/3.

36. "Mexico Halts Repatriation," *Brownsville Herald,* July 25, 1939; "Beteta to Cárdenas," AGN, Cárdenas, 711/203; "Informe," Ramón Beteta, AGN, Cárdenas, 503.11/3.

37. Jorge, interview with author, Empalme, Tamaulipas, 1998; "Balboa to Cárdenas," AGN, Cárdenas, 656.4/346; Efrén Covian Martinez, *Valle Hermoso, Un Triunfo del Hombre,* 16.

38. "Sindicato to A.C.," AGN, Ramo Presidentes, Avila Camacho, 503.11/1; "Chávez to Cárdenas," AGN, Cárdenas, 503.11/3; "Mexico Planning Another Colony," *Brownsville Herald,* October 11, 1939; "Chávez to Cárdenas," AGN, Cárdenas, 508.1/490.

39. "Chávez to Cárdenas," AGN, Cárdenas, 508.1/490.

40. "Colonia Nicolas Lenín to Cárdenas," AGN, Cárdenas, 508.1/490; "Sánchez to Cárdenas," AGN, Cárdenas, 508.1/490; "Acuerdo," AGN, Cárdenas, 503.11/3; "Memorandum," AGN, Cárdenas, 580.1/490; "Sindicato Unico to A.C.," AGN, Ávila Camacho, 503.11/1.

41. "Liga to Cárdenas," AGN, Cárdenas, 503.11/3-1.

42. "Sagahón to Cárdenas," AGN, Cárdenas, 508.1/178; "Esquivel to Cárdenas," AGN, Cárdenas, 503.11/3-1.

43. "Chávez to Cárdenas," AGN, Cárdenas, 508.1/490; "Chávez to Gallardo," AGN, Cárdenas, 503.11/3-1.

44. "Colonos to Cárdenas," AGN, Cárdenas, 508.1/490.

45. "Sánchez to Cárdenas," AGN, Cárdenas, 503.11/3-1; "Lombardo to Cárdenas," AGN, Cárdenas, 503.11/3-1; "Almazán Party Proclaims Revolution," *Brownsville Herald,* September 5, 1940; "Houses of Almazanistas," *Brownsville Herald,* September 19, 1940; "Cárdenas Warns Almazán," *Brownsville Herald,* October 5, 1940; "Sindicato Unico to Cárdenas," AGN, Cárdenas, 508.1/490.

46. "'New' Valley Is Seen by Cárdenas," *Brownsville Herald,* February 19, 1936.

47. L. Cárdenas, *La Irrigación del Nordeste: Plan Económico,* 23.

48. "Giant Border Development Planned," *Brownsville Herald,* February 18, 1936.

49. "Palabras Pronunciadas por el Director," Eduardo Chávez, AGN, Cárdenas, 508.1/490.

50. "Sociedades de Crédito to Cárdenas," AGN, Cárdenas, 508.1/490.

51. "Sindicato SCOP to Cárdenas," AGN, Cárdenas, 508.1/490.

52. "Rivera to Rivera," AGN, Cárdenas, 503.11/3-1.

53. Ibid.; "Castro et al. to Cárdenas" (4-23-39).

54. "Gallardo to Gómez," AGN, Cárdenas, 503.11/3-1.

55. "Colonia Agricola '18 de Marzo,'" *El Regional,* March 18, 1944.

56. Ibid.

57. "Cristalizando los Anhelos de la Revolución," *El Regional,* March 18, 1944.

58. "Chávez to Gallardo," AGN, Cárdenas, 503.11/3-1; "Parres to Cárdenas," AGN, Cárdenas, 503.11/3-1.

CHAPTER 8

1. Judith Irvine, "When Talk Isn't Cheap: Language and Political Economy," *American Ethnologist* 16.2 (1989): 248–67.

2. Mary Kay Vaughn, *Cultural Politics in Revolution: Teachers, Peasants, and Schools in Mexico, 1930–1940;* Elizabeth Emma Ferry, *Not Ours Alone.*

3. "Development South of Rio Foreseen," *Brownsville Herald,* April 2, 1937.

4. S. D. Myres, "Texas: Nationalist or Internationalist?" *Arnold Foundation Studies in*

Public Affairs 4.1 (1935); "Visit to the U.S. Cotton Belt," *International Cotton Bulletin* 16(1): 78; "Markets Lost to American Cotton," *International Cotton Bulletin* 15.2 (1936–1937): 254–56; "Proposed Subsidy for U.S. Cotton Exports," *International Cotton Bulletin* 17.3 (1938–1939): 309–10.

5. Mexico, Secretaría de Agricultura y Fomento, *Cultivo y Comercio del Algodón en México*, 325.

6. "Report to the International Cotton Advisory Committee," SRE, Algodón, III-403-1; "Ávila Camacho to Gómez," AGN, Ávila Camacho, 523.8/16; Juan M. Rulfo, *El Futuro del Algodón Mexicano*, 286.

7. Julián Rodríguez Adame, "El Algodón. Conferencia Sustentada en la Universidad de Sonora" (1941), 29.

8. "Ortiz to Ávila Camacho," AGN, Ávila Camacho, 565.1/17; "Memorandum de la Central Financiera Algodonera," AGN, Ávila Camacho, 565.1/17; "Gaxiola to Ávila Camacho," AGN; Presidentes, Ávila Camacho, 705.2/188; "Gaxiola to Ávila Camacho," AGN, Presidentes, Ávila Camacho, 523.8/16; "Memorandum para el Sr. Presidente," AGN, Presidentes, Ávila Camacho, 705.2/188.

9. "Fleming to Ávila Camacho," AGN, Ávila Camacho, 565.4/609; "Ávila Camacho to Fleming," AGN, Ávila Camacho, 565.4/609.

10. Francisco Argüello Castañeda, *Problemas Económicos del Algodón*, 62–63, 141–144, 212–214; Tomás Rodríguez Cázares, *Las Colonias Agrícolas 'Anáhuac,' '18 de Marzo' y 'Magueyes' en Tamaulipas: Su Agricultura y Economía*, 22; Mexico, Secretaría de Agricultura y Fomento, *Plan de Movilización Agrícola de la República Mexicana: Cotejo de los Resultados Obtenidos en 1943 y Modificaciones Impuestos para 1944 y Años Subsecuentes*, 10–15; Mexico, Secretaría de Agricultura y Fomento, *Plan de Movilización Agrícola de la Republica Mexicana: Cotejo de los Resultados Obtenidos en 1944 y Modificaciones Impuestas para 1945 y Años Subsecuentes*, 5–6.

11. Tomas Leal Moreno, *Rendimientos del Algodón en el Valle Bajo Río Bravo*, 5; Martínez Cerda, *El Algodón*, 79–83; Argüello, *Problemas Económicos*, 61; Rodríguez, *Las Colonias Agrícolas*, 10.

12. "Empleados Federales," *El Regional*, June 19, 1943; "Habrá Convención Comunista," *Heraldo de Brownsville*, December 20, 1944; "Hoy es la Convención," *Heraldo de Brownsville*, December 24, 1944; "SJOI to Ávila Camacho," AGN, Ávila Camacho, 432/63; "Liga Feminil to Ávila Camacho," AGN, Ávila Camacho, 503.11/1.

13. Cited in Ralph Milliband, *The State in Capitalist Society*, 32.

14. "Longória to Ávila Camacho," AGN, Ávila Camacho, 523.8/16; "Se Organizó la Asociación Algodonera Mexicana," *El Regional*, November 22, 1941; "A.A.M. to Ávila Camacho," AGN, Presidentes, Ávila Camacho, 515.1/117.

15. AGN, Ávila Camacho, 545.22/125.

16. Argüello, *Problemas Económicos*, 137; "Unión Central to Ávila Camacho," AGN, Ávila Camacho, 545.22/125.

17. "Gonzalez to Ávila Camacho," AGN, Ávila Camacho, 513.52/115; "Comite Regional to CNC," AGN, Ávila Camacho, 565.4/1023.

18. "Ruíz Cortines to Ávila Camacho," AGN, Ávila Camacho, 545.22/125; Argüello, *Problemas Económicos*, 142–143; "Gaxiola to Ávila Camacho," AGN, Ávila Camacho, 513.52/115; "Todo el Algodón de Matamoros Congelado," *El Regional*, November 20, 1943.

19. "AAM to Ávila Camacho," AGN, Ávila Camacho, 513.52/115; "Magdaleno Aguilar to Ávila Camacho," AGN, Ávila Camacho, 513.52/115; "Más de 500 Tns de Semilla," *El Regional,* February 12, 1944; Argüello, *Problemas Económicos,* 141; articles concerning the cotton "freeze" filled the pages of the *Brownsville Herald, Heraldo de Brownsville,* and the *El Regional* from February to September of 1944.

20. "Gran Manifestación," *Heraldo de Brownsville,* July 5, 1944; "Matamoros Closed Tight," *Brownsville Herald,* July 6, 1944; "La Vida," *Heraldo de Brownsville,* July 6, 1944.

21. "El Monopolio del Algodón," *El Regional,* June 1, 1944.

22. "Mexico May Confiscate," *Brownsville Herald,* July 7, 1941; "Confiscaran," *Heraldo de Brownsville,* July 7, 1941; "Fijaron el Precio," *Heraldo de Brownsville,* July 9, 1944.

23. "Matamoros May Face New Strike," *Brownsville Herald,* July 10, 1944; "Sigue el Descontento," *Heraldo de Brownsville,* July 10, 1944; " Descontento en la Región," *Heraldo de Brownsville,* July 19, 1944; "Se Esfumó el Nuevo 'Paro,'" *Heraldo de Brownsville,* July 11, 1944; "Protestaron de Nuevo," *Heraldo de Brownsville,* July 28, 1944; "Otra Véz La Pugna," *Heraldo de Brownsville,* September 8, 1944.

24. "Otra Institución de Crédito," *Heraldo de Brownsville,* October 17, 1944; Argüello, *Problemas Económicos,* 145.

25. William Clayton, "The World Cotton Situation," *Proceedings of the First Cotton Research Congress, 1940;* Leslie Wheeler, "Agricultural Surpluses in the Postwar World" *Foreign Affairs* 20.1 (1941): 87–101.

26. Dobney, *Selected Papers,* 9; Argüello, *Problemas Económicos,* 144–145.

27. Amos Taylor, "Cotton and the Postwar World Trade," *Proceedings of the Eighth Cotton Research Congress;* E. D. White, "The Road Ahead for Cotton," *Proceedings of the Eighth Cotton Research Congress,* 11–12; E. D. White, "What's Ahead for Cotton?" *Proceedings of the Eleventh Cotton Research Congress,* 40.

28. White, "The Road Ahead," 10.

29. "Mercados y Productos, Algodón," *Revista de Comercio Exterior* 3.9 (1953): 349–50; "Mercados y Productos," *Revista de Comercio Exterior* 1.2 (1951): 59–60.

30. Dorothy Tercero, "Mexican Irrigation Commission," *Bulletin of the Pan American Union* 80.5 (1946): 265–66; Adolfo Orive Alba, *La Irrigación en México,* tables 10 and 11; "Mercados y Productos, Algodón," *Revista de Comercio Exterior* 2.7 (1952): 268; Martínez, *El Algodón,* 92; Horacio Bervera Alba, "La Producción de Algodón en la República Mexicana," *Revista de Economía* 13.5 (1951): 145.

31. Enrique Gálvez, "La Región Algodonera de Matamoros," *Revista de Economía* 14.5 (1951): 136–40, 146; Martínez, *El Algodón,* 84–85, 117, 171; Luis, interview with author, Río Bravo, Tamaulipas, 1997; Asociación Algodonera Mexicana, *Informe del Desarrollo Agrícola e Industrial de la Región Algodonera de Matamoros,* 6.

32. Martínez, *El Algodón,* 151–156; "El Banco Ejidal Embarga," *La Voz de la Frontera,* August 28, 1948; "Ya No Hay Dinero," *La Voz de la Frontera,* July 21, 1949; "Regresó la Comisión Algodonera," *La Voz de la Frontera,* July 23, 1949.

33. Asociación Algodonera Mexicana, *Informe del Desarrollo,* 1, 39; "Para la Historia de la AAM," *La Voz de la Frontera,* November 12, 1948.

34. Galvez, "La Región Algodonera," 136; "Comisión de Algodoneros," *La Voz de la Frontera,* March 4, 1948; "La Asociación Algodonera," *La Voz de la Frontera,* May 3, 1948; "Actividades de la Asociación Algodonera," *La Voz de la Frontera,* June 19, 1948.

35. Gálvez, "La Región Algodonera," 136; Martínez, *El Algodón*, 40–41; "Ministro de Agricultura," *La Voz de la Frontera*, January 25, 1948; "Fue Terminado," *La Voz de la Frontera*, February 17, 1948; "Se Resolverá," *La Voz de la Frontera*, February 19, 1948; "Utilizase Fuerza Militar," *La Voz de la Frontera*, March 6, 1948.

36. "Revoltosos con Bandera de Socialistas," *La Voz de la Frontera*, July 14, 1948; "Manuel Gil," *La Voz de la Frontera*, July 15, 1948; "Se Esperan Graves Sucesos," *La Voz de la Frontera*, July 16, 1948.

37. Pablo, conversation with author, Valle Hermoso, Tamaulipas, 1998.

38. Manuel Gamio, "Consideraciones Sobre Problemas Del Valle Del Mezquital," *América Indígena* 12.3 (1952): 219.

39. Pablo, conversation with author, Valle Hermoso, Tamaulipas, 1998.

40. "Valle Hermoso Vive Alejado de la Civilización," *La Voz de la Frontera*, March 3, 1948; "Se Cerrarán los Centros de Vicio," *La Voz de la Frontera*, January 26, 1948; "Afluencia de Trabajadores," *La Voz de la Frontera*, June 23, 1948; "Impera la Anarquía en Col. Anáhuac," *La Voz de la Frontera*, June 25, 1950; "Retorno al Gangsterismo," *La Voz de la Frontera*, November 2, 1948.

41. "Los Ánimos Autonomistas," *La Voz de la Frontera*, May 15, 1952; Vidal Covian Martínez, *Valle Hermoso, un Triunfo del Hombre*, 34–36.

42. "Que no Hay Latifundio en Matamoros," *La Voz de la Frontera*, March 23, 1949; "Gran Agitación de los Colonos," *La Voz de la Frontera*, February, 21, 1950.

43. "Colonia 18 de Marzo,'" *La Voz de la Frontera*, March 18, 1949; "Construirán una Compuerta," *La Voz de la Frontera*, February 21, 1950.

44. "Comercio Exterior de México, 1946–1951," *Revista de Comercio Exterior* 2.10 (1952): 375; Guillermo Ramos Uriarte, "La Situación Algodonera" *Revista de Comercio Exterior* 3.11 (1953): 425; "Mercados y Productos," *Revista de Comercio Exterior* 4.6 (1954): 243–44; "Los Negócios en el Mundo. Estados Unidos," *Revista de Comercio Exterior* 3.8 (1953): 298; "Ventas de Excedentes Agrícolas," *Revista de Comercio Exterior* 5.1 (1955): 28; "Mercados y Productos. Algodón," *Revista de Comercio Exterior* 4.11 (1954): 452; "Informe Sobre el Algodón Mexicano," *Revista de Comercio Exterior* 5.6 (1955): 226; Frank Barlow and Grady Crowe, *Mexican Cotton: Production, Problems, Potentials. Foreign Agriculture Report No. 98*, 15, 36–38; "Algodón," *Revista de Comercio Exterior* 5.6 (1955): 243.

45. Julián Rodríguez Adame, "El Algodón," 22.

46. "Algodón. Precios Mundiales," *Revista de Comercio Exterior* 5.10 (1955): 419–20; "Política Algodonera Mexicana," *Revista de Comercio Exterior* 6.6 (1956): 240–41; "Política Algodonera Norteamericana," *Revista de Comercio Exterior* 5.9 (1955): 33–38; "Repercusiones de la Caída del Algodón," *Revista de Comercio Exterior* 5.11 (1955): 438; "Política Algodonera Norteamericana," *Revista de Comercio Exterior* 6.3 (1956): 97; "Notas Sobre el Mercado Algodonero," *Revista de Comercio Exterior* 9.3 (1959): 213; Adalberto Polo Celis, *Matamoros Frente el Algodón*, 63–66; Miguel Manterola, "Los Problemas del Comercio Exterior de México," *Revista de Comercio Exterior* 7.11 (1957): 583.

47. "Comité Consultivo del Algodón," *Revista de Comercio Exterior* 10.6 (1960): 309–10; "Conferencia Internacional del Algodón," *Revista de Comercio Exterior* 10.6 (1960): 294.

48. Lamar Fleming Jr., "Declaración Sobre el Subsidio a La Exportación de Algodón de E.U.A. en 1959," *Revista De Comercio Exterior* 9.2 (1959): 77.

49. Henry Drath, "La Economía de Los Estados Unidos se Beneficia con la Ayuda al Algodón Mexicano," *Revista de Comercio Exterior* 9.5 (1959): 305.

50. "Producción de Sorgo y Maíz en Matamoros," *Comercio Exterior* 14.6 (1964): 401.

51. "Mercados y Productos. Algodón," *Comercio Exterior* 12.5 (1962): 328–30; "Se Espera Mayor Producción," *Comercio Exterior* 9.3 (1959): 133; Polo, *Matamoros Frente el Algodón,* 71; "Solución al Problema Algodonero de Matamoros, Tamaulipas," *Panagra* 3(5): 12–14; Joseph Stevenson, "Auge Algodonero en Centroamérica," *Agricultura de las Américas* 15.5-6 (1966); Robert G. Williams, *Export Agriculture and the Crisis in Central America.*

52. Steven Sanderson, *The Transformation of Mexican Agriculture: International Structure and the Politics of Rural Change.*

53. Jorge, interview with author, Río Bravo, Tamaulipas, 1997.

54. Gregorio, interview with author, Río Bravo, Tamaulipas, 1997.

55. Francisco, interview with author, Río Bravo, Tamaulipas, 1997.

56. Jaime, interview with author, Valle Hermoso, Tamaulipas, 1998.

57. Rodolfo, interview with author, Matamoros, Tamaulipas, 1997.

58. Maria, conversation with author, Valle Hermoso, Tamaulipas, 1998.

59. Don Renato Vázquez, Valle Hermoso, Tamaulipas, 1998.

CHAPTER 9

1. Fausto, Marcelo, and Roberto, interview with author, Poblado Anáhuac, Tamaulipas, 1997.

2. Williams 1977.

3. Marcelo, conversation with author, La Culaca, Tamaulipas, 2002.

4. Harvey 1999; Harvey 2001.

5. Walsh, "Aguas Broncas," 45–60; Vicente Sánchez Munguía, ed., *El Revestimiento del Canal Todo Americano: ¿Competencia o Cooperación por el Agua en la Frontera México-Estados Unidos?* Tijuana: COLEF.

BIBLIOGRAPHY

ARCHIVES

Archivo General de la Nación, Mexico City, Mexico.

Archivo Histórico del Estado de Tamaulipas, Ciudad Victoria, Tamaulipas.

Archivo Histórico de la Secretaría de Educación Pública, Mexico City, Mexico.

Fondo Francisco J. Múgica, Centro de Estudios de la Revolución Mexicana "Lázaro Cárdenas," Jiquilpan, Michoacán, Mexico.

Fondo Juan F. Brittingham, Archivo Histórico "Juan Agustín de Espinoza, S.J.," Universidad Iberoamericana, Torreón, Coahuila, Mexico.

Fondo Luis Montes de Oca, Centro de Estudios de Historia de México de Condumex, Mexico City, Mexico.

Fondo Plutarco Elías Calles, Archivo Histórico Calles/Torreblanca, Mexico City, Mexico.

Rockefeller Archive Center, Tarrytown, N.Y.

United States National Archives, Department of State, College Park, Md.

NEWSPAPERS

The Brownsville Herald, Brownsville, Tex.

El Heraldo de Brownsville, Brownsville, Tex.

El Regional, Matamoros, Tamaulipas.

La Voz de la Frontera, Matamoros, Tamaulipas.

Periódico Oficial del Estado de Tamaulipas, Ciudad Victoria, Tamaulipas.

BOOKS AND ARTICLES

Aboites, Luis. *La Irrigación Revolucionaria: Historia del Sistema Nacional de Riego del Río Conchos, Chihuahua. 1927–1938.* Mexico: Secretaría de Educación Pública / CIESAS, 1988.

———. *Norte Precario: Poblamiento y Colonización En México (1760–1940).* Mexico: El Colégio de México / CIESAS, 1995.

———. *El Agua de la Nación: Una Historia Política de México (1888–1946).* Mexico: CIESAS, 1998.

Adams, Robert McCormick. *The Evolution of Urban Society: Early Mesopotamia and Pre-Hispanic Mexico.* Chicago: Aldine, 1971.

Alimonda, Héctor, ed. *Ecología Política: Naturaleza, Sociedad y Utopía.* Buenos Aires: CLACSO, 2002.

Allen, Ruth. *The Labor of Women in the Production of Cotton.* New York: Arno Press, 1975[1933].

Allhands, J. L. *Gringo Builders.* Joplin, MO: J.L. Allhands, 1931.

Alonso, Ana María. *Thread of Blood: Colonialism, Revolution and Gender on Mexico's Northern Frontier.* Tucson: University of Arizona Press, 1995.

Alonzo, Armando. *Tejano Legacy: Rancheros and Settlers in South Texas, 1734–1900.* Albuquerque: University of New Mexico Press, 1998.

Alvarado Mendoza, Arturo. *El Portesgilismo en Tamaulipas: Estudio sobre la Constitución de la Autoridád en el México Posrevolucionario.* Mexico: El Colegio de México, 1992.

Álvarez, Robert. *Familia: Migration and Adaptation in Baja and Alta California, 1800–1975.* Berkeley: University of California Press, 1987.

———. "The Mexican-U.S. Border: The Making of an Anthropology of the Borderlands." *Annual Review of Anthropology* 24 (1995): 447–70.

———. *Mangos, Chiles and Truckers: The Business of Transnationalism.* Minneapolis: University of Minnesota Press, 2005.

Anguiano, María Eugenia. *Agricultura y Migración en el Valle De Mexicali.* Tijuana: El Colégio de la Frontera Norte, 1995.

Appadurai, Arjun. *Modernity at Large: Cultural Dimensions of Globalization.* Minneapolis: University of Minnesota Press, 1996.

Appelbaum, Nancy. "Whitening the Region: Caucano Mediation and 'Antioqueño Colonization' in Nineteenth-Century Colombia." *Hispanic American Historical Review* 79.4 (1999): 631–67.

Argüello Castañeda, Francisco. *Problemas Económicos del Algodón.* Mexico: Editorial América, 1946.

Asociación Mexicana Algodonera. *Informe del Desarrollo Agrícola e Industrial de la Región Algodonera de Matamoros.* Matamoros, Mexico: A.A.M., 1948.

Balderrama, Francisco E., and Raymond Rodríguez. *Decade of Betrayal: Mexican Repatriation in the 1930s.* Albuquerque: University of New Mexico Press, 1995.

Baran, Paul. *The Political Economy of Growth.* New York and London: Monthly Review Press, 1967[1957].

Barkin, David, ed. *Innovaciones Mexicanas en el Manejo del Agua.* Mexico: Universidad Autónoma Metropolitana, 2001.

Barlow, Frank, and Grady Crowe. *Mexican Cotton: Production, Problems, Potentials. Foreign Agriculture Report No. 98.* Washington, DC: U.S. Government Printing Office, 1957.

Basch, Linda, Nina Glick Schiller, and Cristina Szanton Blanc. *Nations Unbound: Transnational Projects, Postcolonial Predicaments, and Deterritorialized Nation-States.* Langhorne: Gordon and Breach, 1995.

Becker, Marjorie. "Torching La Purisima and Dancing at the Altar: The Construction of Revolutionary Hegemony in Michoacán, Mexico, 1934–1940," in *Everyday Forms of State Formation: The Negotiation of Rule in Modern Mexico,* Gilbert Joseph and Daniel Nugent, eds. Durham, N.C.: Duke University Press, 1994.

———. *Setting the Virgin on Fire: Lázaro Cárdenas, Michoacán Peasants, and the Redemption of the Mexican Revolution.* Berkeley: University of California Press, 1995.

Bennett, Vivienne. *The Politics of Water: Urban Protest, Gender and Power in Monterrey, Mexico.* Pittsburgh: University of Pittsburgh Press, 1996.

Bernal, Victoria. "Colonial Moral Economy and the Discipline of Development: The Gezira Scheme and 'Modern' Sudan." *Cultural Anthropology* 12.4 (1997): 447–79.

Bervera Alba, Horacio. "La Producción de Algodón en la República Mexicana." *Revista de Economía* 13.5 (1951): 145–150.

Blaisdell, Lowell. *The Desert Revolution: Baja California, 1911.* Madison: University of Wisconsin Press, 1962.

Bogardus, Emory. *The Mexican in the United States*. Los Angeles: University of Southern California, 1934.

Bourdieu, Pierre. *Distinction: A Social Critique of the Judgment of Taste*. Cambridge, Mass.: Harvard University Press, 1984.

———. *The Logic of Practice*. Palo Alto, CA: Stanford University Press, 1990.

Brambila, Alejandro. "Casas Para Colonos." *Irrigación en México* 1.2 (1930): 34–37.

———. "Estudio Agrícola del Proyecto de Riego de Santa Gertrudis, Tamaulipas." Unpublished document, 1930.

Bueno Castellanos, Carmen. *Globalización: Una Cuestión Antropológica*. Mexico: CIESAS/Porrúa, 2000.

Campbell, Linda. *Endangered and Threatened Animals of Texas: Their Life History and Management*. Austin: Texas Parks and Wildlife, 2003.

Cárdenas, Enrique. *La Industrialización Mexicana durante la Gran Depresión*. Mexico, D.F.: El Colegio de México, 1987.

———. "La Política Económica en la Época de Cárdenas." *El Trimestre Económico* 60.239 (1993): 675–97.

Cárdenas, Lázaro. *La Irrigación del Nordeste: Plan Económico*. Mexico: Partido Nacional Revolucionario: Biblioteca de Cultura Social y Política, 1936a.

———. *Resolución del Problema Agrario de la Comarca Lagunera*. Mexico, D.F.: Talleres Gráficos de la Nación, 1936b.

———. *Condiciones Económicas de México*. Mexico, D.F.: D.A.P.P., 1937.

———. *Ideario Político*. Mexico, D.F.: Ediciones Era, 1991.

Cardoso, Fernando Henrique, and Enzo Faletto. *Dependency and Development in Latin America*. Berkeley: University of California Press, 1979.

Cardoso, Lawrence. "Labor Emigration to the Southwest, 1916 to 1920: Mexican Attitudes and Policy." *Southwestern Historical Quarterly* 79.4 (1976): 400–16.

———. "La Repatriación de Braceros en la Epoca de Obregón: 1920–1923." *Historia Mexicana* 26.4 (1977): 576–95.

Carr, Barry. "Las Peculiaridades del Norte Mexicano: Ensayo de Interpretación." *Historia Mexicana* 22.3 (1973): 321–46.

———. *Marxism and Communism in Twentieth Century Mexico*. Lincoln: University of Nebraska Press, 1992.

Carreras de Velasco, Mercedes. *Los Mexicanos que Devolvió la Crisis*. Mexico: Secretaría de Relaciones Exteriores, 1973.

Castañeda González, Rocío. *Irrigación y Reforma Agraria: Las Comunidades de Riego del Valle de Santa Rosalía, Chihuahua 1920–1945*. Mexico: CIESAS/Comisión Nacional del Agua, 1995.

CEPAL (Comisión Económica para América Latina). *Economic Survey of Latin America, 1949*. New York: United Nations Department of Economic Affairs, 1951.

Cerutti, Mario. *Burguesía y Capitalismo en Monterrey (1850–1910)*. Mexico: Claves Latinoamericanas, 1983.

Chávez y Barragán de Martín, Lucrecia. "El Retamal." *XVII Jornadas de Historia de Occidente: Lázaro Cárdenas en las Regiones, 26–27 De Octubre 1995*. Compiladores Luis Prieto Reyes and Carolina Figueroa. Mexico: Centro de Estudios de la Revolución Mexicana Lázaro Cárdenas, A.C., 1996, 154–208.

Ciolek-Torrello, Richard. *Early Farmers of the Sonoran Desert: Archaeological Investigation at the Houghton Road Site, Tucson, Arizona.* Tucson: Statistical Research Inc., 1998.

Clayton, William. "What Price Cotton?" *International Cotton Bulletin* 8 (1930): 475–80.

———. "The Struggle for the World's Cotton Markets." *International Cotton Bulletin* 9 (1931): 345–51.

———. "Our National Cotton Policy." *International Cotton Bulletin* 12 (1934): 444–55.

———. "The World Cotton Situation." *Proceedings of the First Cotton Research Congress,* 1940.

Clifford, James. "Diasporas." *Cultural Anthropology* 9.3 (1994): 302–38.

Coalson, George. *The Development of the Migratory Farm Labor System in Texas: 1900–1954.* San Francisco: R and E Research Associates, 1977.

Coatsworth, John. *Growth against Development: The Economic Impact of Railroads in Porfirian Mexico.* Dekalb: Northern Illinois University Press, 1981.

Comisión Nacional de Irrigación (CNI). *El Desarrollo de la Irrigación en México. Publicaciones de la Comisión Nacional de Irrigación, Número 10.* Mexico: CNI, 1928.

———. *Estudio Agrícola y Económico, Sistema de Riego "Río Salado."* Miguel Yepez Solarzano and Alejandro Brambila. Mexico: Editorial "Cultura," 1930a.

———. "La Labor del Colono en los Sistemas de Riego." *Irrigación en México* 1.4 (1930b): 5–8.

———. "Ley Federal de Colonización." *Irrigación en México* 1.5; 6 (1930c): 74–75, 89–90.

———. "La Política Agrícola de la Comisión." *Irrigación en México* 2.4 (1931a): 293–95.

———. "Nuestro Concepto de la Colonización." *Irrigación en México* 2.5 (1931b): 389–91.

Compañía Agrícola del Río Bravo, S. A. *Constitución de la Cía Agrícola del Río Bravo.* Mexico, D.F.: Impresa E. I. Aguilar, 1912.

Cook, Scott. *Mexican Brick Culture in the Making of Texas, 1880s–1980s.* College Station: Texas A&M University Press, 1998.

———. *Understanding Commodity Cultures: Explorations in Economic Anthropology with Case Studies from Mexico.* Lanham, MD: Rowman and Littlefield, 2004.

Córdova, Arnaldo. *La Política de Masas del Cardenismo.* Mexico: Era/Serie Popular, 1974.

Coronil, Fernando. *The Magical State: Nature, Money and Modernity in Venezuela.* Chicago: University of Chicago Press, 1997.

Covián Martínez, Vidal Efren. *Valle Hermoso, Un Triunfo del Hombre.* Valle Hermoso, 1977.

Cowen, M. P., and R. W. Shenton. *Doctrines of Development.* London and New York: Routledge, 1996.

Cox, A. B. "New Cotton Areas for Old." *International Cotton Bulletin* 5 (1927): 554–61.

Daddysman, James. *The Matamoros Trade: Confederate Commerce, Diplomacy, and Intrigue.* Newark: University of Delaware, 1984.

De la Cadena, Marisol. *Indigenous Mestizos: The Politics of Race and Culture in Cuzco, Peru, 1919–1991.* Durham, N.C.: Duke University Press, 2000.

Dobney, Fredrick, ed. *Selected Papers of Will Clayton.* Baltimore: The Johns Hopkins Press, 1971.

Dozal, Fortunato. "La Irrigación en México." *Estudios Publicados en los Números 9 y 10 del Volumen 1 de la Revista Mexicana de Ingeniería y Arquitectura.* Fortunato Dozal, Agustin Aragón, and Ignacio López Bancalari. Mexico: Empresa Editorial de Ingeniería y Arquitectura, S.A., 1923, 1–10.

Drath, Henry. "La Economía de los Estados Unidos se Beneficia con la Ayuda al Algodón Mexicano." *Revista de Comercio Exterior* 9.5 (1959): 305–306.

Enge, Kjell, and Scott Whiteford. *The Keepers of Water and Earth: Mexican Rural Social Organization and Irrigation.* Austin: University of Texas Press, 1989.

Escobar, Arturo. *Encountering Development: The Making and Unmaking of the Third World.* Princeton: Princeton University Press, 1995.

Espeland, Wendy. *The Struggle for Water: Politics, Rationality and Identity in the American Southwest.* Chicago: University of Chicago Press, 1998.

Fallaw, Ben. *Cárdenas Compromised: The Failure of Reform in Postrevolutionary Yucatán.* Durham, N.C.: Duke University Press, 2001.

Ferguson, James. *The Anti-Politics Machine: "Development," Depoliticization, and Bureaucratic Power in Lesotho.* Cambridge: Cambridge University Press, 1990.

Ferry, Elizabeth Emma. *Not Ours Alone: Patrimony, Value and Collectivity in Contemporary Mexico.* New York: Columbia University Press, 2005.

Fiege, Mark. *Irrigated Eden: The Making of an Agricultural Landscape in the American West.* Seattle: University of Washington Press, 1999.

Fierro, Juan B. *Informe Relativo a la Utilización que Debe Darse a las Cortinas Llamadas Rompevientos del Distrito de Riego del Bajo Río Bravo, Tamaulipas.* Mexico: Comisión Nacional de Irrigación, 1943.

Fitzgerald, E. V. K. "Restructuring through the Depression: The State and Capital Accumulation in Mexico, 1925–1940," in *Latin America in the 1930s: The Role of the Periphery in World Crises,* Rosemary Thorpe, ed. Oxford: MacMillan Press/St. Anthony's College, 1984.

Fleming, Lamar Jr. "Declaración sobre el Subsidio a la Exportación de Algodón de E.U.A. en 1959." *Revista De Comercio Exterior* 9.2 (1959): 77.

Foley, Neil. *The White Scourge: Mexicans, Blacks and Poor Whites in Texas Cotton Culture.* Berkeley: University of California Press, 1997.

Fradkin, Philip L. *A River No More: The Colorado River and the West.* New York: Knopf, 1981.

Galarza, Ernesto. "Life in the United States for Mexican People: Out of the Experience of a Mexican." *Proceedings of the National Conference of Social Work.* Chicago: University of Chicago Press, 1929.

Gálvez, Enrique. "La Región Algodonera de Matamoros." *Revista De Economía* 14.5 (1951): 136–140.

Gamio, Manuel. "Consideraciones sobre Problemas del Valle del Mezquital." *América Indígena* 12.3 (1952): 217–23.

———. *Hacía un México Nuevo: Problemas Sociales.* Mexico: Instituto Nacional Indigenista, 1987[1935].

Garside, Alston. "Domination of American Cotton Threatened." *International Cotton Bulletin* 9 (1930): 351–55.

Gayol, Roberto. *Dos Problemas de Vital Importancia para México. La Colonización y la Irrigación.* México, D.F.: CIESAS/IMTA, 1994.

Geertz, Clifford. *Negara: The Theater State in Nineteenth-Century Bali.* Princeton: Princeton University Press, 1980.

Gelles, Paul. *Water and Power in Highland Peru: The Cultural Politics of Irrigation and Development.* New Brunswick, N.J.: Rutgers University Press, 2000.

Gilly, Adolfo. *El Cardenismo: Una Utopía Mexicana.* Mexico: Cal y Arena, 1994.

Glennon, Robert. *Water Follies: Groundwater Pumping and the Fate of America's Fresh Waters.* Washington, D.C.: Island Press, 2002.

Gould, Jeffrey. *To Die in This Way: Nicaraguan Indians and the Myth of Mestizaje, 1880–1965.* Durham, N.C.: Duke University Press, 1998.

Gould, Steven Jay. *The Mismeasure of Man.* New York: Norton, 1981.

Gramsci, Antonio. *Selections from the Prison Notebooks.* Quintin Hoare and Geoffrey Nowell Smith, eds. and trans. . New York: International Publishers, 1971[1928–1935].

Grandin, Greg. *The Blood of Guatemala: A History of Race and Nation.* Durham, N.C.: Duke University Press, 2000.

Greenberg, James, and Thomas K. Park. "Political Ecology." *Journal of Political Ecology* 1.1 (1994): 1–12.

Griswold del Castillo, Richard. "The 'Mexican Problem': A Critical View of the Alliance of Academics and Politicians during the Debate over Mexican Immigration in the 1920s." *Borderlands* 4.2 (1981): 251–74.

Guérin-Gonzales, Camille. *Mexican Workers and American Dreams: Immigration, Repatriation and California Farm Labor, 1900–1939.* New Brunswick: Rutgers University Press, 1994.

Gupta, Akhil. *Postcolonial Developments: Agriculture in the Making of India.* Durham, N.C.: Duke University Press, 1998.

Gupta, Akhil, and James Ferguson. "Beyond 'Culture': Space, Identity, and the Politics of Difference." *Cultural Anthropology* 7 (1992): 6–23.

Guy, Donna. "'El Rey Algodón': Los Estados Unidos, la Argentina y el Desarrollo de la Industria Algodonera Argentina." *Mundo Agrario: Revista de Estudios Rurales* 1 (2000). www.mundoagrario.unlp.edu.ar/nro1/guy.htm.

Haber, Stephen. *Industry and Underdevelopment: The Industrialization of Mexico, 1890–1940.* Stanford: Stanford University Press, 1989.

Hale, Charles. *Mexican Liberalism in the Age of Mora.* New Haven: Yale University Press, 1968.

———. *The Transformation of Mexican Liberalism in Late-Nineteenth Century Mexico.* Princeton: Princeton University Press, 1989.

Hall, G. Emlen. *High and Dry: The Texas-New Mexico Struggle for the Pecos River.* Albuquerque: University of New Mexico Press, 2002.

Hamilton, Nora. *The Limits of State Autonomy: Post-Revolutionary Mexico.* Princeton: Princeton University Press, 1982.

Handman, Max Sylvius. "The Mexican Immigrant in Texas." *The Southwestern Political and Social Science Quarterly* 7.1 (1926): 33–41.

Hanna, Agnes K. "Social Services on the Mexican Border." *Proceedings of the National Conference of Social Work.* Chicago: University of Chicago Press, 1935.

Hannerz, Ulf. *Transnational Connections: Culture, People, Places.* London: Routledge, 1996.

Hart, John Mason. *Revolutionary Mexico: The Coming and Process of the Mexican Revolution.* Berkeley: University of California Press, 1987.

Harvey, David. *The Condition of Postmodernity.* Cambridge: Basil Blackwell, 1989.

———. "The Nature of Environment: The Dialectics of Social and Environmental Change." *Socialist Register* 29 (1993): 1–51.

———. *The Limits to Capital.* London: Verso, 1999.

————. *Spaces of Capital: Towards a Critical Geography.* New York: Routledge, 2001.

Haury, Emil. *The Hohokam: Desert Farmers and Craftsmen. Excavations at Snaketown, 1964–1965.* Tucson: University of Arizona Press, 1976.

Hauser-Schaublin, Brigitte. "The Precolonial Balinese State Reconsidered: A Critical Evaluation of Theory Construction on the Relationship between Irrigation, the State, and Ritual." *Current Anthropology* 44.2 (2003): 153–170.

Herrera Pérez, Octavio. "Del Señorío a la Posrevolución. Evolución Histórica de una Hacienda en el Noreste de México: El Caso de la Sauteña." *Historia Mexicana* 63.1 (1993), 5–54.

Hewitt de Alcántara, Cynthia. *Modernizing Mexican Agriculture: Socioeconomic Implications of Technological Change, 1940–1970.* Geneva: United Nations Research Institute for Social Development, 1976.

Heyman, Josiah McC., "The Mexico-United States Border in Anthropology: A Critique and Reformulation," *Journal of Political Ecology* 1.1 (1994): 43–65.

Hirschman, Albert. "The Political Economy of Latin American Development: Seven Exercises in Retrospection." *Latin American Research Review* 22.3 (1987): 7–36.

Hoffman, Abraham. *Unwanted Mexicans in the Great Depression: Repatriation Pressures, 1929–1939.* Tucson: University of Arizona Press, 1974.

Hundley, Norris Jr. *Dividing the Waters: A Century of Controversy between the United States and Mexico.* Berkeley: University of California Press, 1966.

Hunt, Eva, and Robert Hunt. "Canal Irrigation and Local Social Organization." *Current Anthropology* 17 (1976): 389–411.

Hunter, W. D. "The Present Status of the Mexican Cotton-Boll Weevil in the United States." *Yearbook of the Department of Agriculture* (1901): 369–80.

Irvine, Judith. "When Talk Isn't Cheap: Language and Political Economy." *American Ethnologist* 16.2 (1989): 248–67.

Isaacman, Allen, and Richard Roberts. *Cotton, Colonialism and Social History in Sub-Saharan Africa.* Portsmouth; London: Heinemann; James Currey, 1995.

Jones, Anita Edgar. "Mexican Colonies in Chicago." *The Social Service Review* 2 (1928): 579–97.

Joseph, Gilbert, and Daniel Nugent. "Popular Culture and State Formation in Revolutionary Mexico," in *Everyday Forms of State Formation: Revolution and the Negotiation of Rule in Modern Mexico,* Gilbert Joseph and Daniel Nugent, eds. Durham, N.C.: Duke University Press, 1994.

Katz, Friedrich. *La Servidumbre Agraria en México en la Época Porfiriana.* Mexico, D.F.: Ediciones Era, 1976.

————. *The Secret War in Mexico.* Chicago: University of Chicago Press, 1981.

Kearney, Michael. "The Local and the Global: The Anthropology of Globalization and Transnationalism." *Annual Review of Anthropology* 24 (1995): 547–65.

Kearney, Milo, and Anthony Knopp. *Boom and Bust: The Historical Cycles of Matamoros and Brownsville.* Austin: Eakin Press, 1991.

Keremitsis, Dawn. *La Industrial Textil Mexicana en el Siglo XIX.* Mexico, D.F.: SEP, 1973.

Kerig, Dorothy Pierson. "Yankee Enclave: The Colorado River Land Company and Mexican Agrarian Reform in Baja California, 1902–1944." Ph.D. dissertation, University of California, Irvine, 1988.

Knight, Alan. *The Mexican Revolution,* 2 Volumes. Lincoln: University of Nebraska Press, 1986.

———. "Racism, Revolution and Indigenismo: Mexico, 1910–1940," in *The Idea of Race in Latin America, 1870–1940,* Richard Graham, ed. Austin: University of Texas Press, 1990, 78–107.

———. "Cardenismo: Juggernaut or Jalopy?" *Journal of Latin American Studies* 26 (1994a): 73–107.

Kuper, Adam. *The Invention of Primitive Society: Transformation of an Illusion.* London: Routledge, 1988.

La Compañía Agrícola del Río Bravo, S. A. Mexico: E.I. Aguilar, 1912.

Lansing, Stephen. *Priests and Programmers: Technologies of Power in the Engineered Landscape of Bali.* Princeton: Princeton University Press, 1991.

Leal Moreno, Tomás. *Rendimientos del Algodón en el Valle Bajo Río Bravo.* Chapingo, Mexico: Escuela Nacional de Agricultura, 1943.

Lloyd, Jane-Dale. *El Proceso de Modernización Capitalista en el Noroeste de Chihuahua (1880–1910).* Mexico: Universidad Iberoamericana, 1987.

———. *Cinco Ensayos Sobre Cultura Material de Rancheros y Medieros del Noroeste de Chihuahua, 1886–1910.* Mexico: Universidad Iberoamericana, 2001.

Lomnitz, Claudio. "Concepts for the Study of Regional Culture," in *Mexico's Regions: Comparative History and Development,* Eric Van Young, ed. San Diego: Center for U.S.-Mexican Studies, University of California, San Diego, 1992, 59–89.

———. "Barbarians at the Gate? A Few Remarks on the Politics of the 'New Cultural History of Mexico.'" *Hispanic American Historical Review* 79.2 (1999): 367–83.

López Bancalari, Ignacio. *Work Done by the Mexican Government in the Execution of Water Works.* Mexico: Editorial "Cultura," 1929.

Lucas, Paul. "Como Trata la 'U.R.S.S.' de Producir Algodón en su Territorio." *Agricultura* 1.5 (1938): 45–47.

Lucero, Lisa J. "The Collapse of the Classic Maya: A Case for the Role of Water Control." *American Anthropologist* 104.3 (2002) 814–26.

Mallon, Florencia. *Peasant and Nation: The Making of Postcolonial Mexico and Peru.* Berkeley: University of California Press, 1995.

Manterola, Miguel. "Los Problemas del Comercio Exterior de México." *Revista de Comercio Exterior* 7.11 (1957): 580–84.

Marcus, George. "Ethnography in/of the World System: The Emergence of Multi-Sited Ethnography." *Annual Review of Anthropology* 24 (1995): 95–117.

Martínez, Tomás, and Jacinta Palerm, eds. *Antología Sobre Pequeño Riego [vol. I].* Texcoco, Mexico: Colegio de Postgraduados, 1997.

Martínez Cerda, Carlos. *El Algodón en la Región de Matamoros, Tamaulipas.* Mexico: Banco Nacional de Crédito Ejidal, S.A., 1954.

Martínez Saldaña, Tomás. *El Costo Social de un Exito Político: La Política del Estado Mexicano en la Comarca Lagunera.* Chapingo, Mexico: Colegio de Posgraduados, 1980.

———. *La Diáspora Tlaxcalteca, la Expansión Agrícola Mesoamericana,* segunda edición. Tlaxcala, Mexico: Gobierno del Estado de Tlaxcala, 1998.

McCool, Daniel. *Command of the Waters: Iron Triangles, Federal Water Development, and Indian Water.* Tucson: University of Arizona Press, 1994.

McCully, Patrick. *Silenced Rivers: The Ecology and Politics of Large Dams. Enlarged and Updated Edition.* London and New York: Zed Books, 2001.

McKay, R. Reynolds. "The Federal Deportation Campaign in Texas: Mexican Deportation from the Lower Rio Grande Valley during the Great Depression." *Borderlands* 5.1 (1981): 95–120.

———. "Texas Mexican Repatriation during the Great Depression." Ph.D. dissertation, University of Oklahoma, 1982.

McLean, Robert. "Mexican Workers in the United States." *Proceedings of the National Conference of Social Work.* San Francisco, 1929. Chicago: University of Chicago Press, 1929.

McWilliams, Carey. *Ill Fares the Land: Migrants and Migratory Labor in the United States.* Boston: Little, Brown and Company, 1968[1942].

Mead, Elwood. "Making the American Desert Bloom." *Current History* 31 (1929): 123–132.

Melville, Roberto. "Ramon Beteta y la Repatriación de Mexicanos En 1939." 1997.

Menefee, Selden. *Mexican Migratory Workers of South Texas.* Washington, D.C.: U.S. Government Printing Office, 1941.

Mexico, Departamento de Estadística Nacional. *Quarto Censo de Población.* Mexico: Talleres Gráficos de la Nación, 1928.

Mexico, Secretaría de Agricultura y Fomento (SAF). *Estadisticas sobre Algodón, Decenio 1925–1934.* Mexico: Dirección de Economía Rural, Departamento de Estadística Agrícola, Secretaría de Agricultura y Fomento, 1935.

———. *Cultivo y Comercio del Algodón en México.* Mexico: Secretaría de Agricultura y Fomento, 1939.

———. *Plan de Movilización Agrícola de la República Mexicana: Cotejo de los Resultados Obtenidos en 1943 y Modificaciones Impuestos para 1944 y Años Subsecuentes.* México, D.F.: Secretaría de Agricultura y Fomento, 1944.

———. *Plan de Movilización Agrícola de la Republica Mexicana: Cotejo de los Resultados Obtenidos en 1944 y Modificaciones Impuestas para 1945 y Años Subsecuentes.* Mexico, D.F.: Secretaría de Agricultura y Fomento, 1945.

Mexico, Secretaría de Economía Nacional. Dirección General de Estadísticas. *Quinto Censo de Población.* Mexico: Talleres Gráficos de la Nación, 1930.

Mexico, Secretaría de Relaciones Exteriores (SRE). *El Gobierno de México ante los Problemas Sociales y Económicos.* Mexico: Imprenta de la Secretaría de Reláciones Exteriores, 1936.

Meyer, Michael C. *Water in the Hispanic Southwest: A Social and Legal History, 1550–1850.* Tucson: University of Arizona Press, 1996.

Meyers, William K. *Forge of Progress, Crucible of Revolt: The Origins of the Mexican Revolution in La Comarca Lagunera, 1880–1911.* Albuquerque: University of New Mexico Press, 1994.

———. "Seasons of Rebellion: Nature, Organisation of Cotton Production and the Dynamics of Revolution in La Laguna, Mexico, 1910–1916." *Journal of Latin American Studies* 30 (1998): 63–94.

Michel, Suzanne, ed. *The U.S.-Mexican Border Environment: Binational Water Management Planning.* SCERP Monograph Series, no. 8. San Diego: San Diego State University, 2003.

Milliband, Ralph. *The State in Capitalist Society.* London: Weidenfeld and Nicolson, 1969.

Mintz, Sidney. *Sweetness and Power: The Place of Sugar in Modern History.* New York: Viking, 1985.

Mitchell, Brian R. *International Historical Statistics: The Americas, 1750–1993.* London: Macmillan Reference; Stockton, 1998.

Molina Enríquez, Andrés. *Los Grandes Problemas Nacionales.* Mexico, D.F.: Ediciones Era, 1997[1909].

Montejano, David. *Anglos and Mexicans in the Making of Texas, 1836–1986.* Austin: University of Texas Press, 1987.

Myres, S. D. "Texas: Nationalist or Internationalist?" *Arnold Foundation Studies in Public Affairs* 4.1 (1935).

Narotzky, Susana. *Antropología Económica: Nuevas Tendencias.* Barcelona: Editorial Melusina, 2004.

Nugent, Daniel. *Spent Cartridges of Revolution: An Anthropological History of Namiquipa, Chihuahua.* Chicago: University of Chicago Press, 1993.

Nugent, David, "Introduction," in *Locating Capitalism in Time and Space: Global Restructurings, Politics, and Identity,* David Nugent, ed. Stanford: Stanford University Press, 2002.

Omi, Michael, and Howard Winant. *Racial Formation in the United States: From the 1960s to the 1980s.* New York: Routledge, 1986.

Oñate, Abdiel. *Banqueros y Hacendados: La Quimera de la Modernización.* Mexico: UAM Xochimilco, 1991.

Orive Alba, Adolfo. *Ciudades Agrícolas.* Mexico: Publicaciones del Comité Permanente de la Tercera Conferencia Interamericana de Agricultura, Sección 13a, 1944.

———. *La Irrigación en México.* Mexico: Editorial Grijalbo, 1970.

Palerm, Ángel, "The Agricultural Bases of Urban Civilization in Mesoamerica," in *Irrigation Civilizations: A Comparative Study,* Julian Steward et al., eds Washington, D.C.: Pan American Union, 1955.

———. *Agricultura y Sociedad en Mesoamérica.* Mexico: Secretaría de Educación Pública, 1972.

———. *Antropología y Marxismo.* Mexico,: CIS-INAH/Editorial Nueva Imagen, 1980.

Palerm, Ángel, and Eric Wolf. "Irrigation in the Old Alcohua Domain, Mexico." *Southwestern Journal of Anthropology* 11 (1954): 265–81.

———. *Agricultura y Civilización en Mesoamérica.* Mexico: Secretaría de Educación Pública, 1972.

Paulson, Susan, and Lisa L. Gezon, eds. *Political Ecology across Spaces, Scales and Social Groups.* New Brunswick: Rutgers University Press, 2005.

Pazuengo, José D. "La Cooperativa Agrícola dentro de los Sistemas Nacionales de Riego." *Irrigación en México* 2.6 (1931): 536–38.

Pearse, Arno. "Ceará Cotton: The Irrigation Works of Ceará." *International Cotton Bulletin* 1 (1923): 360–65.

———. "New Cotton Districts in the U.S.A." *International Cotton Bulletin* 3 (1924): 260–71.

Peet, Richard, and Michael Watts. *Liberation Ecologies: Environment, Development, Social Movements.* New York: Routledge, 1996.

Peloso, Vincent C. *Peasants on Plantations: Subaltern Strategies of Labor and Resistance in the Pisco Valley, Peru.* Durham, N.C.: Duke University Press, 1999.

Pigg, Stacey Leigh. "Constructing Social Categories through Place: Social Representations and Development in Nepal." *Comparative Studies in Society and History* 34.3 (1992): 491–513.

Pisani, Donald J. *Water, Land, and Law in the West: The Limits of Public Policy, 1850–1920.* Lawrence: University of Kansas Press, 1996.

———. *Water and American Government: The Reclamation Bureau, National Water Policy and the West, 1902–1935.* Berkeley: University of California Press, 2002.

Plana, Manuel. *El Reino del Algodón en México. La Estructura Agraria de la Laguna.* Torreón: Ayuntamiento de Torreón, et al., 1991.

PNR (Partido Nacional Revolucionario). *La Gira del General Lázaro Cárdenas.* Mexico, D.F.: Partido Revolucionario Institucional, 1986[1934].

Polo Celis, Adalberto. *Matamoros frente el Algodón.* Chapingo, Mexico: Escuela Nacional de Agricultura, 1962.

Poole, Deborah. *Vision, Race and Modernity: A Visual Economy of the Andean Image World.* Princeton: Princeton University Press, 1997.

———. "An Image of 'Our Indian': Type Photographs and Racial Sentiments in Oaxaca, 1920–1940," *Hispanic American Historical Review,* 84.1 (2004): 37–82.

Porter, Philip W. "Note on Cotton and Climate: A Colonial Conundrum," in *Cotton, Colonialism and Social History in Sub-Saharan Africa,* Allen Isaacman and Richard Roberts, eds. Portsmouth: Heinemann Books, 1995, 43–49.

Potash, Robert. *El Banco de Avío de México. El Fomento de la Industria, 1821–1846.* Mexico, D.F.: Fondo de Cultura Económica, 1986.

Quiros Martinez, Roberto. "Tamaulipas: Sus Elementos de Riqueza." *Irrigación en México* 5.3 (1932): 249–72.

Raat, Dirk W. *Revoltosos: Mexico's Rebels in the United States, 1903–1934.* College Station: Texas A&M University Press, 1981.

Ramos Uriarte, Guillermo. "La Situación Algodonera." *Revista de Comercio Exterior* 3.11 (1953): 422–27.

Rangel, Moisés. "La Colonización de los Sistemas Nacionales de Riego." *Irrigación en México* 2.6 (1931): 526–31.

Reisler, Mark. *By the Sweat of Their Brow: Mexican Immigrant Labor in the United States.* Westport and London: Greenwood Press, 1976.

Reisner, Marc. *Cadillac Desert: The American West and Its Disappearing Water.* New York: Penguin Books, 1993.

Renique, Gerardo. "Sonora's Anti-Chinese Racism and Mexico's Postrevolutionary Nationalism, 1920s–1930s," in *Race and Nation in Modern Latin America,* Nancy Appelbaum, Anne MacPherson, and Karin Rosemblatt, eds. Raleigh: University of North Carolina Press, 2003, 211–36.

Reyes Heroles, Jesús. *El Lliberalismo Mexicano.* Mexico, D.F.: Fondo de Cultura Económica, 1974.

Richards, Henry. *Cotton and the A.A.A.* Washington, D.C.: The Brookings Institution, 1936.

Rivera Saldaña, Oscar. *Los Longoria; Trabajo, Dedicación y Triunfo.* 1988.

———. *Frontera Heróica. I Colonización del Noreste de México (1748–1821).* Matamoros, Tamaulipas: Impresiones y Publicaciones, 1994.

———. *Historia del PRI en Matamoros: Semblanza de sus Políticos de 1924 a 1947.* Matamoros: Editorial del Seno Mexicano, 1999.

Roberts, Richard L. *Two Worlds of Cotton: Colonialism and the Regional Economy in the French Soudan, 1800–1946*. Stanford: Stanford University Press, 1996.

Rodríguez Adame, Julián. "El Algodón. Conferencia Sustentada en la Universidad de Sonora." Hermosillo, Sonora, 20 Apr. 1956. Hermosillo: Universidad de Sonora, 1956.

Rodríguez Cázares, Tomás. *Las Colonias Agrícolas 'Anáhuac,' '18 De Marzo' y 'Magueyes' en Tamaulipas: Su Agricultura y Economía*. Chapingo, Mexico: Escuela Nacional de Agricultura, 1945.

Roseberry, William. *Coffee and Capitalism in the Venezuelan Andes*. Austin: University of Texas Press, 1983.

———. *Anthropologies and Histories: Essays in Culture, History and Political Economy*. New Brunswick: Rutgers University Press, 1989.

———. "Hegemony and the Language of Contention," in *Everyday Forms of State Formation: Revolution and the Negotiation of Rule in Modern Mexico*, Gil Joseph and Daniel Nugent, eds. Durham, N.C.: Duke University Press, 1994.

———. "Political Economy and Social Fields," in *Building a New Biocultural Synthesis: Political-Economic Perspectives on Human Biology*, Alan H. Goodman and Thomas L. Leatherman, eds. Ann Arbor: University of Michigan Press, 1998a, 75–92.

———. "Social Fields and Close Encounters," in *Close Encounters of Empire: Writing the Cultural History of U.S.-Latin American Relations*, Gilbert Joseph, Catherine Legrand, and Ricardo Salvatore, eds. Durham, N.C.: Duke University Press, 1998b, 518–23.

Rubin, Jeffrey. *Decentering the Regime: Ethnicity, Radicalism, and Democracy in Juchitán, Mexico*. Durham, N.C.: Duke University Press, 1997.

Rulfo, Juan M. *El Futuro del Algodón Mexicano*. Mexico: Secretaría de Agricultura y Fomento; Dirección de Economía Rural; Departamento de Control de la Producción, 1941.

Sachs, Wolfgang, ed. *The Development Dictionary: A Guide to Knowledge as Power*. London: Zed, 1992.

Sánchez Mejorada, Javier. *Obra Social de la Comisión Nacional de Irrigación*. Mexico, D.F.: Comisión Nacional de Irrigación, 1928.

Sánchez Munguía, Vicente, ed. *El Revestimiento del Canal Todo Americano: ¿Competencia o Cooperación por el Agua en la Frontera México-Estados Unidos?* Tijuana: El Colegio de la Frontera Norte/Plaza y Valdés, 2004.

Sanderson, Steven. *The Transformation of Mexican Agriculture: International Structure and the Politics of Rural Change*. Princeton: Princeton University Press, 1986.

Schoonover, Thomas. "El Algodón Mexicano y la Guerra Civil Norteamericana." *Historia Mexicana* 91 (1974): 483–506.

Schwartz, Harry. *Seasonal Farm Labor in the United States: With Special Reference to Hired Workers in Fruit and Vegetable and Sugar-Beet Production*. New York: Columbia University Press, 1945.

Scott, James. *Seeing Like a State: How Certain Schemes to Improve the Human Condition Have Failed*. New Haven: Yale University Press, 1998.

Senior, Clarence. "The Laguna Region: Mexico's Agrarian Laboratory." *Quarterly Journal of Inter-American Relations* 1.2 (1939a): 67–78.

———. "Mexico in Transition." *League for Industrial Democracy Pamphlet Series*. Vol. 6. New York: League for Industrial Democracy, 1939b.

Sheridan, Thomas. *Where the Dove Calls: the Political Ecology of a Peasant Corporate Community in Northwest Mexico.* Tucson: University of Arizona Press, 1988.

Shiva, Vandana. *Water Wars: Privatization, Pollution, and Profit.* Boston: South End Press, 2002.

Simpson, Eyler. *The Ejido: Mexico's Way Out.* Chapel Hill: University of North Carolina Press, 1937.

Snyder, Robert. *Cotton Crisis.* Chapel Hill: University of North Carolina Press, 1984.

Stevenson, Joseph. "Auge Algodonero en Centroamérica." *Agricultura de las Américas* 15.5-6 (1966).

Steward, Julian et al. *The People of Puerto Rico: A Study in Social Anthropology.* Urbana: University of Illinois Press, 1956.

Steward, Julian, et al. *Irrigation Civilizations: A Comparative Study,* Washington: Pan American Union, 1955.

Stonich, Susan. *"I Am Destroying the Land": The Political Ecology of Poverty and Environmental Destruction in Honduras.* Boulder, Col.: Westview Press, 1993.

Striffler, Steve. *In the Shadows of State and Capital: The United Fruit Company, Popular Struggle, and Agrarian Restructuring in Ecuador, 1900–1995.* Durham, N.C.: Duke University Press, 2002.

Tamayo, Jorge L. "Las Aguas Internacionales del Norte de México y el Tratado de 1944." *El Trimestre Económico* 12.47 (1945): 467–87.

Taylor, Amos. "Cotton and the Postwar World Trade." *Proceedings of the Eighth Cotton Research Congress.* 1946.

Taylor, Lawrence Douglas. *La Campaña Magonista de 1911 en Baja California: El Apogeo del Partido Liberal Mexicano.* Tijuana: El Colegio de la Frontera Norte, 1992.

Terán, Manuel. *Agua, Tierra, Hombre: Semblanza de Eduardo Chávez.* Mexico: Ediciones Desfiladero, 1985.

Tercero, Dorothy. "Mexican Irrigation Commission." *Bulletin of the Pan American Union* 80.5 (1946): 265–66.

Thorpe, Rosemary, ed. *Latin America in the 1930s: The Role of the Periphery in World Crises.* Oxford: Macmillan Press/St. Anthony's College, 1984.

Topik, Steven and Allen Wells. "Introduction: Latin America's Response to International Markets during the Export Boom," in *The Second Conquest of Latin America: Coffee, Henequen and Oil During the Export Boom, 1850–1930,* Steven Topik and Allen Wells, eds. Austin, Tex.: University of Texas Press, 1998, 1–36

Trawick, Paul B. "The Moral Economy of Water: Equity and Antiquity in the Andean Commons." *American Anthropologist* 103.2 (2001): 361–79.

———. *The Struggle for Water in Peru: Comedy and Tragedy in the Andean Commons.* Palo Alto: Stanford University Press, 2003.

Tsing, Ana. *Friction: An Ethnography of Global Connections.* Princeton: Princeton University Press, 2004.

Turner, John. *White Gold Comes to California.* Fresno: Book Publishers Inc., 1981.

Tutt, Ernest L. "Marketing Cotton in South America." *International Cotton Bulletin* 5 (1927): 117–127.

United States Department of Agriculture (USDA). *1921 Yearbook of Agriculture.* Washington D.C.: U.S. Government Printing Office, 1921.

————. *The World Cotton Situation: Foreign Cotton Production (Preliminary)*. MS, 1935.

United States Department of the Interior (USDI). Bureau of Reclamation. *Rio Grande Federal Reclamation Project: New Mexico-Texas.* Washington D.C.: U.S. Government Printing Office, 1936.

Urquidi, Victor. *Otro Siglo Perdido. Las Políticas de Desarrollo en América Latina (1930–2005).* Mexico: El Colegio de México/Fondo de Cultura Económica, 2005.

Valdés, Dennis Nodín. "Mexican Revolutionary Nationalism and Repatriation during the Great Depression." *Mexican Studies / Estudios Mexicanos* 4.1 (1988): 1–23.

Vargas-Lobsinger, María. *La Hacienda de "La Concha": Una Empresa Algodonera de la Laguna, 1883–1917.* Mexico: UNAM, 1984.

Vaughan, Mary Kay. *Cultural Politics in Revolution: Teachers, Peasants, and Schools in Mexico, 1930–1940.* Tucson: University of Arizona Press, 1997.

Vázquez del Mercado, Francisco. "Irrigation in Mexico." *Bulletin of the Pan American Union* 71.3 (1937): 255–67.

Vélez-Ibañez, Carlos. *Border Visions: Mexican Cultures of the Southwest United States.* Tucson: University of Arizona Press, 1996.

Vinson, Curtis. "Can America Retain Cotton Leadership?" *International Cotton Bulletin* 12 (1933): 277–80.

Wallace, Henry. "The World Cotton Drama." *Foreign Affairs* 13.4 (1935): 543–56.

Walsh, Casey. "Aguas Broncas: The Regional Political Ecology of Water Conflict in the Mexico–U.S. Borderlands." *Journal of Political Ecology* 11 (2004a): 45–60.

————. Eugenic Acculturation: Manuel Gamio, Migration Studies, and the Anthropology of Development in Mexico. *Latin American Perspectives* 31.5 (2004b): 118–145.

Walsh, Casey, and Elizabeth Ferry. "Introduction: Production, Power and Place" in *The Social Relations of Mexican Commodities: Production, Power, and Place,* Casey Walsh et al., eds., San Diego: Center for U.S.-Mexican Studies, 2003, 19–54

Ward, Evan. *Border Oasis: Water and the Political Ecology of the Colorado River Delta, 1940–1975.* Tucson: University of Arizona Press, 2003.

Warman, Arturo. *La Historia de un Bastardo: Maíz y Capitalismo.* Mexico: UNAM IIS/Fondo de Cultura Económica, 1988.

————. *El Campo Mexicano en el Siglo XX.* Mexico: Fondo de Cultura Económica, 2001.

Weber, Devra. *Dark Sweat, White Gold: California Farm Workers, Cotton, and the New Deal.* Berkeley: University of California Press, 1994.

Wheeler, Leslie. "Agricultural Surpluses in the Postwar World." *Foreign Affairs* 20.1 (1941): 87–101.

White, E. D. "The Road Ahead for Cotton." *Proceedings of the Eighth Cotton Research Congress.* Dallas, Tex., 1947.

————. "What's Ahead for Cotton?" *Proceedings of the Eleventh Cotton Research Congress.* Dallas, Tex., 1951.

Whiteford, Scott, and Roberto Melville, eds. *Protecting a Sacred Gift: Water and Social Change in Mexico.* La Jolla, San Diego: Center for U.S.-Mexican Studies, 2002.

Williams, Raymond. *Marxism and Literature.* Oxford: Oxford University Press, 1977.

Williams, Robert G. *Export Agriculture and the Crisis in Central America.* Chapel Hill: University of North Carolina Press, 1986.

Wissler, Clark. "Final Report of the Committee on Scientific Problems of Human Migration." *Reprint and Circular Series of the National Research Council* 87 (1929).

Wittfogel, Karl. *Oriental Despotism: A Comparative Study of Total Power.* New Haven: Yale University Press, 1957.

Wolf, Eric. *Europe and the People without History.* Berkeley: University of California Press, 1982.

Worster, Donald. *Rivers of Empire: Water, Aridity, and the Growth of the American West.* New York: Pantheon Books, 1985.

Yerkes, Robert. "The Work of Committee on Scientific Problems of Human Migration, National Research Council." *The Journal of Personnel Research* 3.6 (1924).

INDEX

Note: references to illustrations and photographs are *italicized*.

ISBN-13: 978-1-60344-013-4
ISBN-10: 1-60344-013-5